REDNECK HEAVEN

REDNECK

PORTRAIT OF A VANISHING

BANTAM BOOKS

New York
Toronto
London
Sydney
Auckland

HEAVEN
CULTURE

Bethany Bultman

REDNECK HEAVEN

A Bantam Book/December 1996

Library of Congress Cataloging-in-Publication Data
Bultman, Bethany.
Redneck heaven : portrait of a vanishing culture / Bethany Bultman.
p.   cm.
Includes bibliographical references
ISBN 0-553-37804-X
1. Rednecks.   2. United States—Social life and customs—1971-
1. Title.
E169.04.B84   1996
973.929—dc20   96-12719
                                                     CIP
Published simultaneously in the United States and Canada

Bantam Books are published by Bantam Books, a division of Bantam Doubleday Dell Publishing Group,
Inc. Its trademark, consisting of the words "Bantam Books" and the portrayal of a rooster, is Registered in
U.S. Patent and Trademark Office and in other countries. Marca Registrada. Bantam Books, 1540 Broadway,
New York, New York 10036.

PRINTED IN THE UNITED STATES OF AMERICA

FFG 10 9 8 7 6 5 4 3 2 1

For Lois Gore,

my third-grade teacher, who taught me the power of words,

and

for Gwyther, Tristan, Delia, Karl, and Andrew,

in hopes they grow to adulthood better than our generation, and humming

the country song "You've Got to Stand for Something or You'll Fall for Anything."

Author's Note

In the course of my five years in redneck country, I met self-styled rednecks from every part of America, from Alaska to the Southwest to the Deep South to Maine and everywhere in between. I interviewed hundreds of cowboys, bikers, factory workers, professional fishermen, truckers, country music singers, hairdressers, snake wrestlers, preachers, politicians, and moonshiners. These good people had plenty to say, and I've let them say it in their own words so you can encounter them more or less as I did. To protect the innocent, or sometimes the guilty, I've used pseudonyms and changed certain identifying details for some people. The first time those people are encountered, their names appear in italics. Every quote in the book is from a real person—proud rednecks all.

Contents

BOB SCHATZ

SUE ROSOFF

STEPHEN COLLECTOR

Five Years in Redneck Heaven

I'M NOT EXACTLY THE MOST CULTURALLY COMPETENT PERSON to have spent five years chronicling redneck culture. For most of my life I practiced the double standard that historian C. Vann Woodward observed: I was one of those Southern liberals who go ballistic at the "n word" yet had no qualms about dishing out the term "redneck" as a synonym for dumber-than-spit hair-trigger racists. As a child raised in Anglo-Southern comfort in Natchez, Mississippi, a community that boasts of being a place "where the Old South still lives," the only times I can remember having a sunburned neck were from pruning camellia bushes or spending too many hours dancing in front of the stage at a jazz festival. To be honest, I didn't know the difference between Jack Daniel's and Charlie Daniels. And even though I'm a devoted Southerner, Hank Williams's "If Heaven Ain't a Lot Like Dixie" only evoked disquieting visions of oppressive hoop skirts and the business end of a bullwhip.

My preoccupation with rednecks was precipitated by a confrontation with ethnic bias. In the beginning I was determined to confront

Whether a redneck hails from the hill country of Pennsylvania or a row house in Detroit, his struggle for independence has made Dixie, and all it has come to symbolize, the heartland of his antiestablishment views. Today, more Confederate flags are displayed on the back windows of trucks at the Boeing plant outside Seattle than were ever carried by the rebel fighters who met defeat at Gettysburg.

In the South, the debate over the banner of Dixie rages on. Flying over statehouses and serving as the symbol of numerous football teams (including those with African American players), it remains a potent and controversial icon.

Michael Westerman, a nineteen-year-old redneck from Todd County, Kentucky, kept Confederate flags on proud display: one hung in his living room, one was tattooed on his arm, and one waved from the back of his bloodred Chevy four-by-four truck. Freddie Morrow and Damien Darden, two eighteen-year-old African Americans, saw the flags as banners for people who support slavery, and fatally shot Westerman in the heart as he drove through town one night flying his proud emblem behind him. The shooting incident occurred on a weekend when much of the country was celebrating Dr. Martin Luther King's birthday. In Morrow and Darden's hometown of Guthrie, an hour north of Nashville, a local honky-tonk was hosting a pool tournament to celebrate "Thank God for James Earl Ray Day."

Westerman was buried in a Confederate-flag-draped coffin. Today the grave is seen by many as a shrine to a martyr of ethnic pride. Morrow and Darden were convicted of attempted kidnapping, felony murder, and civil rights intimidation and sentenced to life imprisonment.

Redneck Bumper Stickers

Rednecks have never been hesitant to use their bodies and vehicles as political billboards. Wherever I went, I was given the opportunity to join these folks in proclaiming redneck opinions on the rear bumper of my car. My collection now covers items spanning numerous elections, wars, and political issues.

★ IF THEY KNEW THEN WHAT WE KNOW NOW, THEY WOULDN'T HAVE VOTED FOR LINCOLN

★ I'LL FORGIVE JANE FONDA WHEN THE JEWS FORGIVE HITLER

★ MORE PEOPLE DIED AT CHAPPAQUIDDICK THAN LOVE CANAL

★ MAKE WELFARE AS HARD TO GET AS A BUILDING PERMIT

★ GENERAL SHERMAN, WHERE ARE YOU WHEN ATLANTA NEEDS YOU?

★ I DON'T BRAKE FOR GAYS, LIBERALS, OR ANTI-GUNNERS

★ IF I'D KNOWN ABOUT THIS I WOULD HAVE PICKED MY OWN COTTON (NEXT TO A PICTURE OF THE CONFEDERATE FLAG)

- ★ IMPEACH EARL WARREN

- ★ THE HANOI JANE OR SADDAM HUSSEIN URINAL TARGET (WRITTEN ON A BULL'S-EYE TARGET)

- ★ WE CAN LICK BUSH IF WE WANT TO (FAVORED ONLY BY LIBERAL REDNECKS)

- ★ SADDAM HUSSEIN, YOUR FLY IS OPEN AND YOUR CAMEL IS OUT

- ★ VOTE FOR THE CROOK (A PRO-EDWARDS BUMPER STICKER ADVOCATING THE LOUISIANA GOVERNOR AGAINST HIS OPPONENT, DAVID DUKE, IN THE 1991 GUBERNATORIAL RACE)

theirs; ironically, I had to confront my own. As a member of a political action committee called the Coalition Against Nazism and Racism, I'd gone to observe a Republican political rally for David Duke in 1991. A former grand wizard of the Klan and a Nazi sympathizer, Duke was running for the office of governor of Louisiana. In this time of ethnic sensitivity, I was surprised by Duke's choice of an unofficial campaign song— "What the World Needs (Is a Few More Rednecks)." I snickered at the thought of how the song might be received at one of my ACLU (American Civil Liberties Union) meetings. It wouldn't be too long before I had a hunch that the actual sentiments of the song were much more in line with the philosophy of the ACLU than the far right.

One thing became apparent to me as I watched the crowd at that Duke rally: they embraced both the label "redneck"and the song as if they were their mantra. From the first bars, the audience members were on their feet stomping the heels of their boots on the linoleum, waving shirts, baseball caps, and small babies with Duke bumper stickers on their diapers. This frenzy of pride over being called rednecks made me wonder whether they were offering a reactionary political philosophy complete with its own dress code or simply displaying the marks of a cerebrally disadvantaged caste.

By the song's finale, a burly man in front of me with "FRIGIDAIRE" overstitched on his shirt pocket gave a concerned pat to his gray-haired mother's arm. "Mama, you look tired. I'll carry you home and come back for Glenn Rae and the kids," he leaned down to whisper.

"No, son," she replied as she wiped away her tears. "I've been waitin' a long time for God to send us rednecks hope of gettin' our freedom and dignity back."

This simple expression of vulnerability so devoid of hate and so filled with hope was not what I had expected. Obviously there was far more to redneck culture than the bigotry I had so long maligned. Thus began my search to acquaint myself with who or what a redneck is.

The first time I tried to type the word "redneck," spell-check flashed a warning: "Pejorative." It was then I realized I'd never move past the stereotypes until I enlisted the aid of some knowledgeable guides to help me find my way into the heart of redneckdom.

Randy Newman, a singer/songwriter who made an album defending rednecks, started me off. "I define rednecks as a bunch of independent working guys," he said. "They're white Christians who like to do and hate the same things. For instance, they hate guys who wear silk underwear and tweed jackets. They like country music, pickup trucks, Harleys, sex, God, and Mama. They may look tough, but their hearts are tender."

An ATF (Alcohol, Tobacco and Firearms) agent who participates in the Good Ole Boy Round-Up also spoke of the values that lie at the core of redneck identity. "You'll meet redneck wanna-bes who drive pickups, call themselves Bubba, and wear cowboy boots, but they haven't got a clue. Hell, rednecks aren't a fraternity. Rednecks aren't a race you get born into and have to stay in. It's a code. It's showing up for family and friends and freedom."

Rednecks clearly have a strong set of beliefs. However, this stubborn strength and rigid ideology can often be misinterpreted. *Sister Bernadette*, former director of a social services agency in Texas, showed sympathy for rednecks. "The first time I heard the word 'redneck' was in the song 'Up Against the Wall, Redneck Mother.' One of my fellow sisters told me it meant 'narrow-minded' and 'prejudice against outsiders.' I understood. Rednecks are just folks like Archie Bunker, people who are a lot like my friends and Catholic family from Brooklyn. People who've been oppressed themselves, so they'll persecute other minorities. But you know, that oppression has also endowed them with a remarkable gift of empathy. It causes them to be the first to rush to the aid of perfect strangers when there's a crisis."

Archie Bunker personifies the juxtaposed redneck characteristics of intolerance and compassion. According to Norman Lear, producer of *All in the Family*, "The only difference between Archie Bunker and another redneck guy in Montgomery, Alabama, or Butte, Montana, is the accent. Archie epitomized the contradictory strands in the human psyche. He's a man who feared what he didn't understand. He was ill-informed, not vicious."

As I continued my search, I became aware of the vast number of rednecks that exist outside of Dixie.

"I was amazed to discover rednecks are not Southern! I might be in Michigan, but these folks are about as redneck as I am, and I'm from rural Georgia. After all, I'm performing in a comedy club attached to a bowling alley with valet parking," said Jeff Foxworthy, comedian and author of *You Might Be A Redneck If*—(a series of humorous paperbacks).

"Daddy drove to work in a pickup truck, listenin' to country music, but he was an IBM executive," continued Jeff. "You can't tell me these same cultural impulses can't be found from Alaska to Florida. The guys and gals behind the wheels of cabs in Manhattan, the rodeo cowboys from New Jersey, the Washington State fishermen, and the charter boat captains in Hawaii find beer and country music a lot more thrilling than watching *Masterpiece Theater* while sipping Beaujolais!"

Although there may be rednecks everywhere, some claim that Southern rednecks carry a certain distinction. "All Southern rednecks can address each other like homeboys. Maybe it's because they fought and lost a war together," said Russell Hebert, a Colorado lawman. "In the rest of the country, rednecks don't have that brotherhood. A Coloradan talking to a Nebraskan, he could give a shit! Or a cowboy and a New England fisherman. Their culture has taught them that the only way to protect their independence is to be suspicious of anyone who isn't just like them."

A Chicago police officer married to a Southerner added, "In the South the people who call themselves rednecks are hospitable, generous, and practice good old easy violence and social illiteracy. Yankee rednecks aren't particularly hospitable or generous. They vote just alike, though—for the guy who wants to control big government's power, not rednecks' guns."

Charlie Daniels seemed like a good person to ask about rednecks, since he wrote the song used at the Duke rally. Daniels is a bear of a man

THE REDNECK CODE

According to the rednecks I interviewed, adherence to the following values, habits, and behaviors is the litmus test that sets rednecks apart from lower-than-snake-spit white trash (aka poor white trash, or PWT). White trash, by redneck definition, is the lowest form of life, useless, valueless, Godless creatures, lower on the food chain than albino cockroaches. In the words of Miss Ida, a Kansas grocery-store clerk, "White trash are easy to spot. They'll lie on credit, while a redneck uses the truth for cash."

While the contradictions in the redneck code are many, one thing is for certain. To paraphrase the famous quote by Texan Jim Hightower, "The only thing that's in the middle of the road is a yellow stripe and dead armadillos" but never a redneck.

The Value System

★ Protect Mama, family, small children, dogs, property, and country—even if it means killing someone.

★ Never accept a handout, 'cause if you do, you're white trash.

★ Don't give an inch in an argument, even if the person you disagree with is your boss.

★ Happiness, good fortune, and grudges are to be shared and savored.

★ It's more honorable to be brave than rich.

★ "Scruples" ain't two words.

★ Anything worth having is worth having now, so never wait in line.

★ Stand up for the Bill of Rights, especially the Second Amendment, which protects the right of every American to bear arms.

with inscrutable eyes as cold and blue as the North Sea. When I mentioned Duke's use of his song, he unholstered a glare that could intimidate the devil.

Thankfully, this elder statesman of hillbilly rock chose not to kill the

* Never squeal to the law or give information to an outsider about a friend or relative.
* Mind your own business, unless the business involves a machine or vehicle belonging to a person incapable of fixing it or someone who needs you and your powerful vehicle to pull him out when he's stuck.
* Never flaunt your formal education or pay for anyone else's expertise.
* Be proud America is the only industrialized nation in the world with the death penalty; stand up for it.
* Salute the flag, bow your head for prayers, and tip your hat to a lady, even if it's merely a mental gesture.
* Don't stand too close to people when you talk to them, especially when they're chewing tobacco.
* Pay the debts you rightfully owe; screw the ones you don't.
* If you can't convince, confuse.
* Never lie, unless it's to give an alibi for a buddy, but exaggerate all you want when it adds sizzle to the steak.
* Buy American, and never own a machine or appliance you can't repair yourself.
* Keep up your auto and burial insurance payments.
* Pursue expensive leisure activities requiring lots of equipment and little skill.
* Recycle machinery, plastics, motor oil, and soda to their fullest extent.
* Anyone who doesn't understand "Don't Tread on Me" deserves to get bitten.

messenger. Instead, he turned philosophical. "If there's one thing I hate, it's a racist! You know, I grew up in a Jim Crow society in the North Carolina timber country. But I realized somethin' when I was just a kid: God didn't love me better 'cause I'm white. He loves everybody the same. And it's up to rednecks, the hardworkin' common man, to have the guts to set the example for freedom and equality in America."

That night at a honky-tonk, Charlie dedicated the song to me with wishes for success in my adventure. He also predicted I'd return from my journey to redneck heaven a far different person. By the time the song had ended, I had no doubt that rednecks might have a helluva lot of contradictions, but beneath it all there was a strong sense of character and pride.

Charlie also helped me see how country music serves as a cultural keyhole into the redneck value system. A self-effacing quality mingles with an in-your-face ethos, as illustrated by the title of one of Waylon Jennings's albums, *Too Dumb for New York City, Too Ugly for L.A.* Earthy parables are told by cultural bards in lines such as "rearranging deck chairs on a ship that's goin' down," "I met her in the washateria and we went out with the tide," "you're just a button off my shirt," "you could turn a redneck green," "from the gutter to you, ain't up," "if today was a fish, I'd throw it back," and "you ain't much fun since I quit drinkin'."

I soon found myself humming along with "Rednecks, White Socks and Blue Ribbon Beer" and "Red Neckin' Love Makin' Night," "Redneck! (The Redneck National Anthem)," "Longhaired Redneck," "(I'm Just a) Redneck in a Rock and Roll Bar," and "High-Tech Redneck," to name but a few.

These songs synthesize an oral tradition of philosophy, psychology, and spirituality and somehow create real, honest music for real, honest folk. As one musician in Nashville advised, "Darlin', to write a good redneck song you gotta be a working stiff and put you some twang where the funk is in the blues. We're writing for guys and gals like us who use elbow grease to acquire elbow room from the pussies who wear suits and ties to work."

REDNECK–THE ARMY THAT FIGHTS FOR DIGNITY

Standing on a UMW (United Mine Workers) picket line in Tuscaloosa, Alabama, I experienced the true meaning of the term "redneck." Leering with unmodulated belligerence beneath their picket signs, the brawny men could have passed for the bad guys in *Deliverance*. Sam, a night-shift miner in the deepest coal mine in North America, walked the picket line in camouflage overalls with a red bandanna tied around his neck. As we walked, he filled me in on the history of the miners' union and its relationship to the word "redneck." "In the old days miners worked in poison air, got terrible physical disabilities, and lived in constant fear because they worked in a place filled with the sounds of crackin' and poppin' as the mountain threatened to come down on them," Sam told me. "The coal companies owned the miners, body and soul.

"When the miners began to complain about the conditions, the coal company imported workers from Greece and Italy. But they were uncooperative, too, so the company brought in black railroad workers to do the mining. But the thing that the company didn't bargain on," Sam continued, "was that the miners would put aside their distrust of one another to fight for a better life, together.

"The union thing had been brewing since about 1890. When all the trouble blew up in 1921 on Blair Mountain, West Virginia, near the Kentucky border, it quickly turned into a civil war involving tens of thousands of miners and their families. The rebels didn't have uniforms, just their work coveralls or their World War I service uniforms. They tied red kerchiefs around their necks and called themselves the Rednecks—the Army That Fights for Dignity.

"By the time the revolt was over, these union men, now called Rednecks, had taken over five hundred square miles. The coal company hired a private police force to fight the miners. They even had a couple of biplanes drop bombs on them. When President Warren G. Harding sent in federal troops, the miners surrendered, because their battle was not with the U.S. government. As the Rednecks said, the fight 'wasn't for profit, it was for dignity.' It's like Dr. King preached—your dignity should always come first. It's the only thing worth going to jail or even dying for."

THE HIERARCHY

In the redneck world, the heart always overrules the head, a behavior style that guarantees rednecks a reputation as ornery outsiders. I could identify with them. My society taught me to be polite for peace, so I did my best to let my head win out over my heart's lifelong inclination to fight for justice. But then I encountered the redneck ideology . . . and became reconnected to my root instincts.

On closer observation I discovered other bold and thorny wildflowers hidden among some lavish but unlikely bouquets. Self-described rednecks presented themselves—from major players on Wall Street and partners in L.A. law firms, to literary agents and editors in New York, and lesbian executives in country music. They all proudly claimed that greed wasn't behind their success, but rather "a genetic inability to kiss butt" and a natural competitiveness that had driven them to achieve just enough power so "they'd be left alone."

I also began to notice that as varied as rednecks might be, they seemed to fall into three socioeconomic classes. By observing a set of parameters (if it walks like a duck, quacks like a duck . . .) for each group, my redneck sources helped me identify some philosophical kinsmen.

Good Solid Folk: The Good Ole Boy and the Good Ole Girl

Definition: "Blue collar, an outdoorsman, a patriot, something of a populist, basically conservative—a man's man . . . the good ole boy is someone who rides around in a pickup truck, drinking beer and putting his empties in a sack" (Ingram Parmley, *Encyclopedia of Southern Culture*). A good ole boy will always act humble first, but when provoked, will become cocky as hell. The purists among them, however, don't drink, cuss, smoke, dance, or gamble. Even the worst good ole boy will show up at church when it seems important to his good ole girl, who inevitably has to be there to teach Sunday school. Good solid folk are the mainstays of the Kiwanis and Elks Clubs, the VFW, the Welcome Wagon, and *The 700 Club*. But they are still rednecks. For example, an Illinois-based chapter of Dads against Drugs once sponsored a car wash featuring topless dancers soaping up automobiles for ten dollars a car.

> ***Good Ole Girl Hall of Fame:*** Cousin Minnie Pearl, who died in 1996 at the age of eighty-three, was America's first successful female stand-up comedian. Born Sarah Ophelia Colley, she was a graduate of a fashionable finishing school, yet made her living portraying the hayseed spinster from Grinder's Switch. One of her classic quotes regarded female pallbearers: "If those ol' boys won't take me out when I'm-a-livin', I sure don't want 'em taking me out when I'm dead."
>
> ***Professions:*** Foreman, preacher, heating and air-conditioning contractor, law enforcement officer, teacher, farmer, fisherman, rancher, salesman, conductor, or bus driver
>
> ***Life's Goals:*** See that kids finish high school, children and grandchildren stay close to home, own an RV
>
> ***Courting Style:*** Stencil each other's names on their belts and/or have them embossed in the velour headrests of the automobile
>
> ***Home:*** Blond-brick ranch house, matching his and hers La-Z-Boy recliners as soft as catcher's mitts, riding mower, satellite dish
>
> ***Art:*** Home hobby crafts, bumper stickers
>
> ***Dream Vehicles:*** Ford or Chevy pickup, sturdy Buick or Oldsmobile kept in pristine condition

Recreation: Fishing, hunting, golfing, bowling

Good Ole Boy Hall of Fame: Country and gospel music legend Jimmie "You Are My Sunshine" Davis served as the governor of Louisiana in the early sixties. When the press mocked him for having a telephone installed in his office limousine, he became furious. Just to show his constituents he hadn't "gotten above himself," he brought his horse, which had been grazing behind the capitol, into his office. When the press caught up to the governor he was sitting at his desk with his horse reading the mail over his shoulder. Questioned as to what had possessed him to bring his horse to work, Davis replied, "He was about the best friend I'd ever had, and I realized he'd never been in my office."

Likely Good Solid Folk Candidates:

Loretta Lynn, queen mother of country music

President Harry Truman

Willard Scott, folksy weatherman

Wilford Brimley, actor and Quaker Oats pitchman

Will Rogers, late humorist

Nolan Ryan, baseball legend

Paul Harvey, news commentator

Fannie Flagg, comedian and author

Miz Lillian Carter, Peace Corps volunteer and mother of the former president

Fictional Characters: Forrest Gump and Popeye and the characters in *The Honeymooners, The Andy Griffith Show, The Beverly Hillbillies, Mayberry R.F.D., Gomer Pyle,* and *Hee Haw*

Classic Good Solid Folk Quotes: "I get 435 channels in my livin' room in East Fork, Mississippi. In my fancy hotel suite in New York City I can only get seven; and they call *me* a hick!" (Jerry Clower, comedian)

Shit Kicker

Definition: Given the choice between cocky and humble, he'll try cocky until he's beaten into humble. He's the over-the-top, adrenaline-powered knight known for taking life on two wheels. He's every bit as likely to chew tobacco as to own a powder-blue suit studded with beads. He can become involved in a bar fight of biblical proportions one night and play Santa to hundreds of critically ill children the next day. Women in this group are described as hellcats with hearts of gold or "every redneck's wet dream and worst nightmare rolled into one," as one welder put it.

Favorite Shit-Kicker Professions: Rodeo cowboy, athlete, bounty hunter, arms dealer, wildcatter, deep-sea diver, musician, oil-field fire fighter, entertainer, demolition expert, fighter pilot, stuntman

Life's Goals: Have fun, make a fortune, or die trying

Courting Style: Will paint the name of a loved one on a water tower, a commercial fishing boat, or have it tattooed on his buttocks

Home: On the road—in the saddle, on the back of a Harley, or the bed of a pickup

Art: Airbrushed design of Confederate flags, unicorns, or hunting scenes on vehicle; tattoo of favorite cartoon character, brand of beer, Harley-Davidson, or pro-gun slogan

Dream Vehicles: Anything fast and/or a Harley with a phone and state-of-the-art sound system

Recreation: Hunting, fishing, stock-car racing

Shit-Kicker Hall of Fame: Country music legend George Jones, nicknamed Possum, once rode his ten-horsepower riding mower 8 miles into Beaumont to the liquor store. Jones claims he was provoked into doing it because his former wife, Shirley, poured out all the liquor in the house and hid the car keys to prevent him from drinking. When his drinking exploits gave him a reputation for missing concert dates, he renamed his touring bus and had new license plates emblazoned with his other nickname, NO SHOW.

Likely Shit-Kicker Candidates:

Janis Joplin, late, busted-loose Pentecostal rock and roller

Jerry Lee "Killer" Lewis, former preacher, and rockabilly legend

Evel and Robbie Knievel, daredevils

Richard and Kyle Petty, race-car drivers

President Andrew Jackson

Sam Kinison, the late comedian

Wild Bill Hickok and Annie Oakley

John Kruk, baseball star

Hank Williams Sr. and Jr., Patsy Cline, Tanya Tucker, David Allan Coe, and Willie, Waylon, and the boys, country musicians

Willie Morris, James Lee Burke, Carolyn Chute, Larry McMurtry, Rita Mae Brown, Molly Ivins, Tom McGuane, writers

Dennis Hopper, Don Johnson, Nick Nolte, Jack Nicholson, and the late Steve McQueen, actors

Brett Butler, comedian

Don Imus, shock jock

Bruce Springsteen, Melissa Etheridge, ZZ Top, John Mellencamp, Keith Richards, former and present members of the Allman Brothers and the Fabulous Thunderbirds, rock and rollers

Fictional Characters: Just about anyone ever portrayed in film by James Dean or Bruce Willis

Classic Shit-Kicker Quotes:

★ Andrew Jackson was said to have fought many duels and been in more than a hundred fights. Obviously he'd heeded his mother's advice: "Never sue anybody for slander or assault and battery. Always settle them scores yourself!"

★ "Sometime after the review we came into possession of her [the reviewer's] latest book. [My wife] took it out into the backyard and shot it with a pistol and so did I." (Pulitzer prize–winning author Richard Ford, *British Esquire,* July/August 1995)

Definition: The redneck millionaire is not to be confused with British royalty–emulating robber barons of the nineteenth century such as Rockefeller, Astor, and Vanderbilt. The Sir Bubba's world is one of risk and bravado, where Old World pretensions—not bankruptcy—carry the burden of shame. To make his point, this shit-kicker-made-good will down beer out of the can at fashionable corporate parties. Once his vocal cords are lubricated, the Sir Bubba (even if he happens to be a graduate of Princeton) will deliver a linguistic elbow jab to the ribs of polite society by sprinkling an "ain't" and a cuss word or two into his conversation.

Favorite Sir Bubba Professions: Surgeon, contractor, oil tycoon, defense or personal injury attorney, poultry processor, car dealer, televangelist, real estate developer, media mogul, commodities trader, entertainer, S and L president

Life's Goals: Own large tracts of land, buy a new home for Mama, own a top-of-the-line bass boat, give a Rolex to friends, employees, the crew of the boat that won the fishing rodeo for him, the roadies for his band, or his favorite coach from high school, own a professional sports franchise, provide a Redneck Ivy League education for his kids at a school like Baylor or Coca-Cola U. (Emory)

Courting Style: Propose via billboards, klieg lights, skywriters

Home:

✳ Baronial log cabin on a five-hundred-acre ranch or new Tara-style mansion in a gated community with a name like Druid Hills or Camelot Estates

* Mansion with a lot of bathrooms—bathrooms are the most important status symbol in redneck homes
* An air-conditioned doghouse for his faithful old hunting dogs, designed as a scale model of Sir Bubba's own house

Art: Remington sculpture, Civil War or Old West memorabilia

Dream Vehicles: Lexus with a gun rack and CB, Jeep with a fax machine, king cab pickup with surround sound and a refrigerator

Recreation: Hunting, fishing, golfing, polo, snow skiing

Sir Bubba Hall of Fame: Gerry Spence, "the [self-described] best trial lawyer in America," has never lost a trial since 1969. Standing more than six feet tall and dressed like Buffalo Bill, complete with flowing hair, he addresses the jury with the fearless indignation of Stonewall Jackson. His jury victories include a $10.5 million judgment against the Kerr-McGee Corporation for the family of Karen Silkwood, the nuclear plant worker contaminated by radioactivity.

Likely Sir Bubba Candidates

Dolly Parton and Elvis, queen and king of redneckdom

T. Boone Pickens, Wall Street tycoon

Bill Gates, New Age techno tycoon

President Thomas Jefferson

Gene Autry

Sam Walton, the late founder of Wal-Mart

Ann Richards, Harley-riding farmer's daughter from Hogjaw and former governor of Texas

Reba McEntire and Garth Brooks, crown princess and prince of country music

Jimmy Swaggart and Tammy Faye Baker, televangelists

Ted Turner, media mogul and owner of the Atlanta Braves (and in the ultimate act of defiance, the husband of Jane Fonda, star of the bumper sticker VIETNAM VETS AIN'T FONDA JANE)

Mary Kay Ash, founder of Mary Kay Cosmetics

John Grisham, lawyer turned author

Tommy Lee Jones, John Wayne, and Robert Duval, actors

Fictional Characters: J. R. Ewing of *Dallas* and Rhett Butler of *Gone with the Wind*

Classic Sir Bubba Quotes:

★ A young air force officer once pointed to a helicopter L.B.J. was about to board and said, "Mr. President, that will be your helicopter over there."
President Johnson winked and replied, "No, son, they're all mine!"

★ "When people say less is more, I say more is more. Less is less. I go for more." (Dolly Parton)

"JUS' CHOP OFF MY LEGS AND CALL ME SHORTY

—Exclamation of surprise expressed by a cowboy in an
Abilene, Texas, honky-tonk

I realized that to be a redneck involved a dedication to a well-established and often contradictory code of conduct, but I still wondered whether this was the result of heredity or environment. I had a hunch that it wasn't environment after my meetings with antiracist rednecks such as Charlie Daniels and Jerry Clower, who rebelled against some of the opinions of their kinsmen while remaining firmly rooted in the culture. A lapsed son of redneckdom, author Pat Conroy (*The Great Santini* and *Prince of Tides*) seems to wrestle with his redneck demons in print, though he often takes himself out of the culture.

If the redneck system can be attributed to heredity, *what* heritage? According to rednecks they're nothing but 100 percent mongrel American. I decided that rednecks might be some WASP (White Anglo-Saxon Protestant) mutation. It was Dr. Hunter S. Thompson who planted the grain of doubt in my oyster of certainty. We sat in the kitchen-cum-den at his compound in Woody Creek, Colorado. It was soon obvious that Dr. Thompson didn't want to be interviewed about ethno-culturalism. He just wanted to wax poetic about his guns, his brushes with the law, and the attributes of his favorite automobiles. In frustration I abandoned my mission, but teased him by composing a mock *House & Garden* headline: "At Home with the King of the Rednecks!"

After an awkward pause, Hunter responded in the cadence of sporadic automatic weapon fire, ". . . By your definition, bikers and biker gangs are rednecks too. I rode with the Hell's Angels for two years," he recalled while adroitly juggling a cigarette, a margarita, and a ketchup-oozing hamburger the size of a UFO. "It didn't take more than a few hours with 'em to get a sense of déjà vu for Scots-Irish clans. There's that same sulking hostility toward outsiders, that honor code, and those long bodies that never look natural unless they're leaning on something."

Hunter's insight led me to reexamine my own WASP gene pool. My ancestors were from Scotland and Wales, not Anglo-Saxon at all. They were, in fact, the rugged, stormy Celts, the avowed enemy of the Anglo-Saxons, who referred to Celtic Wales as "the land of strangers."

Most Celtic scholars wanted nothing to do with my theory about a common Celtic-redneck culture. Before he hung up on me, one professor in Wisconsin scoffed, "About all we know is that the Celtic tribes sacked Rome in the fourth century B.C. and then turned around and left. They spoke the same mother language; they were skilled at farming, fighting, and making things with metal; they fought to prove superiority, never to conquer, because they hated cities and outsiders; and they ate a lot of pork!"

I reminded myself that few scholars spend time at tractor pulls, rodeos, and honky-tonks—in fact his argument to disparage my theory had the opposite effect.

Continuing my research, I found that in the four hundred years between Herodotus (the mid-fifth century B.C.) and Julius Caesar (101–44 B.C.) the Greeks and Romans began to notice striking similarities among certain barbarians. These tribes, which they called Celts (after Keltas, "People of Strength," as some tribes called themselves), spread from Spain to Asia Minor and looked exactly alike—golden haired, blue eyed, white skinned, big, and dangerous—and all had clan-based political organizations, a common language, powerful women, similar religious practices, and characteristically exuberant patterns of behavior.

Despite their common bonds, however, the Celts never thought of themselves as anything but diverse clans. The tribes seemed to loathe each other even more than they disliked their Greek and Roman enemies. When I turned to the work of classical writers who had observed the Celts, I discovered that when my kinsmen weren't repelling invaders, they were practicing their pugilistic skills on one another. For this reason, the Romans eventually succeeded in pushing them into the rugged outlands of Brittany in France (ancestral home of the Cajuns in southern Louisiana) and Galicia in Spain (the ancestral homeland of Fidel Castro's father). The largest concentration of Celts, however, went to the British Isles: Cornwall, the Isle of Man, Ulster, Wales, the Hebrides, and Highlands of Scotland.

Once established, the heroic Celtic clans withstood enslavement, rape, and the outlawing of their music, religion, and language by the Romans and Anglo-Saxons for more than sixteen centuries. Then in 1603, James I succeeded, Queen Elizabeth to the throne of England. He was a Protestant empire builder, but before he conquered the world, he knew he had to get rid of those damn Celts. In retaliation, the rebellious Guy Fawkes conceived of the Gunpowder Plot to blow up the House of Lords during King James I's opening of Parliament on November 5, 1606. Fawkes failed. Soon after, my own Welsh ancestors chose to join the mass emigration of Celts to the New World rather than face cultural castration.

And thus, I believe, out of reach of British tyranny some of these Celtic clans became determined to accumulate enough power and wealth to out-Anglo-Saxon their Anglo-Saxon counterparts in Britain, while others established that alternative state of mind called redneck heaven.

CHAPTER ONE

Hey, Good-Lookin'

In The Aeneid, BOOK 8 *(c. 20* B.C.*), Virgil commented on the Celts: "Their hair is gold, their clothing was of gold and light stripes brightened their cloaks. Their milk-white necks had gold collars around them." Other observers of the period noted that the Celts' fine wool cloaks were patterned with multi-colored squares or pin stripes and adorned with tinkling bells, heads, precious gems, eagle feathers, beaks, feet, and fur. The Romans also marveled at the Celts' shoes, which were of tanned waterproof leather with thick soles "excellent for kicking."*

It doesn't matter if you win or lose, it's how you look when you climb off the bus.

—Advice from Texas cowboy Lionel Bevan

WITHOUT A DOUBT, REDNECK STYLE GOES BEYOND mere fashion statement. It's more like a twenty-one-gun salute. But what is sometimes unclear is where the style stops and the statement begins. A truck stop on the Kansas–Missouri border provided the ideal spot to start the quest for an answer.

Charlayne, a lady trucker sitting at the lunch counter, is willing to share her own fashion secrets in a little girl-talk. "When a cowboy asks me to go out after a rodeo, I'll fix myself up." Charlayne explains that the glove compartment of her Chevy truck doubles as a tiny closet; it holds a metallic tube top, two rhinestone barrettes that spell RODEO and DIXIE, and three colors of nail enamel for her fingernails, which are as long as carrots. In a Zip-Loc bag are perfume samples from issues of *Cosmo.* "I look so good you'd kiss my mama for just bringin' me into the world. But no matter what I wear, I remember what Mama always says: 'Never let your makeup write a check your body won't cash.' "

Charlayne's sense of style isn't anything new. Redneck women have always been known for their distinctive way of outfitting themselves. In the 1760s, the writings of Charles Woodmason, an Anglican missionary who visited the descendants of the Celts in the Carolina backcountry, included this description: "The young women have a most uncommon practice, which I can not break them of. They draw their shift as tight as possible round their Breasts, and slender waists (for they are generally finely shaped) and draw their Petticoat close to their Hips to show the fineness of their limbs . . . indeed nakedness is not censurable or indecent here . . . rubbing themselves and their hair with bears' oil and tying it up behind in a bunch like the Indians—being hardly one degree removed from them."

The women who choose to dwell within redneck heaven obviously know that for centuries their sex has been judged on precisely that—sex. And in the time-honored tradition of Celtic women, when they play, they play to win. That doesn't mean they don't pray for the end of the game, though. There's the famous quote from country singer Lacy J.

PHOTO ON PAGE 25 BY SUE ROSOFF.

Dalton: "Wouldn't it be great to be a woman and be just like Willie Nelson? I've often thought, 'God, would that be great, to be the first woman out there on the stage with wrinkles and not have to cover 'em up.' "

Not that redneck women still don't take delight in defying the rules. As Charlayne likes to say, when she dresses up she prefers to stand out like "a hair in a biscuit." Another noteworthy example is the Zodiacs, a ladies' bowling league from Louisiana who claim Liberace as its spiritual mentor. The league recently celebrated its twenty-fifth anniversary. One of the Zodiacs' high points came in 1969, when the Women's International Bowling Congress banned miniskirts and pants from tournaments. Offended by the concept of a dress code, the ladies showed up at the tournament in California in full-length sequined evening gowns and matching bowling bags. When it was their turn to bowl, they stripped off the long skirts to reveal their miniskirts. Then in 1973 in Las Vegas they bowled braless and in hot pants. Today the costumes of the Zodiacs are on permanent display at the Bowling Hall of Fame in St. Louis.

Many rednecks think of singer and actress Dolly Parton as the premier icon of fashion, style, and femininity.

Charlayne says: "That Dolly's a pistol! I heard someone ask her if it hurt her feelings when people told dumb-blonde jokes. She just smiled and said, 'Of course not. In the first place, I know that blondes aren't dumb. In the second place, I know I'm not really a blonde.' "

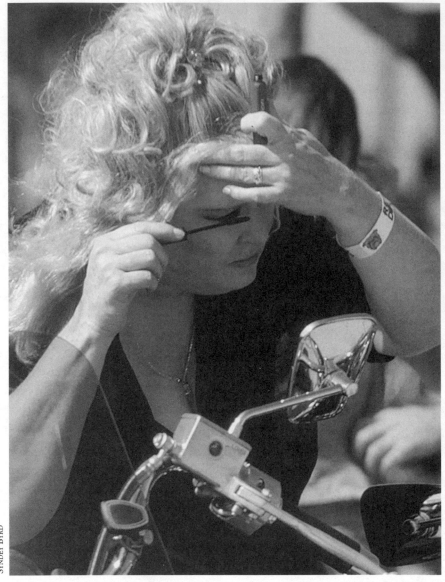

SYNDEY BYRD

BEAUTY TIPS FROM THE HONKY-TONK

In the First Century a.d., *Diodorus Siculus remarked that Celtic women not only painted their eyebrows with berry juice but put roses in their cheeks with herbs.*

Within the female shit-kicker redneck culture there are clear parameters: Looking ladylike is reserved for appearances at church, funerals, or court. The rest of the time is a full-tilt opportunity to flaunt one's womanliness to mankind.

Wasting money on store-bought beauty aids is for fashion victims—and no self-respecting redneck woman would ever be a slave to anything!

* Rub sperm into your scalp to stimulate hair growth. (Whipped egg whites can be substituted when sperm is unavailable.) The best shampoo is Mane and Tail from the feed store.
* The only weight-loss incentive that works is to carry a bag of flour (or sand) of the poundage you want to lose with you in a backpack everywhere you go for one week. At the end of the week you'll be so tired of lugging the extra pounds of flour that you'll stop eating.
* Tone the skin with a wash of one-fourth Pepto-Bismol (any generic pink stomach remedy is fine) and three-fourths beer. Leave it on until it dries, then rinse it off.
* Once a week, give your man the night out and sleep completely coated with Vaseline. Sleep on a rubber sheet or a shower curtain and cover your body with garbage bags and your hands with rubber gloves. Your skin will be like satin.
* If you want to catch a lover, wear Estee Lauder perfume. If you want to catch a husband, place a dab of lemon Pledge on a piece of cotton concealed in your bra. As the evening heats up, you'll begin to remind him of the scent of a nice clean home.

Hey, Good-Lookin'

* For skin the color of a magnolia petal, rub a cotton ball saturated with full-strength lemon juice or peroxide onto the skin.
* Mix Comet with water for a paste to whiten teeth. Brush it on gently with a small paintbrush and leave it on for five minutes. Be careful not to swallow or rub into gums. If you do swallow some, drink a glass of water to dilute it, as the Comet container recommends.
* For strong fingernails, stick your nails into a raw potato for fifteen minutes every day. Rub in horse-hoof cream from the feed store as part of the manicure. For special occasions have your astrological sign and favorite cartoon characters airbrushed on your nails.
* A Visine-soaked cotton ball will remove the red from a pimple. Turn the blemish into a semi permanent beauty spot with a black laundry marker. At night apply a dab of toothpaste to heal the pimple. (If, however, you like the location of the beauty spot, have it permanently tattooed.)
* For soft skin, exfoliate once a week by making a paste of sugar and lard or Crisco, or mix natural, fresh kitty litter with Mazola oil to make a greasy clay paste. Rub the mixture on your body from forehead to toe. Cover with black garbage bags, secured tightly with duct tape. Leave on for fifteen minutes before showering. (To prevent suffocation, use Saran Wrap on the face, leaving breathing space.)

THE HAIR APPARENT

No Muff Too Tuff

—Sign outside the Curl Up and Dye,
a Woodville, Mississippi, beauty parlor

As early as the fourth century B.C., *Roman writers were criticizing the flamboyance of the women of the Celtic tribes. By the first century* B.C., *Diodorus, generally finicky when it came to the uncivilized Celts, conceded they had the habit of regularly washing their bodies and hair with soap, a custom the Greeks and Romans did not adopt for several centuries. He described how the Celtic women not only piled thick braids and cascades of curls atop their heads in elaborate structures, but also decorated these assertive hairdos with tinkling bells and chains.*

Dolly's oversize hairdo is, of course, emblematic of the redneck woman's style. And Big Hair requires a great deal of attention. Some women keep their hair poofy and manageable by conditioning it with mayonnaise, using beer as a setting agent, and rolling their hair on jumbo orange-juice cans. To keep the hairdos in place between trips to the beauty parlor, they sleep on satin pillowcases (which also reduce facial wrinkles), wrap their hair in yards of toilet tissue, and then secure it with a pair of men's Jockey shorts, worn upside down.

Sometimes Big Hair makes for big problems, too. A Vietnamese-born biochemist confirmed what has often been suspected about women with Big Hair—it might serve as a deterrent to intimacy. "When

Hey, Good-Lookin'

Charlayne's West Texas Rodeo Sheet Cake

Honky-tonk women often express pity for fashion models because they look more like prepubescent boys than real women. Eating fats, they say, not only rounds out a woman's finer points, but also leads to glowing hair and skin. "When you gain a few pounds," says Charlayne, "your woman parts just get bigger. I mean, you don't gain weight in your *feet*."

Cake:

2 cups Swans Down cake flour
2 cups sugar
½ stick oleo
1 cup butter-flavored Crisco
3½ tablespoons Hershey's cocoa powder
1 cup Coca-Cola
2 large eggs, beaten
1 teaspoon baking soda
½ cup buttermilk, or 1 teaspoon vinegar mixed with ½ cup plain milk
Pinch of salt , pinch of cinnamon
1 teaspoon vanilla extract

1. Preheat oven to 400°.
2. Grease and flour a 12½ × 9 × 2–inch pan.
3. Sift flour and sugar.

4. Boil oleo, Crisco, cocoa, and Coca-Cola and mix into the dry ingredients.
5. Add 2 eggs and beat.
6. With mixer running at medium speed, add soda, buttermilk, salt, cinnamon, and vanilla.
7. Bake for 20 minutes.
8. Cool in pan for 30 minutes.

Icing:

½ cup butter-flavored Crisco
6 tablespoons Eagle brand condensed milk
¼ cup cocoa powder
1 pound box confectioners' sugar, sifted
2 tablespoons vanilla extract
Pinch of salt
1 cup chopped nuts
1 cup brickle pieces and/or chocolate chips

1. Put Crisco, milk, and cocoa in a pot and bring to a boil.
2. Pour into a mixer with box of confectioners' sugar, vanilla, salt, and nuts.
3. Spread on cake and top with brickle and/or chocolate chips. Charlayne uses the topping to spell out the cattle brand of her current cowboyfriend.
4. Cover with foil and chill in the refrigerator for 2 hours. Cake freezes well.

Makes 40 cake squares

I first came to America and saw redneck ladies with lots of hair," he recalled, "I thought they must be very wealthy. You know, like Marie Antoinette, Elizabeth Taylor, and Ivana Trump. They had a certain grace about them. Then I fell in love with this girl down in Atlanta. When I kissed her, she'd get very cross if I touched her hair. Some American girls don't want you to touch anything from their neck down. Not girls with Big Hair.

"One time when she was asleep, I touched her hair. It felt like a shellacked Brillo pad. It smelled worse. Like a model airplane. I guess Big Hair is better from a distance."

"My Long Hair Don't
Cover Up My Redneck"

—*Song by David Allan Coe,*
outlaw biker and country musician

First century B.C. *historian Diodorus Siculus (Historical Library, book 5) noted: "The [male] Gauls are tall with moist white flesh; their hair is not only naturally blond, but they also make artificial efforts to lighten its color by washing it frequently in lime water. They pull it back from the top of the head to the nape of the neck, drying it into stiff spikes. . . . It was capable of impaling apples." Diodorus also commented that most Celtic men possessed lavish, drooping mustaches, through which "drink passes, as it would through a sort of strainer."*

As important as hair is to women, it's an equally crucial element of style for redneck men. Taylor Hackford, director of films about the working-

"Bein' from the country, I know what it's like: you dress square. But your hair is your glamour. Nowadays I still do my own hair," said Chris Owens, the legendary Bourbon Street entertainer, of her childhood in Stamford, Texas. "Proper maintenance of Big Hair is really important to a woman. In that dry sun sometimes it'll just break off, it gets so brittle."
FROM THE COLLECTION OF
CHRIS OWENS.

Hey, Good-Lookin'

class culture he was raised in (*Dolores Claiborne* and *An Officer and a Gentleman*), shared some of his thoughts on hair. "Redneck culture was always extremely hair conscious. It reached the high-water mark when Elvis stood up on stage waving that greased-up pompadour around, hollering, 'I am who I am, and I'm hotter than a firecracker.'"

However, the King's carefully coiffed do is not the real symbol of redneck masculinity. The contemporary preferred style leans toward the hairy antiestablishment look. *Radelle,* a third-grade teacher from West Virginia, took a long drag on her Virginia Slim and expelled her opinions along with a tornado of smoke. "To me, guys with short hair look like accountants. I prefer a man to look like a buffalo—big, strong, and with a good head of hair on him. You know, a frontiersman, like Bosephus [Hank Williams Jr.], looks sexier than a man who gets his hair styled at a beauty parlor and all."

One reason redneck men sport their long, untamed locks is suggested by Philip Carter, the son of Hodding Carter and a former *Newsweek* bureau chief who grew up in the Mississippi Delta. He bases his opinion on years as a chronicler of rednecks. "Maybe it's subliminal, but if you see a redneck guy on a tractor, there isn't much that would distinguish his appearance from that of the average Confederate volunteer in the 1860s. They're just boys off the farm who get a haircut once a year. They don't have to worry about shaving if they grow a beard. When it's cold, all that hair keeps you warmer. It also lets the world know a woman doesn't dress you, and you don't do an establishment-type job."

But redneck men haven't always had long hair. Pride in the military victory of World War II prompted a whole generation to replace shaggy antiestablishment hair with snappy buzz cuts. Filmmaker Taylor Hackford points out that hair remained a signal of values—or lack there-

"Cheyenne Bodie" at the Mountain Man Rendezvous in Colorado in his homemade frontier finery. STEPHEN COLLECTOR.

Hey, Good-Lookin'

of—to rednecks: "In the final scene of the 1969 film *Easy Rider* two long-haired bikers, played by Dennis Hopper and Peter Fonda, are traveling through the rural South. A redneck in a pickup shoots the bikers for no apparent reason. Unless, perhaps, they're killed because of their long hair.

"But a few years later, the hippies—who'd looked down on all rednecks as low-class greasers—were sporting long hair as their symbol of rebellion. By the seventies, this whole hair dichotomy disappeared. Rednecks like the Allman Brothers, Lynyrd Skynyrd, Leon Russell, and Willie Nelson were sporting very long hair. And nobody was shooting *them* from pickup trucks!"

RHINESTONE COWBOYS

Redneck men choose clothes that range from well-worn Wranglers and black leather motorcycle jackets to rhinestone-studded blazers. And although they don't like to admit it, redneck men are to American style what Coco Chanel is to French fashion.

Tuff, a pipeline engineer eating macaroni and cheese at a diner in Louisville, Kentucky, pondered the redneck male's idea of vogue. "Redneck style . . . that's kinda a mind flogger. I gotta admit, some of my buddies sure get theirselves done up in some geegaw duds. Shit, my buddy Otis looks like a downtown Christmas tree. And he smells like a Honolulu whorehouse. And Elvis wore eye shadow at the Opry in the 1950s. But don't you go mistakin' one of us for Liberace or that priss puss Fabio," Tuff warned as he massaged his hubcap-sized belt buckle embossed with an eagle in flight.

Most redneck men tend to make classic, traditional, and practical choices when it comes to clothes. As country singer Charlie Daniels points out, bib overalls work as well on the golf course as they do on a tractor, and black leather jackets are as efficient in a bass boat as on a Harley. But today, many of those elements of redneck style have been appropriated by those who promote "the Western look"—designers such as Ralph Lauren and Calvin Klein. And that fact prompted advice from many cowboys, bikers, farmers, and country singers. Or in the words of Lionel Bevan, "Don't squat with your spurs on, buddy!"

"Hud," a veterinary supply salesman and rodeo fixture, is typical of many white-collar rednecks—his uniform is starched Wranglers and a starched shirt. For special occasions, he isn't shy about donning glittering regalia.
SUE ROSOFF.

Hey, Good-Lookin'

COWBOY BOOTS

Miki de Jean, a Nashville radio producer, recounted the first time she met up-and-coming country star Clinton Gregory. "I complimented him on his red patent-leather cowboy boots. He said, 'Thank you, ma'am, they match my neck.' "

The design of the cowboy boot did not happen by accident. "It evolved," in the words of a spokesman for Acme boots, "as a matter of necessity.

"The softest boots are of elk skin or deer. Ostrich and alligator are pure show dog and thus the most expensive. Snake is the hottest seller in the blue-collar market."

KATHY RICHARD

* Toes of boots are pointed so that the cowboy gets an easy grip on the stirrup.
* The heels are high (at least $1^3/_8$ inches) to make sure the foot doesn't slip through the stirrup. They're also tapered in, for better support.
* Leather helps protect the rider's leg, but allows him to feel the movements of the horse.
* The high leg shaft protects the cowboy from wire and brush burns and from getting chafed by rubbing up against the wet horse.
* Overstitching reinforces the leather.
* The back **V** was developed so that when the cowboy's out mending fences, he doesn't get a blister on the back of his leg.

COWBOY HATS

"If you see two guys working and one has a cowboy hat and the other doesn't, the guy in the cowboy hat can do about one-third more work, since he's protected from the elements," claims famed bronc rider Buddy Simmons. "The different hat styles came from the East and West." In the Old West, a broad-brimmed Stetson could serve as a portable tent to keep the sun out of a cowboy's eyes, as a bowl to carry drinking water, as a fan to swat away horseflies, and even as a decorous covering for his face when he died.

"To this day, each job on the range has its appropriate hat," said Simmons. He explained how every region still uses a hat to provide as much information as a truck driver's "gimme" cap (given away to advertise products such as tractors, gasoline, chewing tobacco, etc.) "The Garth Brooks and the Wynonna Judd hats are working musicians' hats. They were just created to camouflage a lot of microphone wires," he warned. "But out on the rodeo circuit, the bull rider's crease is not something a non–bull rider ought to wear around cowboys. Unless, of course, he plans to hop on a bull."

SUE ROSOFF

Hey, Good-Lookin'

—T-shirt spotted at a rodeo in New Jersey

When the Celts were not going into battle naked, Diodorus Siculus reported, "they wear amazing clothes: tunics dyed in every color and tight trousers that they call Gracae [breeches]."

If Marty Stuart's butt ain't music to your ears, honey, you ain't listenin'.

—Bernice Turner

Manuel, the dashing Nashville-based costume designer for Elvis Presley, Clint Eastwood, and new-generation country music dandies Marty Stuart and Dwight Yoakam, credits the range-riding cowboy with setting the standards for style. "People used to look at Roy Rogers and Gene Autry as hicks on horses. Now those guys are in their eighties. When they make personal appearances they're sharper than a mosquito's toenail."

Manuel points out that it's the rednecks who lived out in the boondocks who created American style. He credits this distinction to their fantasies of flamboyance. Manuel has decided, "It's not money that gives the redneck style. It's the attitude! They're like galaxies making thunder."

"Hawkeye's" curriculum vitae.
SUE ROSOFF.

To crease or not to crease has long been a question answered only by regional tradition. In the South, the mothers of working-class boys have been known to iron a sharp crease into their sons' denims, just to make certain nobody mistakes their boys for white trash. Some moms who don't have electric clothes dryers or the time to iron school clothes, buy wire forms that stretch their boys' sun-dried jeans and guarantee a crisp, scratchy solar-pressed crease.

"In Arizona it was the opposite," recalled Theresa Underdown, a cowgirl and stock-car driver. "Out there, it was the cowboys who wore creased jeans. The town kids wore their jeans right out of the dryer."

Freckles, a cowboy from Guthrie, Oklahoma, speaks for many rednecks who are livid about having their style appropriated by Seventh Avenue. His words rumble from a jaw that looks like it could grind corn. "Shiiiit, jeans ain't nothin' but work clothes. It's getting harder and harder for people like me to get 'em for less than twenty bucks a pair. This company in New York City actually pays fifteen dollars for jeans we broke in—wore out is more like it. The buyer gets a certificate telling how the jeans got the rips. Hell, you got to be dumber and lazier than a buckworm to pay extra to get someone to break in your clothes."

Freckles also complains about boots. "It used to be you got a good pair of boots for twenty dollars," he lamented. "Then some asshole makes a couple of movies and overnight his boots cost one hundred fifty dollars. I need boots to work. I don't spend that kind of money for somethin' that's going to end up in cow shit."

BE CRACK CONSCIOUS, IT COULD SAVE YOUR ASS

— Sign posted at a construction site in a Park Avenue penthouse

They [the Celts] try not to become stout and fat-bellied, and any young man who exceeds the standard length of girdle is fined.

—Strabo, Geography, book 4, c. A.D. 17

There is one element of redneck style that is decidedly not emulated by Calvin Klein and the Gap: the butt crack. This particularly bold fashion statement seems to be unique to the culture.

Rednecks have relaxed their standards of physicality since the time of their ancient forebears and are no longer fined for their bulging bellies. Today, the trousers are simply lowered to accommodate the development.

Giselle, girlfriend of a construction worker, lamented her man's crack problem. "My G.T. swears he wears the same size shorts he did in the marines. Sure . . . he just pulls the waist down around his crotch, hides his gut under a tool belt, and moons the world!"

Another woman in South Carolina explained the origins of her husband's physique—a massive orb of a belly held so high and hard it poked from beneath his gaping shirttail. "Came home from Vietnam lookin' like that." She gestured with her cigarette. "Some guys came home a little sideways. Not my Earl. He jus' grinned, 'I figured the best way to protect my good tool was under a big ole shed!'"

SUE ROSOFF

Hey, Good-Lookin'

—Tattoo that stands for twelve jurors, one judge, and half a chance

Big Hair may lose its poufiness. Jeans that fit as tight as the skin on a grape may rip and fade. And at the end of the day a cowboy's hat and boots will always come off. But there is one element of style that stays with the redneck forever: the tattoo. There are some historians who credit the tattoos of the Celts for motivating the Romans to build Hadrian's Wall in the second century A.D. Their tattoos and pierced body parts were repugnant to fine Roman sensibilities.

Strike, a bearded biker/mechanic/tattoo artist with a pierced nipple, has a shop outside of L.A. filled with the dentist-office hum of tattooing instruments and the smell of burning flesh, incense, disinfectant, and sweat. He clutches his tools in his beefy fists, displaying knuckles spelling out SCREW on one hand, and TAXES on the other. As he carefully inscribes a man with several feet of barbed wire, he speaks of the beauty of branding human flesh.

"Art is a flat dead object. If it's on your body, it breathes, moves, and becomes part of your history," explains Strike. "A tat's a collaboration between the body and the artist. A good artist like me is makin' a picture of a piece of your soul for the outside world. People'll always come up and say, 'Why you got the Pink Panther on your knee?' Next thing you know you're exchangin' life stories. It's like you've made a cosmic connection."

For many rednecks, the tattoo is one of the highest levels of aesthetic statement, and some make their statements stronger than others. "There's this guy in Pennsylvania who's got more than eighty-nine hundred individual tattoos. That biker singer, David Allan Coe, has a tattoo on his body for every day of the year," Strike says as he flips his lower lip to reveal an inscription: FUCK YOU.

"There's one slick nickel we know makes his livin' with his tattoo," chuckled *Pop*, Strike's wife ("Pop" is short for "Popsicle"). "I swear to God, he had two words tattooed on his dick. He goes into bars and starts drinkin' with a bunch of good ole boys. Next thing he'll say, 'I bet you fifty bucks I got your name tattooed on my dick.' People line up with their money and driver's licenses to prove what their names are. Then he drops trou'. Sure 'nough, right on his cooter he's got the words YOUR NAME."

"Hey," she added. "Did my old man show you the tattoo on his ass? He has a *W* on each cheek. When he stands up it spells WOW and when he stands on his head it spells MOM!"

JUST CALL ME NARCISSY

Finally, nowhere is the redneck fashion statement more evident than in their names. One of the great Celtic warrioresses (70 B.C.) was called Velleda. It was the Scottish-Irish settlers in the American backcountry and on the frontiers who adapted the custom of first names as a form of adornment. One warrior clan transplanted from the English border country was the Hogg family. The family continued to thrive in the backcountry of America and eventually became one of the most prominent Texas families. So proud was the family Hogg that the daughters were named Etta and Ima.

The May 19, 1947, issue of the *Oklahoman* quoted Mrs. Hoyette White as explaining that since she looked so like her daddy, her mother made a girl's name out of his name, Hoyt. "When I named my own girls,

I wanted names no one else had, and names nobody would ever want." She conceived of Wilbarine, Arthetta, Yerdith, and Norvetta.

George Wallace's mother was called Mozell, Bob Denver *(Gilligan's Island)* married a girl from West Virginia named Dreama, and actress Jean Harlow was christened Harlean. Country singer Tanya Tucker named her daughter Presley Tanita. One contemporary mother named Linda wanted to name her first daughter after herself, but with some sizzle—and came up with Zinda. Her second daughter is called Krystal because when Linda was pregnant she craved Krystal hamburgers.

"When I was growing up in Arkansas I envied the girls who had lots of first names," recalled Missey Leigh Williams. "I've noticed girls with a string of good first names have more fun than those with two important-sounding last names with a hyphen in the middle. My favorite names were Rexa Lee Joyce Ann and Cuba Sue Mae Teese."

Redneck girls don't put their nicknames in quotes. Singer Jerry "Killer" Lee Lewis's sister, Frankie Gean Terrell, is called Killer-ette by her family. One branch of the Collier family had twin girls known as Tick and Flea. Their father is called "Hound Dawg," and their mother is Kitty-Kat.

The last *i* in a redneck girl's name is often dotted with a heart, a circle, a daisy, or a smile face, but never a peace symbol.

Beulah Pearl	Peola	Mona Louisa	Starla
Feather Faye	Dora Leen	Anita Dix	Itty
Lacey Lou	Saradoll	Ash Lee	Wee Anna
Fanci Dee	Forda	Eulah Lee	Teensie
Goo Gaw	Indy	Bushy	Bama (for "Alabama")
Patches	Chevie	Joya Fay	Dallas
Esoterecka	Nyagra	Trenda May	Tana (for "Montana")
Angel Faye	Bootsie	Terra Jean	Mercimay
Reatha May	Squeezie	Velmetta	Burma Lou
April May	Jeweldeen	Paper Doll	Frenchie Faye
June Bug	Hazeltine	Cinder	Pidge Ann
Daynelle	Chestine	Hillie	Pussie Fay
Darnell	Girleen	Dusky	Justyce
Gladiola	Covina	Shereena	Iola
Magnolia Ann	Meshell	Shine	Ayorta
Roma Fern	Tamela	Sunshine	Valdosta
Florette	Leneena	Starlette	Exstacey

CHAPTER TWO

Looking for Trouble

*All the Galatae [Celts] . . . believe in the soul's immortality,
so they have no fear of death and go out to
embrace danger.*

—Iamblichus, *Life of Pythagoras*, book 30, c. A.D. 300

Mmmm, *adrenaline! The
rednecks' favorite drug—
and we can make it our-
selves.*

—Lionel Bevan, cowboy

THERE'S A JOKE REDNECKS LIKE TO TELL THAT GOES LIKE
this: What are a redneck's last three words? "Hey, watch this!"

At a truck stop outside Atlanta, a trucker in turquoise
Wranglers filled her rig with fuel while trailing a caterpillar-
sized ash off her cigarette. When someone objected, she replied,
"It adds a little sport to my job." Her attitude is shared by most rednecks
and seems to start early—it's not uncommon to see two redneck toddlers
race each other to the top of a telephone pole. Perhaps it's in the DNA—
modern rednecks may have inherited their eagerness to battle from their
legendarily war-prone ancestors and now instinctively seek out dangerous situations to keep their skills sharpened until the next heroic episode
arises.

Work-related activities are frequently turned into sports. Rodeos
are just the tip of the iceberg. The Lumberjack World Championships are
held each July in Hayward, Wisconsin. Skagway, Alaska, is noted for its

annual festival featuring a chain-saw toss, ore-truck pull, downhill canoe race, and ugly dog contest. Beaver, Pennsylvania, hosts an annual Snow Shovel Riding Contest. In New York there's the draft-horse pull in La Fargeville and a chain-saw sculpting contest (part of the Woodsman's Days) in Tupper Lake. Sturgis, South Dakota, is the site of a Steam Threshing Bee. Kansas is the home of the National Barbed Wire Museum and a myriad of related events.

PLAYING WITH FIRE

Firemen Have Longer Hoses

—Bumper sticker and slogan on a baseball cap

Hazardous occupations can indeed provide as much excitement as a sport. "Fightin' those oil-well fires over in Kuwait was more fun than bein' a red fox in a henhouse!" mused a ruddy-faced man in a honky-tonk in Amarillo, Texas. "It was like goin' back to the Old West. We made us some memories!

"The temperature was over a hundred degrees," he told a group of rapt strangers at the bar. With bony, sun-blistered fingers he arranged a few bottles on the bar to re-create the scene. "There'd be these hot sand-storms that'd hit us at sixty miles an hour. Completely shut us down. We'd wrap two hundred to three hundred pounds of explosives that'd darn near blow the tin off a bulldozer. Many of them wells had ground fires the size of five football fields. Some of 'em had one-hundred-twenty-foot flames that'd darn near overrun the road.

"You shoulda saw us, a bunch of good ole boys out listenin' to Willie Nelson tapes in our Ford four-by-four trucks on them A-rab roads." He laughed. As 6 million barrels of oil flooded into the atmo-

PHOTO ON OPPOSITE PAGE BY SYNDEY BYRD.

sphere every day and scientists predicted global disaster, three American well-fighting teams from Texas—Red Adair, Boots and Coots, and Wild Well Control—were sent over to work with international teams to put out 732 blazing wells. Predictions were that it would take from two to four years to extinguish the blazes. But it seems they didn't figure in the redneck factor. . . . The Texans helped get the job done in eight months.

RUNNING WILD

At *Mudbugs,* a giant honky-tonk located in a defunct discount store, two agile bartenders compete for attention. Both bartenders can open five Dixie longnecks with one hand. They juggle them into the customers' hands without spilling a drop on the sheaf of ten- and twenty-dollar bills fanned between their fingers.

Polly, a biker, has been a day-shift bartender for ten years. She is of the opinion that most of her regulars keep coming back because they, too, like to show off. "One-upmanship is *it* at a honky-tonk," said Polly. "There'll even be propellers in the urinal. God bless 'em, guys just love to show off their aim! You know, even really old guys find things to brag about—their tomatoes and their bowel movements.

"The men in the bar constantly mouth off about politics," she continued. "When someone on TV calls Clinton a redneck, the guys go ballistic. 'Shiiiiiiiiit,' they'll say, 'the man's got him a pussy for an asshole. He don't stand up for his friends, sure 'nough don't stand up to his enemies. Can't be no redneck, no way, no how!'

"But I don't put up with nonsense," Polly asserted as she used a knife to flip the cap off a bottle of Red Wolf beer she'd snuck in under her shirt. "No sir . . . I can smell trouble a mile away. So when I see 'em

Sometimes the Celts fight duels during their feasts. Though they are always armed at these gatherings, they engage in mock combat and spar among themselves with fists; they still sometimes end up with wounds, and then, becoming angry, if bystanders do not separate them, they go on to get killed.

—Posidonius, Histories, book 23, c. 70 B.C., quoted in Athenaeus, The Deipnosophists, book 4, c. A.D. 200

Welders, farmers, and oil men
relaxing after a hard day in the bar
frequented by three generations of
their families in Boston, Louisiana.
KATHY RICHARD.

REDNECK INGENUITY: HOW TO WEAR A BASEBALL CAP

Hats become an extension of the body and value system. "I finally figured out why all the men hate to take their hats off," said Kathy Richard, a honky-tonk regular. "They all suffer from hat head. That's what happens when you wear a baseball hat so long it alters the contour of your head. Strips of hair get all mashed and mangled. But the worst is the horrible red scar on the forehead.

"Mama told me when the hat gets so dirty wearing it in public that it becomes a health-code violation, it's gotta be washed. Put it on the top shelf of the dishwasher so it keeps its shape. Then run over it with your car so it won't look new."

coiled and rattlin', I warn 'em. I tell 'em I'll call the FBI 'bout their death threats against the president and her husband! Now that cuts 'em off like a busted outboard."

J.C., one of the bartenders flipping bottles of beer, wears his thin yam-colored hair pulled back with a band cut from the ankle of a woman's flesh-colored panty hose. He claims it's competition over women that gets the men in his establishment riled up. "In your smaller honky-tonks it's a mistake to let in them types who look like they were born wearin' pink starched shirts. The first thing they do is start demandin' French wine. Before long, they're hittin' on your women. And if you knuckle-face the motherfuckers, they either sue you or try to get you to therapy."

According to J.C. and Polly, many honky-tonk patrons are endowed with an innate ability to hear someone giving them the finger. *Bart,* a trucker, proved to be a wealth of information on this phenomenon. "You know, we work hard outside. We're tougher'n steel. When you get off work on Friday you start drinkin'. I'll tell you one thing, it don't take much to provoke a tired, drunk guy to kill you.

"I used to run this ole place, Dance Land. You could just watch what'd happen when some guy bought a bottle of V.O. and six Cokes. At two A.M. the band quit. That's when fightin' started up." Bart was getting into the story, swiveling on his bar stool like a turret gunner. "Maybe one old guy'd look at another guy's old lady. Maybe her husband had cussed her out all week. Shit, that night she was Cinderella. All it took was for the other guy to say, 'Rella's lookin' good,' and that's all she wrote, Jack. It doesn't matter if a guy's wife is fat and uglier than a bowling bag. Bang! The free-for-all was off'n runnin'. A week's worth of shit got settled, and that's a fact!

"In the rough bars," he continued, jerking the bill of his cap lower to match his confidential tone, "everybody knows everybody's hat. It's how they dress every day. We'd keep the bar door open. Say a guy wanted to come in, he'd toss his hat into the bar. If it came flyin' back at him, he'd better git, fast. If the other guys in the bar wanted to see him, somebody'd go to the door and say, 'Come on, why you standin' out there like an asshole?' "

Walt Garrison, former rodeo cowboy and Dallas Cowboy, reminisced about his wild old days. "The only thing tougher than rodeo cowboys is the bars where they hang out." Walt stated. "There's this hold-'em-and-hit-'em place I used to go a long time ago called Rustler's Rest in Fort Worth. Wednesday night was the prayer meetin' night. You brought a knife and four dollars. It was all-you-could-drink beer. It's the kind of bar where they check you for a gun when you go in—and if you ain't got one, they give you one."

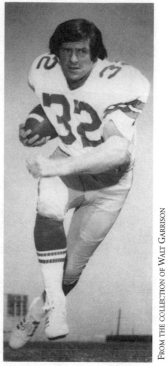

ANYTHING YOU CAN DO, I CAN DO BETTER

Not all competitions are charged by random outbursts of redneck adrenaline. Some barroom contests are organized events where proud individuals come to display a unique and often awe-inspiring skill. From beer funneling to female mud or Jell-O wrestling to midget tossing, rednecks love to flaunt their talents, challenge their opponents, and prove their superiority in their particular métier. The attraction of these seemingly humble activities is easily underestimated. Walt Garrison, offered one example.

"One night I took my teammate Charlie Waters to see this little

Tobacco-spitting contest at a state fair. SYNDEY BYRD.

four-foot eleven-inch guy named "Bear Creek." You could stack a case of beer on that guy's gut. His claim to fame was layin' on his back and spittin' tobacco twelve feet up at the ceiling. You know the whole bar turned out when the announcer said Bear Creek was gonna spit. He laid on his back and goes pah-too-wee! Splat up on the ceiling. A lot of the guys in the crowd turned their flashlights to the ceiling. They were screamin', 'There it is!' There'd be this big glob of spit. 'There it is!' You'da thought they'd struck oil, they were so excited.

Honky-Tonk Sports

If Assholes Could Fly, This Place Would Be an Airport

—Slogan on Maryland honky-tonk bartender's baseball cap

* Bear and/or oil wrestling
* Beer gut contest
* Belching contest
* Best wristwatch (involves running over the watches in the parking lot)
* Body bowling
* Buddha belly bump
* Squealing like a stuck pig
* Velcro jumping (from a running jump, sometimes with the help of a small trampoline), Velcro-encrusted contestants hurl themselves at a similarly covered wall in an effort to become affixed. The winner is either the one who sticks the highest or the one who can hit the wall with the most finesse.
* Chicken drop (the indoor version of the flossy flop). A contest involving live animals with a floor marked off in a checkerboard. Participants bet upon which square the animal will choose to leave a deposit.
* Chicken-(Live) throwing contest
* Frozen turkey and beer bottle bowling
* Hog's breath contest
* Mechanical-bull riding (sanitized version of oil-derrick riding)
* Metal-folding-chair sling
* Nickel (Contestants bet whose nickel a fly will land on.)
* Porno video Academy Awards
* Ugly tongue contest
* Top dog (involves measuring the male member)

"Charlie couldn't believe it. He told me, 'They didn't cheer that loud when I ran interception for a touchdown in the Redskins game.' "

UN-HEALTHY COMPETITION

Warning: Hassling Me about My Smoking Will Be Hazardous to Your Health

—T-shirt and bumper sticker

Bear Creek's amazing spitting spectacular is just one example of a competitive tobacco trick. Big companies host numerous tobacco-spitting contests and also sponsor rodeos and bass tournaments to appeal to their redneck patrons. Chewing tobacco is a long-lived redneck pastime, originally passed on to the first white settlers by the Indians. Today, Copenhagen, which has been around since 1822, holds the distinction of being the world's oldest consumer product.

Oral tobacco accounts for about 10 percent of the tobacco market. Despite the health warnings, it continues to be a redneck favorite, especially convenient for a farmer who might accidentally burn his barn down with a cigarette or a factory worker who doesn't have his hands free. But perhaps the real reason rednecks continue to chew is that this hazardous substance supplies them with yet another way to duel with the Grim Reaper.

Walt Garrison is a longtime chewer; indeed U.S. Tobacco signed this former Dallas Cowboy star and professional bulldogger (steer wrestler) to be their spokesman.

Garrison is the first to admit chewing tobacco is not for the weak. "Back in my pro ball–playing days I tried to get my teammate Roger

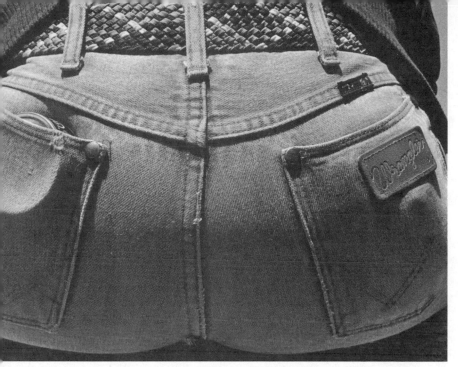

Most cowboys' wardrobes are made up of three pairs of Wranglers: a regular pair in their accurate size, a riding pair in a size larger, and a bar pair in a size smaller. The unmistakable ring of a Copenhagen/Skoal can in the back pocket often causes the pocket to be the first part of the bar or regular pair to wear out.
SUE ROSOFF.

Staubach to try snuff. It didn't occur to me to tell him to spit it out," Walt said slyly. "Well, Roger swallows it! He got so sick his hair began to sweat. Had to run out of the team meetin'. I swear he puked his guts out into the rosebushes. Poor guy, missed two days of practice."

Iler, a former Southern belle, thought snuff dipping looked so cool she used to practice her spitting by mixing up a sweet goo of cocoa and sugar. When her grandmother caught her, she was whipped for acting like a "redneck." The experience actually broke her desire to chew, but led her to a lifelong habit of smoking unfiltered Picayunes and embracing other redneck pastimes at every opportunity.

Missey Leigh was every inch a little lady during the week, but on the weekends she became a consummate tobacco spitter.

Missey Leigh Williams, a former Future Farmers of America Sweetheart, has a special affinity for chewing tobacco. "My childhood summers were spent in Booneville, Arkansas. You might say that's where I did my redneck apprenticeship. Each Saturday, my cousins and I went into town to see a matinee at Miz Fern and Mr. Eunice Savage's picture show. We'd take our cap guns to shoot up the bad guys, along with Hopalong Cassidy or Tom Mix.

"Uncle Berry, the town bootlegger from up in the hills beyond Golden City, was always sittin' on the curb," Missey said. "His rig had big rubber truck tires, so it was pretty slick. Everybody knew he rode into town on Saturdays to deposit his bootleg money. He'd be jus' showin' off his spittin' and watchin' his mule team.

"Every Saturday, I went over and sat right down next to him. I don't remember if I said much of anything. Uncle Berry looked kinda like God or Santa Claus. His long white beard covered the top of his overalls and all. I just watched him chewin' his tobacco. He'd pull plugs of Bull of the Woods out of the pouch. This delicious-smelling brown juice dripped from his mouth into his wrinkles and his beard. He'd move his bottom lip slowly. He sorta got a rhythm goin'. The Bull of the Woods worked back and forth while he told me some sort of old-man tale. Then, right in midsentence, Uncle Berry would stop, purse his lips, and spit all the way across the street. He'd hit whatever speck he aimed at fifty feet away dead-on.

"It took weeks of my imitating him with a Tootsie Roll before he took pity on me. Finally he shared some Bull of the Woods. Of course, I practiced hard every Saturday. I still dripped juice all over my nice cotton shirts. But try as I may, my record is still seventeen feet," she conceded.

ACID RAIN BURNS MY BASS

—Bumper sticker

Even fishing, an activity generally associated with peace and quiet, patience, and the serenity of the great outdoors, gains a competitive edge when rednecks pick up their fishing poles.

It all begins with the equipment. "Just ogling the equipment at fishin' and boatin' shows is almost as fun as the actual ripping the face off the bass," said Matthew Johnson, the producer of Fat Possum Records (a gut-bucket blues label based in Oxford, Mississippi) and a self-described aspiring redneck millionaire. Matthew swigged an early-morning Turbo Dog while straddling the fin of his vintage Cadillac. "The noble bass virtually demands that you buy outlandishly expensive equipment. The redneck's dream boat is a red-and-silver low-riding Bass-Master boat with a one-hundred-and-fifty-horsepower engine. Or there's that Ranger boat from Arkansas . . . starts at 'bout thirteen thousand dollars and goes as high as thirty thousand dollars for one fully tricked out with a trolling motor, a fish locator, and a depth sounder."

Once the equipment is taken care of, the fish itself becomes a competitive item. "The largemouth bass is the Lincoln Continental of redneck fishery," said Matthew. "There are big-money bass tournaments everywhere. Merle Haggard used to host a tournament in California. But, you know, the Cadillac of the workingman's tournaments is the one sponsored by Red Man chewin' tobacco. It attracts over twenty thousand eager bassers. All of 'em goin' for that one-hundred-thousand-dollar purse. To win, you gotta use expert judgment. Especially about things such as travelin' speed, distance, and all.

"It's hard to say what a world-record bass is worth today," he theorized, scratching his head with the neck of his beer bottle. "These days, catchin' the right bass'd easily be worth two million dollars, maybe seven, depending on how much a guy knows about marketing his fish. That's why redneck fishermen'll wake up early on the weekends to watch *Bassmasters* and *In-Fisherman* on TV. It's why we study *Bass*, the official publication of the Bass Anglers Sportsman's Society."

Expert Fishermen Are Master Baiters

—Bumper sticker

One of Matthew's buddies, a former Florida game warden called *Whitey*, spoke of a more adventurous form of fishing, known as grabblin' or noodlin'. "Lotsa us rednecks like it. It means you get to mix huntin' and fishin', " began Whitey, a dead ringer for Abe Lincoln. "There are some big old mean fish or alligators you jus' can't catch with a rod, a stick of dynamite, or a gun. Catfish are smart. You gotta match wits with 'em. Jus' put on your hip boots and go stalkin' in real shallow water.

"You gotta look for rotten logs and holes in the bank. Once you sight a good hole, one that's in less than three feet of muddy water, stick your arm inside." Whitey illustrated the technique with elaborate gestures performed with hands as long as canoe paddles. "At this point, you're hopin' the hole don't belong to a water moccasin or a snappin' turtle. What a grabbler wants is to put his hand in the mouth of a big old cat. He yanks that fish out from down under the water and squeezes hard on its stomach. That'll paralyze it. Then jus' wrestle that big ole fish to the bank. Man, it's a lotta fun."

Arkansas bank president "Long John" Williams, (standing far left) father of tobacco-spitting Missey Leigh, was told by his doctor that he had to fish in order to relax. So fish he did, until he caught the season's limit in one afternoon. FROM THE COLLECTION OF MISSEY LEIGH WILLIAMS.

A COMPETITIVE NATURE

A little princess and her frog at the Rayne Frog Festival.
SYNDEY BYRD.

When rednecks aren't actually fishing they're enjoying one of a plethora of wildlife-related competitions such as the Toad Suck Daze, held in Conway, Arkansas, in which amphibians leap gamely over a fifty-yard course. President Clinton once paid homage to this event by wearing a Toad Suck Daze T-shirt on his morning jog.

South Carolina has its own Jumping of the Bull Frogs on the Saturday before Easter in Springfield. One year the AP flashed the head-line across the wire, "Limber-Legged Strom Thurman Wins Frog Jump." Thurman, a bullfrog, came close to the sixteen-foot record. The beauty contest at this annual event crowns not only Ms. Frog Jump, but also Junior Miss Frog Jump, Ms. Tadpole, and Ms. Mini Tadpole.

California hosts the famed Horned Toad Derby in Coalinga, the Worm Races in Clearlake, and the Yellow Banana Slug Races in Orick. Texas presents the annual East Texas Fire Ant Festival in Marshall. Ocean City, New Jersey, is the home of the Miss Crustacean U.S.A. pageant and, in August, the World Championship Hermit Tree Crab Race.

In Ripley, Ohio, cow-chip throwing is one of the most popular activities during the annual Tobacco Worm Races. The World Cow Chip Throwing Championships are held each spring in Beaver, Oklahoma. In Alaska, the Talkeetna Moose Dropping Festival combines dropping and tossing contests with wilderness women's events; the winners get to bid on eligible bachelors.

Some of the most amazing stories of the special creativity of rednecks have to do with rattlesnakes—hunting them, harnessing them, and using them for protection, profit, food, or good honest fun.

A story from Punxsutawney, Pennsylvania, tells how in the summer of 1912 James Stener was found dead with several large rattlesnakes nearby. Their repeated bites were obviously the cause of death. According to a newspaper account, a lawman at the scene noted, "The man was swole up like biscuit dough." Mrs. Stener was unfazed by the news of her husband's demise. She told the paper, "It was bound to happen. My James was terrible jealous." Evidently he thought men would come courting her in his absence. Not only had he forbidden his wife to leave the house for the previous five years, but he'd booby-trapped the footbridge leading to their remote cabin. Instead of a watchdog, however, he'd employed a tried-and-true redneck method: he'd tethered a pack of rattlers to the base of the bridge with leather thongs. "He was bad to drink, and he come home drunk now and then," said Mrs. Stener, shaking her head. "I guess he fell into his own trap."

Dr. Deborah Adcock revealed she paid part of her medical school tuition through snake hunts. These events—part country fair, part Kentucky Derby—are generally sponsored by civic groups such as the Jaycees and embraced with gusto by the entire community. A marquee in front of a Baptist church in Texas advertised vacation bible school and then wished success to those competing in the local rattlesnake roundup.

The charities sell the live rattlers to skinners, the venom to pharmaceutical suppliers, and the meat (which tastes like a cross between catfish and chicken and is served fried) to food brokers. The viper roundup festivities

Tony and Carolyn in their Florida reptile garden with their prized, 13-foot, 100-pound Burmese python. Tony is a professional snake catcher who specializes in ridding homes of reptiles. SYNDEY BYRD.

include beauty contests, greased pole climbs, snake races, snake daredevil acts, country music and dancing contests, and prayer services. Several of the most popular rattlesnake hunts take place in Whigham and Claxton, Georgia; Opp, Alabama; and in Texas at Big Spring, Sweetwater, and Freer.

At just such an event, three devotees of snake hunting, *C.C.* and his brothers *T.C.* and *R.C.*, wore matching homemade black rubber

sandals the size of tractor tires. They sat on the back of a man-made lake rimmed with artificial sand, eyeing a tethered cigarette boat that shimmered offshore. "You know, rattlers are a lot like us rednecks," T.C. later mused. "I guess we pretty much like to stay to ourselves. Hell, we don't hurt nobody 'less we're cornered, then, shit, no mercy!" But R.C. and his brothers admitted they rarely hunt anything but snakes anymore: "I guess it's more of a fair contest with the animal and all. And it's damn near the only form of *legal* huntin' you can make money doin'."

While the price for western and eastern diamondback rattlers fluctuates like the gold market, it is not a good idea to hoard snakes in hopes of getting a better price. The prices vary from \$4.50 to \$6 a pound, to a flat rate of $25 to $40 for uninjured snakes more than three feet long. A large cash bonus is paid to the winner and to the one with the longest and heaviest snake.

The brothers recommended the following supplies for a snake hunt:

* Protective leggings (similar to those worn by a baseball catcher)
* A five iron or snake catcher (a 4-foot-long pole with a tension gripper on the end) for clubbing purposes
* A sturdy snake carrier—a wooden box or a converted truck oil filter covered with a small-gauge wire screen
* A snakebite kit
* A valid hunting license
* A white pillowcase, which can be tied to your belt, to hold the snakes. (Vipers can't see white. Beware: Burlap is dangerous, as a snake's fangs can penetrate it as easily as flesh.)

DON'T HIT ME NO MORE, MISTER, I'M DYIN' AS FAST AS I CAN

—Cowboy expression

In addition to their simplicity and exuberance the Gauls [Celts] have a propensity for empty-headed boasting and have a passion for personal adornment. . . . Their vanity therefore makes them unbearable in victory, while defeat plunges them into deepest despair.

— Strabo, *Geography*, book 4, c. A.D. 17

Rednecks seem to prefer the raw excitement of straightforward, hard-core, one-on-one competitions. But for sheer flamboyance, nothing can match the combination of bar fight, morality play, and choreographed ballet found in professional wrestling. As a bus driver commented, "Wrestling is as exciting as *Monday Night Football*, but shorter." Devotees of this sport are said to have included some distinguished company, notably writers Eudora Welty and Walker Percy, and Miz

Lillian, mother of former President Carter.

The individual wrestlers are as colorful as the event itself. The heaviest American pro-wrestler was Happy Humphrey, William J. Cobb of Macon, Georgia, who was all the rage in the 1950s and weighed 802 pounds. "Dr. D" Shults quit the sport to be a .38-caliber-revolver-carrying bail enforcement officer, the redneck term for "bounty hunter." Other wrestlers quit to serve God. Gorgeous George, the Hulk Hogan of the 1950s, is now a Fundamentalist preacher wrestling with a greater enemy. Still others wrestle on for years. Lou Threfz won his first six titles in 1937 and was still winning international matches in 1992.

Bill Mikulewicz, a gentle giant of a man, is an off-Broadway set designer who creates the elaborate sets for televised wrestling extravaganzas. A New York liberal, he thought he knew all about racism in the South. "I was once in Jackson, Mississippi, and went to a wrestling show in a small armory. This was in the late 1970s. The black professional wrestler, J.Y.D. [Junk Yard Dog], was still wrestling for the Crockett group. 'The Dawg' was up against a white opponent. This was the title match of the evening. They must've drawn out the action for half an hour. Sweat and teeth were flying twelve feet in the air. The crowd was in a frenzy. You know, when 'The Dawg' won, I knew a race riot was going to erupt. That was until I turned around. There was a black guy and a white guy, both in bib overalls. So, they throw their arms around each other and start dancing in circles. I thought to myself, 'My God, is this Jackson, Mississippi?' "

Watching professional wrestling on TV might be entertaining, but to get the full thrill of the sport, one must experience a live match. One popular arena (until 1994, when it became a temporary casino) was the Municipal Auditorium, the same stately venue where the old society of New Orleans once

"It's *far better to be pissed off than to be pissed on.*"

—Redneck aphorism

held its exclusive Mardi Gras balls. The ringside seats were eight feet from the ring behind a well-guarded police barricade, but still close enough so that a few droplets of sweat could fly into the onlookers' faces.

At one tournament, a large family sat in the front row. By the looks of them—the father and sons in their open-collared white shirts and Sansabelt dress pants, the mother and her daughters with elaborate hairdos atop unpainted faces, the hampers of home-fried chicken at their feet—they could have been Pentecostals going to an afternoon

Redneck Ingenuity: What's in the Purse

The redneck woman's purse is part office, part workshop, part diner, and part beauty shop. To be ready for any eventuality, many redneck women advise carrying the following items:

* Combination brag book, with lots of wallet-sized photos of babies and girls in prom dresses, address book, and appointment book
* Autographed program from a country music concert, protected in a Zip-Loc bag
* Zippo lighter in a case containing a photo of the man in her life
* Needle, assorted minispools of thread, and fold-up scissors
* Miniscrewdriver set
* Plastic rain hat and a collapsible umbrella
* Pouch with Band-Aids and packets of disinfectant
* Several packets of Goody's headache powder
* Two or three premoistened towelettes
* Plastic double caddy for tampons
* Packet of Planters peanuts
* Stick of beef jerky
* Toothpicks
* Tube of 5-Second nail glue
* Tube of Erase
* Imitation-Giorgio atomizer
* Small can of firm-hold hairspray
* Rat-tail comb for emergency hair poufing
* Combination pocket knife/bottle-and-can opener
* A mini-Bible or a copy of *Our Daily Bread*
* Wallet with a mace canister and a personal alarm built in
* Lady Smith revolver

At redneck sporting events, the line to get the tortilla chips submerged in yellow cheese dip is longer than the one for the bathroom. In fact, when you ask redneck kids about their favorite home-cooked foods, almost all of them contain some form of Velveeta.

Erleen's Velveeta Stomp Appeteasers

1 loaf Bunny bread or other soft white bread
½ cup oleo, melted
½ pound Velveeta slices (peanut butter may be substituted)

1. Preheat oven to 350°.
2. Remove crusts from bread.
3. Flatten bread by rolling with a mayonnaise jar.
4. Lightly brush on both sides with oleo.
5. Top with Velveeta slices (or spread with peanut butter).
6. Roll slices around cheese.
7. Arrange slices on cookie sheet about 2 inches apart.
8. Bake for 10 minutes, or until brown.

Makes 3 to 4 dozen hors d'oeuvres

Sandi's VV Casserole

2 4-ounce cans Vienna sausage
3 large eggs, beaten
1 1-pound can cream-style corn
1 12-ounce can evaporated milk
1 teaspoon salt
¼ teaspoon pepper
Slices of Velveeta to cover casserole

1. Preheat oven to 350°.
2. Cut the Viennas into ¹/₄-inch-thick slices.
3. Mix about two-thirds of the sausage slices with everything else and pour it all into a shallow 1¹/₂-quart casserole.
4. Put casserole in pan of hot water and bake for 40 to 50 minutes, or until a knife inserted into center of casserole comes out clean.
5. Arrange remaining Vienna sausage and Velveeta slices attractively over top and bake for another 10 minutes.

Serves 6

Taffi's Six Pounds of Velveeta Fudge

1 pound Velveeta
1 pound oleo
4 boxes confectioners' sugar (4 pounds)
1 cup cocoa powder (optional)
2 teaspoons vanilla extract
4 cups chopped nuts and/or whole mini-marshmallows

1. Melt cheese and oleo together in the microwave or over low heat on the stove.
2. Sift sugar and cocoa (optional).
3. Stir sugar and cocoa into the cheese mixture. Add the vanilla, nuts, and/or marshmallows.
4. Pour into two rectangular 9 × 13-inch pans lined with greased wax paper.
5. Refrigerate overnight.

Makes 6 pounds or 3 to 4 dozen squares

baptism. The oldest daughter clutched an armful of roses, each wrapped in its own colored-tissue nest. When an elderly black couple sitting behind the family complimented her on the flowers, she told them she'd saved her allowance for a month to pay for them. As she spoke, she divided the flowers into three half dozens, each wrapped and separated by color code. "The red tissue is for Sting. The blue is for Elegante. The orange is for Johnny B. Badd," she told them proudly.

The national anthem crackled from the sound system and the front-row family was the first to its feet. In the auditorium there was a low rumbling, out of which arose the voice of the blond tuxedo-clad announcer: "Ladies and gentlemen, the first match of the evening: Ricky Morton versus Johnny B. Badd."

The daughter readied her orange-wrapped bouquet. Each parent grabbed a younger child by the shoulder, pulling them up onto their feet. The rumble in the auditorium swelled to a roar. The eight of them raised their fists and began chanting: "Rick-y sucks! Rick-y sucks!"

Johnny B. Badd made an unlikely good guy with his headful of long black tendrils and a penciled-in mustache. His caramel-colored body had been waxed hairless. Badd exemplified that homegrown, pelvic-grinding arrogance that Elvis employed to incite girls to squeal the enamel off their fingernails. B-A-D-D was spelled vertically on the back of each of his black vinyl boots in bold hot-pink paste-on letters. A pair of pink lips leered from the seat of his gold spandex bikini pants, which he topped off with a red ribbon–fringed G-string. He had pulled a dozen frilly crayon-colored garters onto each thigh.

In contrast, Ricky Morton was a stringy-haired bottle blond with the attitude of a convenience-store robber. Badd surprised his opponent with a modified "DDT," and then dazed him with an "Irish whip." Johnny B. Badd had his foe pinned on the mat. As he tugged at Morton's fleshy white arm, the family in the front row chanted, "Break it, break it!"

However, this was to be Ricky Morton's night. He slammed Johnny into the mat a few times and clotheslined him to the ropes. Johnny staggered across the ring, his ribbons hanging flaccid, his garters drooping, as the referee jerked Morton's right arm up into the spotlight.

In the front row, the youngest of the three boys burst into tears. "But Ricky sucks! Ricky sucks!" he cried. His mother broadsided him with her program. Then she grabbed a pastel pink tissue out of her capacious brown vinyl shoulder bag to dab at the boy's face, as she admonished him, "Young man, you watch what you're sayin'. That little varmint won fur and square. Sting's gonna be out here in a minute. What's gonna happen when he sees you blubberin'?"

COME AND GIT IT

Women can compete, too. Some honky-tonks even host contests in which women can make up to five hundred dollars exhibiting the womanly art of orgasm faking.

Bourbon Street was shrouded in mist after midnight on a cold Sunday. The artificial smoke concealing the courtyard of the bar from the street finally cleared, revealing a Macy's Thanksgiving Day parade–sized crowd. Inside there were men and women who, on an average workday, looked to be secretaries, nurses, teachers, and lots and lots of union auto workers in town for the Saints–Bears game.

At the stroke of one, Meg Ryan's face, moaning through the fake-orgasm scene of *When Harry Met Sally*, burst forth from dozens of chicken-wire-sheathed televisions located above the cavernous dance floor. The scene held the crowd's attention for less than a minute. There was an edgy commotion. They began to boo at Meg as they hurled Dixie-beer cans at the screens.

The emcee asked for male volunteers to be judges. The men who rushed the stage were instructed to drop trou'. The five guys in bikini briefs won; the rest, duly humiliated, climbed down off the stage and tried to vanish into the crowd.

Contestant number one came out wearing a pair of white fringed cowboy boots, a halter top, and hot pants. The emcee announced that she was an elementary-school teacher named *Cody.* The audience soon grew tired of her garden-variety heavy breathing and groaning. Once Cody got tuned up, her hips started to snake around, and she did give Ms. Ryan a run for her money. Unfortunately her finale was lost on a lot of the audience, who had taken a bar or bathroom break.

Angel, the second contestant, had a head full of springy yellow curls and lips the color of a baboon's posterior. She got off to a noble start—slinking onto the floor, flapping her legs as if she were doing a Jane Fonda aerobic pelvic workout. But in the middle of her writhing she passed out. After a few seconds, the emcee grabbed her by the ankles and slid her inebriated body off the stage, announcing that if she came to she could have another shot at the title.

Darlene, a housewife from Chicago, made a comment about Southern girls being passive, and the locals began to get riled. Things degenerated quickly. Bets were made. The next three or four contestants were Bears fans, and they were ruthless. Breasts were bared. In the audience, one shocked school principal wearing a powder-blue pants suit and a floral scarf commented, "I wish I had a can of Lysol spray. That'd clean up their language."

The next contestant looked as if she had stumbled out of a Junior League meeting. Since Northern women don't usually wear two-piece sleeveless sailor suits with culottes, she was assumed to be Southern. From her first maneuver with the cordless microphone, it was obvious that the audience was in the presence of a diva, a sort of groaning combination of Joan Sutherland and Magda the Snake Woman. Then she unleashed her secret weapon, her long red-as-a-turkey-neck tongue. Nimbly, it encircled the tip of the microphone. The crowd was hushed as

BIKER BABES

The *women of the Gauls are not only like men in their stature but they are a match for them in courage as well.*

—Diodorus Siculus, Historical Library, book 5, c. 50 B.C.

Jo Ann is a tugboat dock manager and a die-hard biker. "Riding a Harley with your husband is a wonderful way to keep a relationship together. I took up riding the Harley after I won the Fisherette of the Year grand prize for the four-hundred-forty-nine-pound blue marlin I landed at the Grand Isle Tarpon Rodeo. Fishing just wasn't a challenge anymore.

"When I turned forty, Dickie, my husband, gave me my own 883 Harley Sportster. Dickie put the loudest tailpipes on it so that people can hear me coming. I tied two red bandannas on the handlebars so I can be seen, too.

"One time Dickie and a bunch of longhaired wild bikers decided to push it real hard to make a straight seven-hundred-mile run from Daytona. It was so cold I put Baggies over my socks and put yellow plastic Playtex rubber gloves under my leather gloves. I couldn't take anymore by the time we got outside of Pensacola. I was about to freeze my ass off! Believe me, I'd tried my damnedest to be a good sport, since I was the only woman and I didn't want to embarrass Dickie, but I threw down my helmet and said, 'Fuck you, Dickie! Fuck Daytona! I'm going to get a motel room!' That's when the big bad bikers started cheering. Turns out they were cold, too!"

the courtyard was overcome with her slurping sounds. By the time her performance was over, the audience was spent. It took several seconds for the foot stomping and chanting to begin: "Encore, encore!"

The Junior Leaguer and one Chicago female auto worker made it to the runoff, but there was no contest. The audience knew what the judges didn't need to tell them: they had seen an orgasm virtuoso.

Jo Ann's mother insisted she join the Homemakers Club so she could meet nice ladies. Now after sixteen years, she's the vice president. "We just had a luncheon to show off the clothes we made," says Jo Ann. "I drove up on my bike, in my dog collar and the leather skirt I shortened all by myself. They loved it!" MIKI DE JEAN.

Happy Trails

First of all they [Celts] drive about in every direction hurling their javelins: the fear engendered by the horses and the din of the wheels [of their chariots] is usually enough to disorder the enemy ranks.

—Julius Caesar, *Commentaries on Gallic War*, book 4, 51 B.C.

| *Never Drive Faster Than My Guardian Angel Can Fly*

—Bumper sticker

THE TRUCK IS THE VENERATED SYMBOL OF REDNECK prowess—part office, part home, part workhorse, and part pet. And like a mythical beast, this vehicle is endowed with human characteristics, given names, and surrounded by a powerful aura. Some classic truck names include *HITCH D, BIG MS. TK, C.U.N. HVN, UP L NTE, MISTER BLASTER, DIXIE'S REVENGE,* and *BORN TO OOZE.*

Trucks are so special, in fact, that one waitress bases her relationships on them. She figured she'd met many a guy who fancied himself a ladies' man. "But I got to thinkin' about it. You know, I got more between these rattlesnake-head earrings than mascara and blue eye shadow," she said as she swirled up a cyclone in her coffee. "I realized 'bout the only permanent relationship he'd ever had was with his truck. That's why I never give a man the key to my heart, till he trusts me with the key to his truck."

A well-endowed truck can become a real emblem of redneck status. Ninety thousand dollars will get a professional trucker the ultimate cab for his big rig, complete with surround sound, sleeping quarters, and an air-cushioned ride. The independent operators can have a traveling office with cruise control, temperature-controlled air and heat, a cellular phone, a fax machine, and a portable computer. With the advent of couples trucking together, manufacturers are designing cabs with room to stand up and change clothes; some of the new cabs feature closets and a double-bed compartment behind the cab complete with a window.

Those men who drive the biggest rigs are seen as hypostatic highwaymen, loved and loathed with equal vehemence. These road warriors survey their country at high speed from the cockpits of forty-ton freight-hauling chariots. There are more than 2.5 million professional truck drivers in the United States; 93 percent of them are men. In an average year, American truckers deliver more than $225 billion worth of freight. The average trucker makes an annual gross income of $25,611. The typical trucker is a 41-year-old cigarette smoker with a wife and 1.5 kids at home. He's logged eighteen nights on the road every month for 12.2 years. During that time a guy can get lonely, so 30 percent of all truckers take their wives or girlfriends along for the ride at least once a year.

Although they are a definite minority, there are some lady truckers. "My sister and I got laid off from our jobs making GMC pickups about the same time our husbands and kids decided they'd outgrown us," explained *Blue* and her sister, *Miss Red*. "That's when we got it in our heads to go back to school to learn to drive us a twelve-ton rig. Now we're over sixty and going strong twice a month from Grand Blanc, Michigan, down to Guanajuato, Mexico, in our little home away from home called *Blu By U*. One of us crochets while the other drives. Half the

PHOTO ON OPPOSITE PAGE BY
SUE ROSOFF.

THE REAL McCOY'S RULES OF THE ROAD

Rule 1: An Ounce of Prevention

"If you pull out of a truck stop with problems, you could lose two days in a row. A haul deadline is like an appointment you've gotta keep. That's why most trucks'll have four batteries, not one. A good truck stop'll have CB repairmen, full-time mechanics, and any kind of tire you can think of, twenty-four hours a day."

Rule 2: Know Your Truck Stops

"Truckers don't like to eat a heavy meal because it will make them sleepy. Things like chicken stew look like the bottom of the swamp, without the cypress knees. To be safe, stop at the Iron Skillet Petro; coast to coast it has the best sandwiches in the world. They've got everything from a suit coat and a tie to the best prices on fuel and tires. Petro is the greatest. They can park about five hundred trucks. There's a shoe-shine parlor to get your boots cleaned and a fancy, nice motel. That Tom Bodette's Motel 6 is a joke next to this."

Rule 3: Keep a Pipeline to Cash

"Say you blow an engine—that costs eight grand to rebuild. A flat tire is four hundred dollars plus–apiece. At Petro your company can have the money there before you're even parked. ComChek's crucial and faster than Western Union. Their computer takes your secret code number and spits out the check."

Rule 4: Watch Your Weight

"Truckin' is pretty much governed by DOT, the Department of Transportation. In most states the weight limit's about eighty thousand pounds gross. You can't be over 13.6 feet high or 8 feet wide. That's with no overhang. Used to be you could have an 8-foot overhang if you'd red-flag it in the daytime. Now you can't have no overhang at all without a permit and a designated route."

Rule 5: Walk

"Every three hours on your log book you gotta show T.C.—that's tire check. You gotta hop out of the truck and beat on the tires, all of them, and make sure you ain't got a flat. Especially when you haul them explosives and flammable material. It's probably a good thing to check, because if you've got one gettin' hot, the son of a bitch will pop and catch fire. I've had it happen."

Rule 6: Nap

"The safe way to make a cross-country run is to take another driver with you. If you have a cabin, DOT says you can run ten hours or five hundred miles, whichever comes first. Then you have to take an eight-hour break. If you don't have a cabin—you know, a sleeper—you gotta produce a motel receipt when they stop you. They don't allow sleepin' on the steering wheel or on the seat."

Rule 7: Keep in Touch

"CBs're still big-time on the road. Better to have a cellular phone, though. If you listen to the *On the Road Gang*, WWL 870 AM, you're never alone out on the road, either. Say there's an emergency at home. I can be in Wyoming or New England. They'll broadcast they're lookin for The Real McCoy drivin' for Dresser Industries. They tell you over the air who's callin'."

Rule 8: Don't Miss Rush

"Rush Limbaugh is on every day from one to four. You can look in the car windows of guys on the road and tell everybody is listenin' to the guy. Like today, Rush was laughin' and beatin' on his desk, ravin' 'bout the liberals, global warming, the environmentalists, and the spotted owl. Says he wrote a special song for 'em. Then you hear a machine gun and a chain saw."

day we listen to old radio shows on tapes we buy at the Cracker Barrel. The rest of the time we plug in tapes we borrow from the library so we can learn Spanish."

Truckers view themselves as a clan—a family in which brotherhood collides with economic reality. "Out on the road truckers keep an eye on each other," stressed a trucker known as "The *Real* McCoy" (because he's been hauling hazardous materials "longer, safer, and faster" than any other trucker on the highway). "When somebody blows up at you or calls you up on the radio and says, 'You got smoke, boy,' well, you jump out of your cab with the fire extinguisher. You keep it right under the seat. But that's how it is: everybody's a brother on the road.

"I grew up in a large family—eight boys and two girls. We had ten chiggers eatin' out of one can of beans—and those were the *good* times. My uncle had a cane farm, and his two boys was off in the service, so I moved out with him when I was still a young boy to drive his farm machinery for him. I was driving them cane trucks, them tractors, and them cane loaders. I just loved to drive anything. The bigger the machine, the better."

EAT HERE/GET GAS
— Flashing sign outside a small Arkansas truck stop

For those without the means for a shiny new luxury rig furnished with all the deluxe features, there is the truck stop—a combination corporate headquarters and home away from home. Here, the trucker can pull off the road into a lot with hundreds of other metal-and-chrome stallions. Lading bills can be truckfaxed to him at his temporary truck headquarters. He can plug his credit card into a phone and sit down at a cubicle in a battered burnt-orange swivel chair to do business. Back outside, at the service island, he can borrow a telescoping squeegee to drag across the sludge on his picture-window-sized windshield. When the road conditions deteriorate he can trade war stories with brother and sister truckers over endless cups of coffee and plates of home fries and over-easy eggs or fried chicken livers and large hunks of crisp fried potatoes called potato logs.

Truck stops function like communities. Gloria grew up in a truck stop in the 1960s at the intersection of Highway 90 and Highway 11 near New Orleans, "but not close enough," she quipped. "There was a poem we read at Daddy's funeral that went somethin' like this: 'Let me live by the side of the road and be a friend to man.' Growing up in a mom-and-pop truck stop kept me humble. You know, all of humanity passed through my life.

"I had to fill in for whoever didn't make it to work. One day I'd pump diesel. The next I'd be the cook. There was a problem for the waitresses, though, because they lived and worked in an environment with horny truckers. They didn't start out as hookers. They didn't think of themselves as hookers. But I've gotta admit there were a couple Daddy put out of business."

Some of these oases are legendary, such as Jubit's, a family-owned and-operated truck stop in Portland, Oregon. Besides giving away free mud flaps to truckers, Jubit's has one of the largest honky-tonks in the Northwest—big enough to hold seven hundred. One of the Jubit family's proudest moments was when George Bush made a campaign stop there during the Reagan-Bush campaign in the 1980s.

Two of the busiest truck stops in the world are part of the Truckstops of America franchise—one in Ontario, California, and one in Gary, Indiana.

The other is a Petro in Fort Chissom, Virginia. Part mall, part industrial food court, these emporiums are so crowded they have the atmosphere of the Super Bowl. Each services more than twenty thousand big rigs a day.

According to many long-haul truckers, the Taj Mahal of truck stops is the Perlis truck stop in Cordele, Georgia, at Exit 31 on I-75, about four

---

FEED 'EM OR LOSE 'EM

—A slogan on a short-order cook's apron

Food terms overheard in truck stops:

Armored cow: Artificial milk, canned or powdered.

Breakfast of champions: A six-pack and a bar fight.

Broken arm: Leftover food.

Calf slobber: Meringue on pies.

Cape Cod turkey: Codfish.

Cowboy coffee: Throw in a horseshoe. If it sinks it's not fit to drink.

Colonel Sanders's dawn patrol: Unrecognizable meat.

Deer suicide: Venison killed out of season.

Hat rack: A skinny animal that died a natural death.

Hen fruit: Eggs.

Hunk of skunk: Mysterious meat.

Kentucky oyster: Any edible internal part of a pig.

Lawn mower: Lamb.

---

hours north of Orlando, Florida. In the mid-1980s it even had a fancy French restaurant, but as one employee put it, "It was *way* ahead of its time. They had menus the size of saloon doors, but our customers ain't sophisticated enough to spend one hundred bucks to order food they can't pronounce."

Lighthouse: Bottle of ketchup.

Nigger heads: Tri-tips, cut of meat.

Noah's boy: Canned ham products that come in an ark-shaped can.

Pig it: Slow-cooking method, such as stewing or roasting.

Pig salve: Lard.

Poodles 'n' noodles: Hamburger Helper.

Possum on the half shell: Road kill.

Red noise: Tomato soup.

Rib stickers: Beans.

Salt horse: Corned beef.

Sea gull: Canned poultry product.

Seven-course meal: A six-pack and a possum.

Smear of deer: Slur against the meat of another hunter, indicating that it was "road kilt."

Stool pigeon: A customer who sits for hours nursing one cup of coffee.

Texas turkey: Armadillo.

Tire patch: Pancake.

Yard bird: Chicken, served as meat.

TEN THINGS TO DO WITH COLA
WITHOUT ACTUALLY DRINKING IT

Coca-Cola is a popular choice for a tired driver trying to keep alert on a long haul. But in the hands of the ever-resourceful redneck, Coca-Cola is far more than a mere beverage. The marriage of Coca-Cola and redneck ingenuity has created a diverse catalog of problem-solving tips.

1. "Cola is the secret to a glowing all-over tan," claims a nurse/dancer in San Diego. "Sometimes my hands get all sunburned. If I'm going to wear a tube top, I just put on rubber gloves and soak my arms in cola. It's a little sticky, but it looks better than that old orange artificial-tan stuff from the drugstore."

2. "If you get a real bad sunburn, a bath in cola is an ideal way to soothe the pain."

3. One Oklahoma native swears that Coke is the most efficient way to remove mortar from brick.

4. "It'll clean rust off anything from the toilet to clothes," said one Texas housewife.

5. Room temperature cola splashed on Razorback Red (marijuana) while it's hung will help dry the greenery into tight knots for clean bricks.

6. Several truckers advised that Coke is invaluable for cleaning road film that accumulates on the windshield or inside the engine.

7. Many also swear that Coke poured over a car battery will neutralize the acid.

8. In many redneck homes, Coke is used in the base of Christmas trees.

9. Several capfuls in cut roses keep them fresh.

10. Some biker chicks swear that a bottle of room-temperature Coke shaken up and aimed at the proper orifice just *before sex* offers an ideal birth control and disease-prevention method.

Cooking with Coca-Cola

* In Maine, one man revealed the secret to delectable baked beans—combine the beans, molasses, fatback, vinegar, and Coca-Cola. Cover the bean pot and bury it in the embers of a fire made in a hole in the rocks.
* Pouring salted peanuts into a bottle of Coke and then sucking them out is a quick meal on the run.
* Mothers get finicky children to drink their milk by adding Coke—thus a "flat float."
* A special hot punch can be made by warming Coke or Dr Pepper, adding a tablespoon of instant coffee, and serving it in a mug with a slice of lemon.
* *K.P.* and *Lee* run barbecue booths at several small rodeos from Wyoming to West Texas. Even though the proportions are a closely guarded secret, they acknowledge their sauce contains the following ingredients: Coca-Cola, liquid smoke, vinegar, chili sauce, Worcestershire sauce, onions, garlic, and jalapeños. Lee added, "When I bake my Christmas ham, I keep a big bottle of Coke by the oven. You pour some right over the ham every fifteen minutes to create a perfect glaze."

Perlis is a massive brick full-service truck facility located on a fifty-acre site nestled in a Georgia pine forest. There's a three-bed garage for big rigs, a communications center, a bus-and-truck wash, a TV lounge, showers, a laundry, a 265-seat restaurant for truckers, and a buffet for tourists in the back. Founded in 1971 by Lamar Perlis, this spectacular place has set the standards for the truck-stop industry ever since.

One of the Perlis mechanics proudly stated, "Mr. Perlis might be a self-made millionaire many times over, he might serve on boards all over the world, but his corporate headquarters are still up there in a second-story motel room in a truck stop in south Georgia."

OLD TRUCKERS NEVER DIE, THEY GET A NEW PETERBILT

— Bumper sticker

When their vehicles are not in service, many truck owners like to show them off. At the Humboldt County Truckers' Christmas Parade, more than a hundred truckers roll through the streets of Eureka, California, with their trucks festooned for the holidays. Santa Nella, California, hosts the annual Big Truck Showdown. The Mid-America Truck Show in Louisville, West Virginia, a gathering of thirty to forty thousand truckers from all over the United States, is one of the largest rallies. Then there's the Mountain Dew eighteen-wheeler outdoor TV screen to show sports events and makeshift churches housed in eighteen-wheelers.

WHEELING AND DEALING

Probably no one knows more about cars than the old-time moonshiners. In fact, it was the marriage of the Southern Appalachian moonshiners and the American auto industry that gave birth to auto racing in this country.

An old mountain man in a rumpled John Deere cap watched his grandchildren play on the swing set outside a McDonald's in Waynesville, North Carolina. He dug into a red paper holster of French fries and the legends of the mountains. "The first thing an ATF agent looked for was a vehicle with no backseat. The whiskey runners couldn't modify a Ford like they could your Chryslers, Pontiacs, and Dodges." He pointed a strip of fried potato at similar models in the fast-food parking lot. "Whiskey haulers'd modified 'em with heavy-duty springs. Add a couple of extra carburetors and sets of shocks. You know we'd bolt in the front seats from Plymouths. Shit, them cars could be jiggered to go one hundred forty to one hundred sixty mph. Loaded. Uphill. Didn't matter.

"The finest car on the road," he said, his knowledge getting the bet-

Sheriff Noles breaking up stills on Sand Mountain in Alabama.

FROM THE COLLECTION OF STEVE NOLES.

ter of discretion. "Easy . . . a '61 Chrysler, 'cept I had to modify the sumbitch to fit the cases of whiskey in her. Three hundred seventy-five horsepower and what a torque that baby could pull. . . . Even loaded with seven hundred and fifty pounds of whiskey, it rode as businesslike as any big-shot judge's car on the way to an execution!"

"Granddaddy," the nickname he preferred to be called, leaned forward, out of earshot of a table of matronly church ladies at the adjoining table. "You lived up here in the winter and you either worked whiskey or you starved. I musta been in the sixth grade when Daddy says, 'Son, you done outgrowed them boots. If you want new ones before the snow falls, there's the Dodge and a load of malt a man wants down in Knoxville. You figure out how to drive it. Make it back safe and I'll give you fifty dollars' And, honey, that was a fortune worth quittin' school for!" He winked, a good storyteller's equivalent of popping a wheelie on a Harley.

But the Treasury men also modified their cars, and that made the liquor business dangerous. "The worst cop on the beat was Jim Malt out of China Grove. Sumbitch drove 'im a rigged-to-fly '59 Pontiac. Had him two bumpers in the front. . . . If he caught you, he'd run your hillbilly ass off the high side of the mountain. One night up on Trap Hill I catch him in my mirror. Don't you know I feel the breeze of the pearly gates openin'. Ole Malt slammed into second and floored it. I don't know whether it was Christ or Chrysler that saved us. Thank God for 'em both, is all I can say!

"Fred Johnson, Junior's brother, was the best driver ever. He quit in the 1960s to he'p Junior in his racin' bidness and at Holly Farms chicken farms. You know 'bout Junior, don't you? The king of the Daytona 500 and the czar of the American chicken industry. If you want to know the truth, the success of Johnson's Holly Farms did more to stop the illegal liquor bidness in Wilkes County than the feds."

The Hollow Men

Rednecks don't have to make moonshine anymore. Even in the dry counties that still pepper the South, the next county—with its cache of state-owned liquor stores—is never far away. Many rednecks, however, *like* making moonshine and wine.

Plenty of nice widow ladies never have to set foot in a liquor store. They continue the practice, passed from generation to generation, of making near-lethal brews from rose petals, dandelions, parsnips, marigolds, carrots, clover, or beets. In Pennsylvania, Calamity Jane is a reputed favorite—rhubarb provides the acid. In the Great Lakes region, they prefer Sneaky Pete, made from potatoes. Near-lethal 100-proof home-brew whiskey flows deep and hot in good thrifty Scots-Irish blood. In rural North and South Dakota, Red Hot is a favorite at weddings—cinnamon candy red hots are dissolved in a punch bowl full of Everclear.

Hints from the Hollow:

* Distilling works best under a full moon—mostly because it helps you keep a lookout for the ATF agents.
* Moonshining is even more fun when all the kinfolks help. Men and boys can do the heavy lifting. Girls and women can wash the jars and keep the children quiet. Older folks should bring their shotguns and watch by the side of the road.

Moonshine

(aka White Lightnin', Tiger Sweat, Swamp Root, Swipe, Monkey Rum, Bug Juice)

50 pounds sugar
25 gallons water
1 bushel cracked corn
4 ounces yeast

1. Dissolve sugar in the water. Ferment for 5 to 7 days. Lye or embalming fluid may be added to keep the brew clear.
2. While the home brew is setting, build a still. Be sure to use copper tubing. If it comes from an old refrigerator, be sure to rinse out the Freon.
3. Distill moonshine approximately 4 hours over low heat.
4. Seal in washed, recycled Mason jars.
5. Do not expect richness of flavor or a woodsy bouquet. Expect a burn—all the way down.

Makes 5 to 6 gallons

CRUISIN' FOR A BRUISIN'

The bond between man and machine makes one's vehicle a particularly vulnerable target. A burly Arkansas festival promoter has his own favorite story: "There's this poultry potentate in Arkansas who has two passions besides making money—expensive foreign sports cars and other guys' wives. One day this ole boy was driving his cement truck past the chicken king's house and he sees his wife's car parked outside of the garage. Well, he goes into a red rage and before he knows it, he's dumped a whole load of concrete into the chicken king's convertible. The weight of the cement popped off all four tires. One even went through the plate-glass window of the guy's house.

"Well, by the time the cement-truck driver got back to his head-quarters he was thinking a little clearer. He realized that not only had he not delivered the cement to the job he had been taking it to, but he also knew that he'd probably go to jail for vandalism. Being an honorable man he told his boss what he'd done. He expected the boss to fire him as he led him into his office and closed the door.

" 'Sir, I'm really sorry,' he said, 'please give me another chance so I can work to pay off the load.'

" 'Hell, man,' the boss replied, 'I'm not going to fire you. We're going to send that son of a bitch a bill for the cement. That man did the same thing with my wife back in April!' "

A curly-headed A&P checkout clerk admits to a disinclination to kowtow to the indiscretions of the man she loves. "My friends were the first ones to tell me that *Conrad* was cheatin' on me. It hurt me bad. I was pregnant with our second child; I realized no other man would want me and all. I knew there was just one thing that my husband loved more than anything,

PHOTO ON OPPOSITE PAGE BY SUE ROSOFF.

Happy Trails

and that was his Camaro. One night I got my friend, and we drove around Boston until we found the motel where he and his girlfriend were shacked up. I had a spare key to the car; I put a quahog [a raw clam] up in the springs under his front seat. The next morning he came home and spent the day ripping out the seats looking for what smelled. By the second day he still hadn't found it, but the car stunk so bad he couldn't drive it. Conrad cried like a baby when the insurance guy told him they wouldn't pay off a claim on a bad smell. He told me it was his dream car. He'd never be able to afford to replace it. All I said was, 'I understand. I know what it feels like to have your dream destroyed.' And he quit seeing that other girl."

Another case in point: A woman encountered her boyfriend's ex-wife in a crowded bathroom. The sheepish younger woman said to the formidable-looking ex-wife, "Gosh, this is really embarrassin', us runnin' into each other. *J.T.* shouldn't have brought me here to celebrate gettin' the divorce papers."

The ex-wife adroitly slapped her gold Zippo against the leg of her strawberry-colored Wranglers to offer a light for the girlfriend's cigarette. With a flick of her head she replied courteously, "Don't mention it. You can have him! And give J.T. a message for me—I wouldn't walk across the street to piss on him if his heart was on fire!"

After the girlfriend left the bathroom, the shaken ex-wife was comforted by two of her friends. One of the friends didn't show much sympathy, though. "*Eunice,* I told you, if you'da wanted J.T. back, all you had to do was fight for him. But, no, you was too proud for that. So he brought that teenager here to rub your nose in it! And what do you go and do? You act like you don't care. So, Sister, she gets J.T. and you get to cuddle up to your cold, hard pride. If I was you, I'd show him I still cared. Go out and key the bastard's car!"

"HUNKA HUNKA BURNIN' LOVE"

— Elvis song and name on "Granddaddy's" customized license
on the front of his '83 Buick Regal

If it can't be an eighteen-wheeler, it's still got to be a pickup. To a redneck, the pickup truck, not the car, seems to be the ultimate cultural icon—a piece of machinery combined with a full-sized luxury car. Trucks make up about 40 percent of U.S. vehicle sales, up from 20 percent a decade ago. Not that the vehicle must be shiny or new to be beloved. No matter what the condition, trucks are often decorated for the holidays with wreaths attached to the hood and Christmas-tree lights operated off the battery. Both Chadron, Nebraska, and Pelican Rapids, Minnesota, feature popular ugly pickup contests.

But the real competition is between Ford and Chevy trucks. To a redneck it's part sports rivalry, part blood feud, part duel. Aside from the obvious fights over women, work, and politics, the universal way to start a fight in a honky-tonk is for one man to claim his Ford or Chevy pickup is a better vehicle than another guy's of the other brand. A few beers later, there's a standoff-at-the-OK-Corral-style four-lane-highway showdown. Another version of the duel features contenders facing away from each other in their respective pickups, a Ford and a Chevy. A chain is hooked between their rear axles, and the drivers shift down into first gear. Gravel will fly, and eight truck tires will blow. In lumbering country, some opponents have been observed jumping from the disabled trucks to continue working out their differences with vibrating chain saws.

When *they [the Celtic warriors] died, these iron warriors were not cremated, but buried with their chariots, wearing all of their finery, as though bound for some further encounter in the afterlife.*

—Edward Rutherfurd,
Sarum

Happy Trails

Johnny and Kathy Richard's Dream Pickup Truck

The pickup truck is expected to fulfill a multitude of functions besides mere transportation, and rednecks often customize them to accommodate their needs.

Johnny and Kathy Richard (see photo on page 177) brainstormed on their dream vehicle, complete with several specially designed items. Johnny's priority was to build an extra-strength grille on the front of his truck like the one his buddy *Billy Ray* had. "Now I built a grille on the front of my truck made out of strong oil pipe," boasts Billy Ray. "I can push anything out of the way with it. Of course, sometimes I get stuck in traffic in my wife *Pattie's* little Honda and yell at somebody, 'Move it, buddy, or I will,' and then I remember I'm not in my truck. That's when I pull her twelve-gauge Remington shotgun out from the special pocket on the front of her seat cover. . . .

"It irritates me when I see people who don't even know which end of a cow to feed putting us guys down because they see the guns in our trucks," argues Billy Ray. "Just last week I was checking on some cows and there was a pack of wild dogs. Thank God I had a gun in the truck."

The Richards' Accessory Wish List

* A Dually with king cab and four doors
* An engine powerful enough to tow a string of double-wide mobile homes across the country
* Heavy-duty tow chain, winch, and trailer hitch

- ✱ Storage for pieces of motors from other vehicles and boats
- ✱ Day Lighters—multiply 2 × 4 × 6
- ✱ Two antennas that can double as lightning rods
- ✱ Sliding-glass back window
- ✱ Bass fish stickers
- ✱ Novelty horn that plays "Dixie" or sounds like a cow
- ✱ A battlefield-sized first-aid kit
- ✱ Mud flaps with slogans (e.g., GET OFF MY ASS) or naked women made of chrome
- ✱ Seat covers made from a saddle blanket with a pouch in the front for a rifle
- ✱ Industrial-sized Igloo water cooler
- ✱ Plastic dashboard drink caddy with four holders for spit, ammo, Big Gulp full of coffee or a soft drink, and a beer
- ✱ Mounted tool boxes with a cushion in the bed
- ✱ Bug bra with a Confederate-flag pattern to keep road-kilt insects out of the radiator
- ✱ Transparent rear-window mural, such as a deer, mountain scenes, cowboys, ducks, or a Confederate flag and an American flag

Redneck *Fuzzy Dice:* *"Two fresh tampons soaked in Lemon Pledge and hung from the rearview mirror —guaranteed to banish nasty odors in your truck."*

—Johnny Richard

TRUCKS ARE LIKE WIVES, IF SHE AIN'T YOURS, DON'T TOUCH

— *Bumper sticker "Hoot" gives the buyers of his used trucks*

At a Gulf Coast used-truck auction, *Hoot,* a stocky grandfatherly man, flashes a prodigious amount of gold and diamond jewelry. "I travel the hick circuit," he confides, in an on-the-spot intimacy.

Happy Trails

REDNECK INGENUITY:
HOOT'S TRICKS OF THE USED-CAR TRADE

* Nobody ought to buy a used vehicle from a guy who is passing through town, someone's brother-in-law, or a man whose buddies call him Speedy, Mustang, or Slick.

* Beware of the Arkansas guarantee. That means if the car breaks into a million pieces on the way home, you own all the pieces.

* Roll up the windows on a hot day and get a good whiff of the vehicle after it's been closed up for an hour. You can tell if someone died in it. You can hide that smell for only so long before it comes back to haunt you.

* A thicker motor oil will hold the engine from rattling at least for a few miles. The favorites are STP and the cheap brand Motor Honey.

* A bad transmission can be brought back to life for a few days by dousing it with brake fluid. Sawdust or oatmeal in the transmission will also dock up the engine and keep it from leaking or rattling.

* To cure a cracked block, lead pellets are put in the radiator. As they rattle around in there, they melt and seal the cracks for a short while.

* Paint looks nice and shiny in the rain, but even on a clear day the exterior can be made to look spiffy after a dousing of WD-40.

LITTO'S HUBCAP RANCH

THIS IS ONE OF CALIFORNIA'S EXCEPTIONAL TWENTIETH
CENTURY FOLK ART ENVIRONMENTS. OVER A PERIOD
OF 30 YEARS EMANUELE 'LITTO' DAMONTE (1892–1985)
WITH THE HELP OF HIS NEIGHBORS, COLLECTED MORE
THAN 2,000 HUBCAPS ALL AROUND HUBCAP RANCH
ARE CONSTRUCTIONS AND ARRANGEMENTS OF HUBCAPS
BOTTLES AND PULLTOPS WHICH PROCLAIM THAT 'LITTO
THE POPE VALLEY HUBCAP KING' WAS HERE

CALIFORNIA REGISTERED
HISTORICAL LANDMARK NO. 939

PLAQUE PLACED BY THE STATE DEPARTMENT OF PARKS AND
RECREATION IN COOPERATION WITH SPACES (SAVING AND
PRESERVING ARTS AND CULTURAL ENVIRONMENTS) A NON-PROFIT
EDUCATION CORPORATION APRIL 5 1987

*American automotive
engineering welded to American
ranch architecture earned a
historical marker for this
exhibition of redneck ingenuity.*
Sue Rosoff.

"My inspiration," Hoot explained, "was this guy in Dallas who had a used-car lot over on Ross Avenue. His slogan was 'Gene Goss, the Tradin' Hoss.' Right in front of his lot was a sign that said WE GUARANTEE OUR CARS 30 DAYS OR 30 FEET—WHICHEVER COMES FIRST. Had him these categories for the vehicles like 'Get-to-work cars,' 'Get-you-to-work-late cars,' 'Excuse-for-missing-work cars,' and 'Temporary-job cars.'

"Life dealing used trucks on the road ain't for them guys that're all hat and no cows. When the auction guys see a vehicle arrive with six guys in it, they know they're plannin' to buy five vehicles they can drive home theirselves. You better believe, God ain't made the redneck yet who'll leave his fifty-dollar investment by the highway. These guys travel with a trunk full of tools and that God-given talent rednecks have for making a motor purr until they got the buyer's cash in their back pocket.

"Way before that damn NAFTA, the Mexicans were hurting our boys on American-made pickups. When an alternator goes bad here, even a redneck will replace it. Them damn Mexicans'll rebuild it. Slick Mexican dealers and their mechanics will come over the border at McAllen [Texas], buy off a border guard, and head for a small-town auction in a place like Monroe [Louisiana]. The thing they all go for is a Ford or Chevy, 1983 to 1986, with your big tires. They outbid us, dish out cash, and by morning they've got fifteen or twenty American trucks to the border. They change out the license plates and have a bunch of Mexican women with American-born children who drive the trucks into the waiting arms of Mexican buyers. There go our American trucks, right out of our market.

"The government isn't doing a thing to he'p us. What might happen, I'm not saying it has, is a couple of Mexican boys'll be found with bullets through their heads. That's how rednecks let outsiders know they don't like to get screwed on a good truck deal."

It was redneck ingenuity that took the American pickup further than any executive in Detroit ever dreamed. The monster truck is a uniquely American passion. Bob Chandler of Hazelwood, Missouri, is now a multimillionaire as the result of his idea to use his four-wheel-drive Ford pickup for recreation. In the mid-1970s he added sixty-six-inch tires off a manure spreader, thus becoming the Thomas Edison of the monster truck. Then in 1981 he used the monster truck to crush a car. Now more than 18 million Americans a year attend monster truck spectaculars.

An employee of Dollywood lamented the passing of the combine harvesters demolition derby, the high end of the sport of crashing expensive machinery in America. "The insurance got too high. So they don't have them anymore. But the coolest thing I ever did was drive a combine in the Combine Harvester Demolition Derby over in Greenville [Illinois]. If you want to see a redneck farmer's wet dream, you go to one of those."

A NIGHT AT THE TRACTOR PULL

The American tractor has served as companion and partner to the redneck since 1918, when John Deere went into production of the two-cylinder Johnny Popper. Today the tractor serves as the farmer's office. Fancy ones are equipped with air-conditioning, color TV, and VCRs. But modern technology hasn't quelled the love affair with the old faithful two-cylinder workhorse that ceased production in 1960. Each year eighty thousand people make a pilgrimage to Waterloo, Iowa, to relive the good old days when they rode the fields on the sunbaked seat of a vintage tractor.

Ohio farmer John Hileman's Ohio Gold *is one of the winningest tractors in America. The first tractor he built was* Old Red *in 1974. It did very well. Then in 1978 he added the second engine and won the 1978 national championship. He sold it and built* Old Red II, *which he raced up until 1988, and won several national championships. When it got time to retire it, John went on a cleaning binge and cut it up so that no one would ever beat him with it.*
ANNE HILEMAN.

Even though many former farmers are city folk now, they haven't forgotten the segment of their lives when they were out in the sun imagining they were in a race with thousands of fans cheering just for them. That's probably why millions of Americans live for the thrill of the tractor pull.

Long before cars even hit the gridlock jam for the parking-lot gate, it's easy to tell which ones are headed for the tractor pull. Behind the wheels of these automobiles are men who rev their engines a lot louder. It's an ironic vision—city folk crowding into downtown stadiums to watch tractors show off. After every start and stop, the drivers, wearing their Stetsons and Resistols, make their Fords and Chevys rear up on the back tires like screeching, bucking broncs.

The enclosed-dome stadium is suffused with the pungent aroma of motor oil. It lubricates the teeth and is carried into the bloodstream with each bite of cotton candy. Many of the men and women in the audience are professionals—truckers, mechanics, auto-body specialists, who proudly wear the names of their companies on their hats and jackets.

The tractor pull is as important a strategic career opportunity as a business dinner or a convention. This is the field of honor where Ford and Chevy and their associated parts will show whose products actually are the best. The lights dim, and the sound of the national anthem fills the hushed stadium. The large screens that hang from the ceiling spring to life with images of American flags. When "and the rockets' red glare" is sung, thousands of Bics flash in the darkness. The song ends with pictures of fireworks, and the crowd members throw their hats in the air.

There's a special excitement tonight because Art Afrons, the Henry Ford of tractor pulling, his daughter Dusty, and John Hileman will all be competing in this USHRA (United States Hot Rod Association) Red Man All-American Pulling Series Event. Down in the pit there are lots of drivers, mechanics, and crews. In the midst of the throng is an elegant blonde who looks more like a network anchorwoman than a tractor-pulling enthusiast. She digs into her large shoulder bag and pulls out an economy-sized bottle of Rolaids.

Tonight, John Hileman, her husband, will be driving his legendary 7,200-pound, 6,000-horsepower modified tractor, *Ohio Gold*. Scale models of *Ohio Gold* are sold in toy stores nationwide. The tractor that John built has been known to move up to 80,000 pounds.

"John hadn't been keen on college or working in a factory before we married, and so we bought a farm in Rockford, Ohio, and settled in. But I knew deep down John wanted to get into competition. Tractor pulling and farming are both business. They get in your blood.

REDNECK INGENUITY: THE TIRE

★ Massive urns can be made from white-painted truck tires cut in half. A chain saw makes short work of cutting their edges into decorative points. Add a few stripes of blue paint and a lot of red geraniums for an impressionistic version of the American flag.

★ Splitting an old tire like a biscuit provides two circular troughs for pets, chickens, and so on. The troughs are weather resistant, easy to clean, and heavy enough to resist movement by pets or wind.

★ A pair of large mudders can be used as a base for a picnic table.

★ Hubcaps hung on the side of a barn or home can trace a Christmas tree or spell out the family's initials.

"We recently had an event in Cleveland, Ohio, and were elated because we had a good win on the first night. On Sunday, the first run was perfect, and we came back for the pull off. I was at the end of the track filming when I saw John hit two holes. The tires sank right into the cement floor, there was an awful smell of burned rubber, and smoke was rolling off the tires. When I turned off the camcorder, I wondered why everyone was looking at the motor.

"As they towed the tractor off the track, I saw the puddle of oil with broken pieces of aluminum lying in it. It felt like our world had just ended.

"Dick McPherson was giving us phone numbers and advice on welding a block repair. Ken Lamont hugged us both and expressed his sympathy for our loss. Curt Poole offered to let us use his spare motor. It meant so much that these were our fierce competitors, but when something happens, we were all on the same team.

"We drove to Rockford in four hours. We didn't know whether we'd lost the entire thirty-thousand-dollar motor.

"Monday morning John called all over the country to have parts shipped in. John and our sons worked night and day rebuilding the engine. By the next day we were ready to run in Charlotte, North Carolina. It was a miracle an engine that was that badly damaged could be repaired so quickly and smoothly. Everything fit but the oil pan."

Ann chews another couple of Rolaids. She confides that the track tonight looks good. "According to John, the perfect track is a combination of clay, topsoil, and moisture. It needs to be six to twelve inches deep. Black soil is the best, red soil usually the worst. A rule of thumb is if the soil is too wet to plant corn in, it's too wet to pull in." Ann says her prayers and picks up her camcorder to record everything their competitors do. She says it's crucial that she remembers to tell John if one of them should change a cut of a tire or a lug.

An hour later the crowd is hushed as the winner's name is announced: John Hileman in *Ohio Gold*.

ON THE ROAD AGAIN

If the Trailer Is Rockin',
Don't Come Knockin'
— *Bumper sticker*

Recreation activities involving vehicles need not be related to fierce competition and stressful contests. Instead, many rednecks use their wheels to traverse the country's paved frontier in a comfortable and relaxing style. Private railroad cars may have been the status symbol of royalty and industrialists in the nineteenth and early twentieth centuries. The Indian maharaja's private railcars, or the Palace on Wheels, can't hold a candle to RVs, the motorized salons of comfort that travel the highways of America with their road warriors and warriorettes behind the wheels.

When country music legend Merle Haggard tours with his nine-person band, the Strangers, they travel back and forth across the country in two shiny, tall, windowless custom touring buses, a sort of Graceland on wheels. On the sides of the Strangers' bus is a Sante Fe Railway logo and an emblem that says SUPER CHIEF. Inside there are three sets of double-decker bunks, a living room and a bathroom in the back, another denlike room in the front complete with TV, VCR, CD player, refrigera-

One resourceful recycler created an RV from an old school bus and then built a flotation barge for it out of oil drums lashed together.
GERARD SELLERS.

tor, microwave, and a trash compactor. Merle's bus has a master bedroom and bunk beds for the drivers, two bathrooms, plush carpet, and a full library of videotapes of *The Andy Griffith Show.*

But these rolling palaces don't even need to stay on the road. *Clara,* a spry, compact AARP member from Florida, claims to have found the ideal way to spend her golden years. "For three years now, my sister, our pink poodles, and I've been takin' our RV on the Caravan Barge Cruise," she said. "We're just two ol' gals lookin' for adventure. There'll be as many as thirty-six RVs on a seven-hundred-fifty-feet-long barge. When it starts

REDNECK INGENUITY:
DRIVE-BY SPLENDOR IN THE GRASS

At the hands of an innovative redneck, the front lawn becomes a public art exhibition extolling the wonders of dual usage. Despite popular joke books that confuse redneck style with white-trash neglect, there are rarely sprung sofas in a redneck's front yard. The challenge is to add to nature's beauty, to accessorize the great outdoors with recycled objects that a less frugal and less imaginative individual might view as trash.

Most lawns are groomed to putting-green perfection with a riding mower kept in a corrugated tin shed located in the middle of the lawn. Satellite dishes can be made to look like boulders, yet most rednecks seem to prefer the Con-Rad Alert System look. (Others would even like to see the satellite dish become their state flower.) Some examples of redneck utilitarianism:

* Old bathtubs and commodes can be turned into backyard seating or upturned to be used as shrines for statues of the Blessed Virgin or Saint Francis of Assisi, even in Protestant yards.
* In New England, front yards bloom at Easter with colored Styrofoam eggcarton bottoms attached to Spanish dagger plants, giant inflated plastic Easter bunnies seated in antique sleighs, and Day-Glo beach-ball-sized plastic Easter eggs dangling from immense fir trees.
* A yellow ribbon, often made out of a strip of recycled police-line tape and permanently tied around a large tree, shows support for our armed forces.
* Box springs are used as a self-standing trellis. Three king-sized box springs can be used to construct a gazebo that looks particularly festive when painted white and festooned with jasmine or morning glories.
* In winter, trees can be decorated by filling the branches with blue and green bottles. Recycled Milk of Magnesia and 7-Up bottles are preferred.

Perhaps it is a carryover from pagan times, but among redneck Catholics the home is protected by the female spirit. The Virgin Mary is the most powerful talisman against harm for anything from the automobile to the gas meter.
GERARD SELLERS.

out, we're all shy and standoffish like. But after supper the first night, us campers start visitin' like home folks. It's just like a neighborhood, floatin' down the mighty Mississip' together, eatin' potluck and playin' shuffleboard."

Seeking adventure behind the wheel of an RV has become a way of life for many redneck retirees. "Dot and me're like gypsies," says Rodney, a retiree. "I tell people—if anythin' happened that I couldn't pay my bills, please take my house. Just leave me my tin-can condo!

"I retired as a school-bus driver fifteen years ago. We bought us an old bus and gutted it. We put in some beds, a bathroom, a shower, and running water to make that old bus homey-like.

"But I figured if I wanted to travel out of state, I had to get better than what I had. I got me a twenty-eight-foot motor home. It's not like roughin' it. We got it decorated real nice, and it's got two TVs . . . got fifty-five thousand miles on it. The only thing I'd trade it for'd be one with a full-sized bathtub."

Dot and Rodney travel with a group of friends. "Just a bunch of recycled teenagers, they call us. We're lucky 'cause we got asked to join up with a very nice RV club. Two very nice things with our group—we're all Christians and no one smokes. In the mornings when we get ready to pull out, we hold hands and say a prayer. No matter where we are, we park on the weekends and find out when the church service is."

On their last trip out west Rodney and Dot traveled 7,598 miles through Kansas, South Dakota, Montana, Wyoming, into Nevada, Nebraska, then up to Vancouver and Victoria Island, then back to Washington, Oregon, and Missouri. "That Corn Palace in South Dakota is the most beautiful thing we ever saw."

CHAPTER FOUR

Don't Anyone Make Love at Home No More?

During ancient times, the Greeks and Romans built elaborate urban villas and mocked the rustic Celts for their rural communities built of timber, mud, and straw. Archaeologists of today, however, marvel at the complexity of Celts' round homes; somehow they managed to construct homes as much as fifty feet in diameter with roofs holding more than sixteen tons of straw.

The Celts slept on straw, usually ate meat and did nothing other than fight.

—Polybius, Roman historian, 140 B.C.

THERE SEEM TO BE TWO TYPES OF REDNECK homemakers—those for whom their home is a source of pride, and those who are oblivious to their surroundings. This second group loves to brag that they throw out dirty dishes and go to a garage sale to buy more when the sink "begins to attract buzzards." The first group complains that every day of their lives is a quest for the perfect cleaning product to assist in their struggle against bodily functions—the smelliness and soil of workingmen, the throw-up of sick

The best of all possible redneck worlds can be achieved when a mobile home in an urban trailer park is surrounded by a few accoutrements of the wild.
SUE ROSOFF.

PHOTO ON PAGE 115 BY SUE ROSOFF.

children, the grime that boys track in on their work boots. To the house-proud woman, fastidiousness is the incontrovertible proof that the home is her domain.

But both camps agree with rednecks at all economic levels that the primary function of their homes is comfort. And the goal of those who choose to entertain visitors is to provide a welcome that the rest of us have rarely experienced.

Sherma Rae is one of the house-proud. She's a school-bus driver for a Christian academy on the Indiana–Kentucky border. She tells first-time visitors to look for her mailbox, which turns out to be a unique piece of roadside art made from used auto parts. A license plate dangles from it, featuring a smoking .38: WE DON'T DIAL 911. Two small plastic Big Wheels stand dry-docked in the front yard of her once-pristine clapboard house. On the porch is an assortment of antique split-oak rockers. Stacks of

Ranch style brought into the urban setting.
SUE ROSOFF.

Don't Anyone Make Love at Home No More?

newspapers reinforce their well-worn seats. Cascades of peppermint-striped petunias spill from hanging planters made from upended orange road cones suspended from the porch ceiling by electrical cords.

Sherma Rae's doormat is homemade out of strips of rubber tires woven together like an oversize potholder. Over this base, wide strips of brightly colored synthetic fabric are appliquéd, spelling out: GET A WARRANT.

Once inside the house, visitors are enveloped in the pungent aroma of pine-oil cleaner. On a rusted TV tray table spread with a crocheted doily, Sherma Rae has set slices of a moist and delicious cake on Big Bird paper napkins. No matter what is said to her, Sherma Rae has the agreeable habit of repeating the popular redneck affirmation, "I heard that."

Sherma Rae's
Lunch-'n'-a-Cake

1 cup Blue Plate mayonnaise
½ cup sour cream
1 10½-ounce can condensed tomato soup (generic brands are fine)
3 large eggs
1 3¾-ounce package instant chocolate pudding mix
1 18-ounce box Duncan Hines chocolate cake mix (dark chocolate or fudge flavor)
½ cup Coca-Cola (it can be flat)
Optional: 1 cup mini-marshmallows, 1 cup chopped nuts, and/or 1 cup chocolate chips
1 cup white frosting

1. Preheat oven to 350°.
2. Grease and flour a tube pan.
3. Beat together mayonnaise, sour cream, soup, and eggs.
4. Mix in dry ingredients, alternating with the Coca-Cola.
5. Fold in optional ingredients.
6. Bake for 45 minutes, or until a broom straw comes out clean.
7. Ice with any fluffy white frosting.

Makes 10 to 12 servings

In Sherma Rae's bedroom, the large dead eye of the color television obliterates the window, bringing a darkened air to the cluttered quarters. The Motorola has been built into a hand-wrought knotty-pine curio cabinet, displaying a treasured series of clown dolls collected over a three-year period of watching the Home Shopping Network. The figurines share space with jars of home-canned produce used as jewel-toned accessories. The labels on the peaches, green beans, and tomatoes are also handmade—GET WELL SOON FROM DIMPLES and U.L. AND GOOD EATIN' FROM CAKEY AND SNOOKY.

Over the ironing board is a makeshift wire shelf that holds a calculator, a twenty-foot tape measure, and a Benjamin Moore book of paint colors. When Sherma Rae irons, she channel surfs between QVC (Quality Value Channel) and HSN (Home Shopping Network). Using her handy tools, she can figure out the shipping size and the exact color of what she wants.

The wall behind the sofa is dominated by mounted deer heads, some wearing sunglasses and baseball caps, and numerous plaques displaying stuffed bass. In one corner there's a painting on velvet of dogs playing poker. Sherma Rae jokes, "Isn't that the tackiest thang you ever seen? My husband says nothing should get hung on your wall unless it's something you kilt, a picture of someone you're related to, or it makes you laugh. I wanted to get me a Velvis [a painting of Elvis on velvet]. *Ed Earl* won't hear of it. He says people will think we was showing off like we was related to Elvis."

BOB SCHATZ

INDOOR WILDLIFE

Kill 'Em All and Let God Sort 'Em Out

— *Bumper sticker, T-shirt, and banner slogan*

Cu Chulainn, the Celtic folk hero, was supposedly a great collector of heads. He was said to have displayed as many as twelve human heads taken in one battle. The Welsh, Scots, and Ulstermen not only practiced beheading their most hated enemies, but by many accounts some of their descendants even continued this practice in the antebellum South. Once they became more civilized, these trophies of victory were no longer dis-

When [the Celts] kill enemies in battle they cut off their heads and attach them to the necks of their horses .... They soak the heads of their most illustrious enemies in cedar oil and keep them carefully in a chest and show them off to strangers.

—Diodorus Siculus, Historical Library book 5, c. 50 B.C.

played in their homes, but on trees and posts. One account describes how the heads of Wiley Harpe and James May were stuck on poles by a Mississippi roadside as "warnings to the highwaymen."

Nowadays, thankfully, the redneck homemaker has less disagreeable male trophies to decorate around. Nevertheless, most redneck homes serve as veritable museums of mummified monuments. In addition to the heads of deer, royal elks, pronghorn antelope, Rocky Mountain sheep, mountain goats, feral hogs, and an old tusker (boar), there are also lamps made of wild turkeys (some in flight), picture frames and light fixtures made of antlers, tabletops sitting atop moose hooves, and deer-hoof candlesticks. Some unfortunate wives have to suffer the shame of the ultimate hunter screw-up trophy, generally awarded by a hunter's buddies—the posterior of the animal mounted with a personalized plaque attached.

I Flushed You from the
Bathroom of My Heart

— *Country song*

Sherma Rae's bathroom provides a medley of scents. The yeasty aroma of fresh paint combines with lemon-lime air freshener to create the scent of lemon custard–flavored yogurt. Then there is a Monet-like palette of various shades of blue—blue water in the toilet bowl; lavender-shaded blue toilet tissue; a powder-blue sink, toilet, and tub; an aqua shag commode seat, tank sham, and bathroom rug set; a pastel-blue eyelet tissue and tampon box cover; and a novelty toilet seat that plays "Blue Hawaii."

REDNECK INGENUITY: THE CLOROX BOTTLE

* ★ Cut out the bottom and set the bottle upright in the ground to make a miniature hothouse for seedlings. Unscrew the cap for easy watering and access to the sun.
* ★ Cover with fabric, wicker, decorative painting, and so on and wire to make a table lamp.
* ★ Slice off the bottom at an angle for a great bailer.
* ★ Float ten to twelve Clorox bottles upside down with a fishhook attached to the handles for a trotline.
* ★ Remove the bottom and the cap to make an ideal funnel.

Since most redneck jobs don't carry medical insurance, the bathroom medicine cabinet doubles as the doctor's office. A worker can't afford to take time off from the job to go wait in line to see the doctor at a clinic, and in the country the only doctor in many communities is a veterinarian. One harried mother confided that she herself consumed the Valium the vet prescribed for her husband's hunting dogs.

SAY "CHEESE" . . . OH, NO, FORGET IT

At all levels of redneck society, the most universally approved dental tools are the toothpick and a wad of Juicy Fruit gum. There are, of course, nongenetic reasons why redneck teeth are vulnerable. First, there's the sweet-tooth, snack-heavy diet rednecks thrive on. Then there's the shit-kicker's tendency to get his teeth knocked out competing in a rodeo or fighting in bar brawls. And using teeth as tools for assisting in such tasks as popping the caps off bottles doesn't help.

Dentists are of course scarce in many rural communities, but even in large cities, dental care is rarely covered by insurance plans. A toothache is dispatched with a handful of extra-strength Excedrin, a shot

---

INSIDE THE REDNECK MEDICINE CHEST

Folk healing herbs have been replaced by creative use of commercial products. Here are the basics.

1 large tin of Bag Balm (bovine teat cream used for dry skin and protection from the cold)

1 bottle Outgro treatment for ingrown toenails

1 bottle cod-liver oil (to drink for healthy hair)

Family-sized pack of Dr. Scholl's corn pads

Assorted packets of Goody's and Stanback headache powders (good for hangovers)

1 box Ex-Lax

1 vintage bottle tincture of iodine with several drops left at the bottom

1 tube Poli-Grip denture adhesive

1 industrial-sized bottle Rolaids

Assorted versions of Preparation H (used both for hemorrhoids and to reduce undereye and chin puffiness)

1 book of matches from Hooter's (for emergency bathroom deodorizing and sterilizing needles)

3 snails of Crest toothpaste (used to clear up pimples)

---

of Wild Turkey, and a pair of pliers. In some parts of rural Maine, in fact, bad gums have become such a fact of life that it is considered the height of good financial sense for a dapper young blade to have his teeth pulled and receive his first false teeth as a wedding present.

---

1 potato peeler for calluses

2 economy-sized jars Vaseline petroleum jelly

1 economy-sized Anacin Arthritis Formula

1 applicator-top bottle Absorbine Jr. (for athlete's foot and, in desperation, jock itch)

1 bottle Compound W wart remover

3 tubes Orajel toothache medicine

1 jar Blue Star ointment

1 container of XS (hangover reliever)

Box of Trojans hidden in a Band-Aid box

1 box Band-Aid sheer strips (variety-pack box, with only the ministrips left)

Stored under the bathroom sink:

1 hot-water bottle

1 hot/cold ice pack

1 rectal syringe

Enough hoarded Rely tampons (now off the market) to last until menopause

1 watermarked spring 1991 Victoria's Secret catalog

REDNECK INGENUITY: JUDE'S WORKSHOP

One of the pleasures of home is the freedom to settle in, spread out, and set up a hobby room or workshop where one's creativity can take flight. What's special about the redneck workshop is its focus: Things You Really Need.

Miki de Jean's dad, Jude, is the son of a farmer/cattleman and a nurse. After completing a tour with the U.S. Marine Corps, he received his master's degree in agricultural mechanics. He is now a corporate executive living in a suburb of Chicago. Torn between the demands of a successful career and his love for his country roots, he finds solace in his "shop" and the creativity learned from his days on the farm. "The idea for a new gadget is only a trash pile away," explains Jude.

"Possibly the most extravagant [mis]use of an item was when a former employee of mine used the four-by-six-foot, four-hundred-pound bucket on a sixty-nine-thousand-dollar front-end loader to squash a mouse. It was very effective, but not recommended for those on a budget."

Here are some of Jude's favorite tips:

* Twist a coat hanger into small **S** curve hooks to support large homegrown tomatoes. To keep the stalks from bending and eventually breaking, the hanger hooks suspend tomato-holding pouches made from old panty hose. (Wire floral stands left abandoned in cemeteries also fill the bill for tying up the plants.)
* A short length of hanger can be made into a tiny screwdriver to repair the small screws in eyeglass frames.
* Discarded welder's leather gauntlets make good fireplace gloves.

- ✳ A large coffee can with holes drilled in the sides and a refashioned wooden stopper fitted with a low-wattage lightbulb inside the can makes a great heater/night-light for motherless puppies. Cover it with an old worn shirt for that personal scent.
- ✳ A metal five-gallon bucket with the bottom removed makes a handy portable, comfortable camping toilet. On a cold, damp day, the camper takes his bucket and a roll of tissue into the woods. After selecting a suitably remote spot, he sets the bucket down and puts a few wraps of tissue in the bucket. He ignites the tissue with a match. In a few seconds, the fire goes out and the can is now warm to the touch. After use, the camper simply lifts the clean, empty, bottomless can by the handle and walks away.

Jude at the farm with his prize-winning yam.
FROM THE COLLECTION OF MIKI DE JEAN.

HOG WILD IN THE KITCHEN

Lovin' Don't Last, Good Cookin' Do

— Redneck kitchen-towel slogan

Several of the early Greek ethnographers noted that the Celts were prodigious eaters and drinkers. Meals would last for days, and included pork, beef, fish, ox, game, cheese and butter, curds, cream, and milk and honey. Even when a dagger was used to hack apart a slab of meat, they ate with their fingers. One observer commented, "They partake in a cleanly but leonine fashion, raising up whole limbs in both hands and biting off the meat."

Travelers in colonial America noted a similar diet among the frontier settlers of boiled and fried pork, griddle cakes, corn bread and grits, potatoes, cushaws (large squash), roasted ears of corn, sallet greens, poke salad, and bear's lettuce. Armed with nothing more exotic than salt and pepper, the frontier wife learned how to make a wondrous assortment of dishes from these basic ingredients. Today, you can still find many of these dishes, plus some industrial-sized bottles of ketchup and A-1 steak sauce, readily available on any well-appointed redneck table. The condiments will be used before anyone even tastes a bite. Second helpings are the best compliment.

Amazingly, a redneck woman rarely brags about the taste of her food. Instead the cook will proudly state that she gets dinner on the table promptly at 6 P.M. nightly and there is enough of it so that her teenagers who eat like fire ants will push away from the table with their systems fueled.

At dinnertime, collards and corn dogs cozy up to mounds of marshmallow-studded sweet potatoes and frozen congealed salads with mini-marshmallows and fruit cocktail. (As a matter of fact, without marshmallows few rednecks will eat fresh fruit.) Sweet juices are sopped up with slabs of spongy white bread slathered with golden butter substitute. Meals are washed down with iced tea as sweet as hummingbird

At the Tehama County Cattleman's Field Day annual steak feed more than 1,000 cattlemen feast on steak, beans, salad, and garlic bread. For dessert, the cattlewomen supply homemade cakes. SUE ROSOFF.

Sign on the back of a truck:
We brake for railroad crossings
and blondes. For red-heads,
We Back up!

THIS IS
GOV. WALLACE
Favorite
Stool

food, scalding coffee, or Technicolor soft drinks in plastic containers only marginally smaller than gas pumps. Quick, easy desserts often employ quarts of Eagle sweetened condensed milk in place of sugar and cream. This elixir is so versatile it can be reduced to a thick custard by boiling it in the can (though the label warns you not to) in a pan of water on the stove (be sure to punch holes on the top of the can), then spooned over pies or canned fruit. Another popular dessert is the hot New Hampshire peach sandwich: sprinkle sugar over drained canned peaches and grill between two slices of buttered bread—or use a waffle iron.

Meat is held in high esteem, and the meat of choice is pork, be it barbecued ribs, pulled-pork sandwiches, smothered or chicken-fried pork chops, cracklins (pork rinds), pickled pigs' feet and snouts, sausage, bacon, or ham. Posidonius, the first Greek to make an ethnographic study of the Celts in 70 B.C. in Gaul, noted, "When the hindquarters of the boar were served, the bravest man claimed the best cut for himself, and if someone else wanted it, the two contestants stood up and fought to the death." In the Celtic culture, boars were revered as a special gift to mankind and an important object of cult worship. Anyone who has ever heard 300,000 University of Arkansas Razorback football fans chant, calling the hogs—"Woooooooooooooo! Pig! Suuuuuuuueeeeeee!"—could easily argue that the Celtic cult worship of boars has not been completely abandoned.

It was the value of hogs that fueled one of the most famous of all backcountry feuds—that between the infamous Scotch-Irish Appalachian clans, the Hatfields and the McCoys. It started when two swine were missing. By the time it was over, more than twenty people had been killed.

(One footnote to this feud involves the family that clearly made the greatest mark on culture, the McCoys. The most famous descendant of

PHOTO ON PAGES 130 AND 131 BY SYNDEY BYRD.

the fearsome Celtic McCoy warrior clan was Jackson Pollock, the painter credited with putting the American modern art movement on the map. He was the hard-drinking, renegade artist son of Stella and LeRoy McCoy, a frontiersman from Tingle, Iowa. LeRoy later changed the family name from McCoy to that of his adoptive father, Pollock. Jackson Pollock rebelled against the dictates of the European art world, creating his masterpieces by sloshing housepaint onto canvas with turkey basters.)

Contemporary competition over the hog rarely leads to death. Several popular pork-related celebrations include Climax Swine Time in Climax, Georgia, and Hillsboro Hog Day in North Carolina. Perhaps the most successful of the hog-product festivals, however, is the Chitlin Strut held on the weekend following Thanksgiving in Salley, South Carolina. The festival honoring chitterlings (hog intestines) features a parade of people dressed like pigs, cook-offs, and recipe, beauty, hog calling, and liar (for the best pig story) contests. The Chitlin Strut is actually a dance in which participants look like slices of bacon frying. One Salley resident acknowledged, "Chitlins have the worst odor of any cooked food. Sort of like cooked waste. But they taste delicious! Fried chitlins taste like okra with the consistency of pigs' feet. Our festival makes so much money for the town we hardly pay property taxes!"

FOOD, GLORIOUS FOOD

To celebrate redneck delicacies, there are poke salat, beer, world's record hamburger, French fry sculpting, alligator, rabbit, catfish, swamp cabbage, muskie, chili, dandelion, waterfowl, home-brewing, smelt, molasses, and possum festivals all across the country, each with beauty contests and recipe cook-offs.

Indiana offers the Valparaiso and the Van Buren Popcorn Festivals. For turkey fanciers there are the McMinnville Turkey Rama in Oregon, the Parkersburg Turkey Trot in Wisconsin, and the Live Turkey Olympics in New Preston, Connecticut. Bill Clinton's hometown of Hope, Arkansas (population ten thousand), holds the record for the world's largest watermelon—260 pounds.

Other Popular Events

✶ Irmo Okra Strut in South Carolina
✶ Luling Watermelon Thump and World Class Seed-Spitting Contest in Texas
✶ Minnesota Sit and Spin (cherry)

BOB SCHATZ

* National Hard Crab Derby in Crisfield, Maryland
* National Peanut Festival in Dothan, Alabama
* Shafter Potato Festival in California
* Tennessee's Polk County Ramp Tramp (ramps are a variety of wild onion)
* Vermont Maple Festival in St. Albans
* World Sheep and Rare Breeding Fest in Bethel, Missouri

REDNECK INGENUITY: COOKING METHODS

Frontiersmen often tenderized meat by the same method the Mongols employed for cooking reindeer—they tucked a slab of meat between their horse's body and the saddle. After a day in the saddle, dinner was ready. A few centuries later, truckers and long-distance commuters realized the potential advantage of the heat from their vehicles' engines. As is amply illustrated in *Manifold Destiny* (Chris Maynard and Bill Scheller, Villard Books, 1989) numerous meals can be prepared right under the hood.

Other Tips

* To cook a large tuna or salmon, wrap it in foil and poach the fish on the top rack of the dishwasher. (Don't use the energy-saving cycle.)
* Get the grit out of collard and mustard greens in the light-rinse cycle of the dishwasher. Clothes dryers double as lettuce spinners. (Note: The lettuce must be secured in a knotted pillowcase or a sealed lingerie drying bag.)

Food not only inspires festivals, but also plays an important role in all redneck social functions. Church suppers, wedding showers, and funerals all
revolve around the choice of menu. If a recipe is new, printed on the package, and contains enhanced everyday ingredients, it's deemed "company fare." Of course the pedigree of a recipe is crucial. One lady heard a

Spam

By the 1940s, American know-how, industrialized food processing,
imagination, and necessity had begun to congeal into a discernible
redneck culinary style. Redneck cuisine is based on a cornucopia of
inexpensive, timesaving processed foods—condensed milk, cake
mix, canned soup, and mayonnaise. These ingredients could be
stored, even when power outages cut the electricity for the icebox.

Spam, created in 1937, became a mainstay of the redneck diet.
Since Spam doesn't need refrigeration, it's the ideal food for
hunting trips and glove-compartment picnics. By now it has sold
more than 4 billion cans in the United States and fifty foreign
countries. There are 40 million people in the world who eat Spam
at least once a month, and 3.8 cans of Spam are consumed every
second of the day. And some swear Spam slices make the best
furniture polish on the market.

Spamboree

To celebrate Spam's anniversary, the George A. Hormel Company
of Austin, Minnesota, throws a Spam Jamboree. There is an All-U-

recipe discussed on a talk show. It sounded so delectable she decided to make a batch for her daughter's drill-team awards night. The preparations involved making small layer cakes out of banana Moon Pies, which were then filled and iced with cream cheese flavored with Wyler's tropical fruit drink powder. Each cake was decorated with M&Ms. At the awards ceremony, one of the mothers expressed horror when she saw the cakes. She'd heard the recipe, too, on a program about the lives of women on Texas's death row.

Can-Eat Spam breakfast, Spam pizza and subs, a Spam-eating contest, a Spam sculpture contest, and even a Spam queen and king.

Spam Fritters

1 can Spam
Yellow mustard
Saltine cracker crumbs
Lard

Sauce:

1 cup Miracle Whip
1/2 cup ketchup

1. Cut Spam into 6 slices.
2. Roll slices in yellow mustard and crumbs, pressing firmly.
3. Chill on wax paper for 2 hours.
4. Fry in hot lard until golden brown.
5. Serve hot with white bread and sauce.

Serves 2

Because food is so important, social events in redneck country take place on female turf. For redneck women, a funeral is a time of communal crisis, a perfect showcase for their "fancy" recipes. Upon news of a death, they spring to action like volunteer firefighters called to a four-alarm blaze. In minutes, they can bake six-dozen rolls and find lodging for carloads of the deceased's out-of-town family. Out of their freezers come green bean and mushroom soup casseroles topped with a fresh, crunchy layer of canned onion rings.

It is these recipes that cause hunger pangs in many of those far removed from the redneck kitchens of their youth. *Patricia Ann,* an executive at a major New York talent agency, returned to Alabama for her great-aunt *Edith Mary*'s funeral. There she found a kitchen full of women far more concerned about having enough food for those who would be attending the funeral than they were about the passing of their elderly relative. "The meal we were gathering wasn't just funeral food. This was a family reunion. We knew we had to make a good showing on Aunt Edith Mary's behalf. A lot of my relatives keep casseroles in their freezers year-round, just waiting for the next funeral.

"Living in the land of sushi and bagels, I'd forgotten completely about how delicious things like deviled eggs, pimento-cheese sandwiches, and banana puddin' tasted," said Patricia. "But my aunts were talking about something called a honey-baked ham. That was new to me. Getting it picked up at the right time so that it would be fresh became a much-discussed issue.

"In the meantime, my great-aunt *Virgie* asked me to drive the only car to the funeral home to view Aunt Edith Mary's body before the mourners got there. It was decided, though, that I, who negotiate multimillion-dollar deals for clients, might not be capable of choosing the best honey-baked ham. My sixty-year-old cousin, *Sarah Beth*, was chosen to accompany me on both errands.

"It took Sarah Beth a good half hour to get that damn ham picked out! Then she refused to leave it in the car while we visited the funeral home. She swore people would smell it through the windows of the locked car and break the glass to steal it. So there we were, going into a funeral parlor carrying a giant, spiral-sliced, glazed ham.

"The next thing we knew, three ladies who worked at the mortuary were unwrapping our ham. 'Look how neatly it's sliced,' 'The glaze is so even,' 'Do you think it'll really serve forty people?' I asked to see our aunt.

" 'Oh, honey,' said one of them, 'you better get that ham home. We jus' put Miz Hall up under the hair dryer. She don't have a stitcha clothes . . . time we get her ready, that ham won't be fit to eat. Miz Hall'll jus' die a shame!' "

FEARLESS FRYING

Not all of the cooking responsibilities fall to the women, especially when it comes to frying. This activity is most definitely the redneck man's domain and is also popular with those who fish. (According to expert fish fryers, the real trick is to marinate the fish in hot sauce, slather it with yellow mustard, and dredge it in cornmeal before frying it in lard. The lard is determined to be just the right temperature when a wooden kitchen match ignites when thrown into the hot oil.)

Some favorite things to fry in large quantity are cow fingers (the sixteen toes that must be harvested before the calf grows hooves), prairie or mountain oysters or calf or rooster fries (testicles), squirrel, nutria (swamp rat), possum, chicken, Cornish hen, muskrat, rabbit pies, duck, turtle, alligator, sliced dill pickles, corn on the cob, potato logs, biscuits, okra, whole onions, gizzards and livers, ice cream, batter-dipped steak, and corn dogs.

Deep-Fried Turkey

To clean the oil between batches, drop in rounds of potatoes, which will make instant potato chips. When the oil cools, strain and store it in the refrigerator.

5 gallons peanut oil

Hot sauce, garlic oil, seasoned salt, spices, and liquor of your choice

2 or 3 12- to 14-pound turkeys

6 bacon slices

10-gallon pot

1 50-cc (carrot-size) equine hypodermic needle (from feed)

Wire coat hangers to truss the birds and to hook over side of oil vat

Meat thermometer

Fire extinguisher

1. In a 10-gallon vat, heat oil to 350° (or until a wooden match ignites on contact) over an outdoor propane burner.
2. Use hypodermic to inject spices and liquor into bird.
3. Slide strips of bacon between the skin and breast meat.
4. Truss turkeys with coat hangers. Lower the birds into boiling fat and loop ends of the hangers over the side of the pot. The turkeys should fry for about 3 minutes per pound. When they're done, they will float to the top and be French-fry golden. The meat thermometer should register 180°.

Makes 10 to 12 servings

Note: Do not attempt this recipe under a carport—the grease might blow up.

PHOTO ON OPPOSITE PAGE BY SYNDEY BYRD.

Happily Ever After

When a couple ties the knot, one of their most challenging endeavors is to get settled in their new home. This is a serious project, and wedding guests must think long and hard about the perfect gift to give. Here are a few suggestions for essential items that will help create a happy redneck home:

Practical Items

* Mr. Bacon electric bacon cooker

* SaladShooter

* Beer mug froster

* Vibra Kleen brass polisher with an automatic sifter to recycle bullet casings

* Chain saw

* Bug zapper

* Subscription to *Reader's Digest* or *TV Guide*

* TV tray tables

* Pump dispensers for ketchup, mayonnaise, and mustard

* Rubbermaid trash-can set

* Framed watercolor pictures of the signing of the Declaration of Independence or the Last Supper

* Clapper for all major appliances

- ★ Doormats with the couple's name woven into the matting
- ★ American flag
- ★ Large quartz novelty clock; for example, an exact replica of a roulette wheel or a cuckoo clock that plays "Dixie"
- ★ Pyrex dishes that look like crystal but are microwave safe
- ★ Year's supply of beer, venison, and/or a side of beef
- ★ Sam's Wholesale Club membership

Pretty Stuff

- ★ Crocheted or quilted covers for the toaster, Kleenex and/or sanitary napkin boxes, recipe boxes, address book, the Bible, *TV Guide,* or toilet seat
- ★ Needlepoint pillows for the bed that say NOT TONIGHT on one side and COME 'N' GET IT on the other
- ★ His and hers camouflage hunting jackets, waders, or gun cases
- ★ Front-of-the-truck and -car matching airbrushed license plates: OLE LADY and OLE MAN or simply, THE BUMILLERS
- ★ Airbrushed toilet seat with the couple's name
- ★ Plastic for covering the living room furniture
- ★ Matching bowling shirts with names embroidered in script-style overstitching
- ★ Birdhouse with the couple's name on it
- ★ Doghouse with the husband's name on it

Who's on the Menu?

Not only is food the woman's domain, it's often her name as well. When redneck girls enter the profession of waitressing, they sometimes add the title "Big" in front of their names, particularly if the name is well suited to a career in food service. Little *Cherry Pie Sanders*, for example, went to work behind the counter in a Montana truck stop. Within a week her name tag read BIG CHERRY.

Popular Names

Cookie	Patta Butta	Possum
Cakey	Velveeta Ann	Goosey
Fudgey	Honey Bun	Lettice
Brownee	Peachie Pie	Olive
Fluffy	Tang	String Bean
Fruitcake	Pepper	Brandi
Patticake	Bassy	Tokay
Candi Bar	Lamb	Piggie
Twinkie	Peaches	Duckie
Tootsie Roll	Fawn	Chop (short for "Lamb
Jelly Ruth	Cheerita	Chop" or "Pork Chop")
Muffin	Punkin'	Barbie Q.
Shortnin'	Melon	Popsicle ("Pop" for
Milky	Pigeon	short)
Biscuit	Squirrely	Porkie Pie

CHAPTER FIVE

I'm the Only Hell
Mama Ever Raised

OF THE MANY ENIGMAS IN CELTIC/REDNECK CULTURE, none is as perplexing as the relationship of parent to child. In church, at football games, and school pageants three or four generations of a redneck family openly share affection and pleasure in each other's company. Yet, oppression and shame shroud many individual histories.

Apparently the paradox is part of a tradition: in the eighteenth century, travelers to the backcountry regions of America denounced the age-old child-rearing practices of the Scotch-Irish settlers. As one journalist reported, "The children run free as wild Indians, choosing the company of bear cubs over school books." Efforts at discipline were "the result of parental rage causing numerous acts of violence and tyranny."

And so it remains, according to *Graz* (pronounced "Gracie"), a barrel racer with a master's degree in sociology. Unlike most women within the culture, she's willing to discuss the negative side of redneck child rearing. "I've seen it so often," Graz offers. "When you step outta line your daddy'll beat you or your mama'll bitch at you for so long you pray for a whippin'. Nobody explains the rules they're imposing. Probably 'cause they're just following their parents' example.

"All most redneck kids think about is bustin' loose from parental control. I guess you could say we need to experience gravity firsthand! So what do we do when we become parents? Try to beat the attraction to wild-ass danger out of our kids. Just like our parents did to us."

WOMANLY WILES

Redneck women have developed their own ingenious tricks. "Our grandmother taught us how to find out the sex of your unborn child," said Julie and Gayla, veteran baby-shower hostesses. "All you do is put one tablespoon of Drano in a cup. Then you take the first catch of the day—that's your most potent urine—and pour it into the Drano. If it turns blue or green it's a boy. If it turns pink or stays the same, it's a girl."

Baby-Shower Advice from Julie and Gayla

★ Baby showers are such fun. The ring test is a surefire winner. You take a wedding band and suspend it over the mother-to-be's ribs on a string. If it turns clockwise, it's a boy, and if it's a girl, it turns counterclockwise.

★ Another game that's always great is the potato game. You get a potato and carry it between your knees to a small pitcher and drop it in.

★ For party favors you can take napkins and fold them very tightly and pin them like diapers. You put mustard in one. The person that gets the nasty diaper wins the door prize.

Graz credits her husband's Apache grandmother, who now lives with them, with improving her parenting skills. "Gran Rosie has made me see kids need love most when they deserve it least," she said.

"She may not have much in common with Dr. Spock, but she knows how to raise good kids, the kind of people parents wouldn't mind being friends with when they grow up. What she says is simple: 'To raise good kids you need to nourish their bodies. You nudge 'em forward when they clutch. You fight alongside of 'em when the world gets in their way. And, above all else, you keep your cotton-pickin' hands off their souls.' "

RED-HOT MAMAS

Redneck mothers display their unconditional love with an intensity that can verge on hellcat fury. One man was unfortunate enough to come up against this legendary fighting spirit from the two women in his life. "The most embarrassin' thing that ever happened to our family was the day Mama and my wife got into a face-slappin', hair-pullin' brawl at the Pee Wee football game," cackled a coach in Ohio. "My oldest son was coachin' one team. I was coachin' the other. My youngest son and my granddaughter were on his team. But our three nephews were on mine. I shoulda knowed better than to get those two women fired up against each other.

"Finally got so bad we stopped the game. Only way I knew to get them apart was to pour a bucket of water on 'em. After that they turned on me. It was so awful nobody in our family's ever mentioned it again."

Some of the children raised in redneck homes have a slightly more positive perspective on redneck mothers. Miki, a country radio producer in Nashville, considers herself an expert on the subject, since she spent most of her life as an only child in a house with her mother, aunt, and grandmother. "My mother was like a warden; my aunt was my mentor. But it was my grandmother who taught me how to survive: 'Gettin' your period is better than not gettin' it, and if you're gonna drink, drink vodka. Then your mama can't smell it on your breath.' "

Perhaps that's why Miki became accustomed to looking to older women for advice. "I used to work with this lady at Opryland. She told me the main thing she taught her daughters: 'Women might get kicked down to our knees by life, but never forget you're in the perfect position to bite the balls off what put you there.'

"Now that I'm an adult, I realize that redneck mothers send their daughters all of these mixed messages."

"You know how mothers'll take their babies to the mall wearing pastel-pink diaper covers, hand-embroidered with sayings like SHIT HAP-PENS or LITTLE DOO-DOO KICKER. Then when the daughter is a little older and says 'shit,' her mother will wash her mouth out with Lifebuoy."

Redneck mothers further confound their daughters with the spec-trum of heroines they enshrine—Reba McEntire, Princess Grace, Joan Lunden, Scarlett O'Hara, Oprah, Vanna White, Ann Richards, Delta Burke, Barbara Bush, Barbara Mandrell, Dinah Shore, Dolly Parton, Elizabeth Dole, Marla Maples Trump, and Tipper Gore. "About the only thing they have in common," Miki points out, "is that they're famous. It's like our mamas aspire to have us be the first lady, a fire-baton twirler, and a queen of country music all at once. But don't forget—you've also gotta run the PTA, teach Sunday school, and save money by making your worn-out jeans into pot holders and quilts!"

Speaking of her own attempts to model herself after female icons, Dolly Parton made the famous statement: "I was always impressed with Cinderella and Mother Goose. It's all we saw when I was a kid. We didn't have TV or movies. I kinda patterned my look after a combination of Cinderella and Mother Goose—with a little of the town hooker added in."

Most of all, redneck mothers are determined to set their daughters on the right course. (Sons, it seems, are allowed more latitude.) Like many mothers, *Belinda,* a nurse near Lexington, Kentucky, feels it's her job to facilitate a career path for her daughter. "The one thing I want for my *Brittany* is that she become a beauty queen. It's what'll give her a chance for a college education and a high-payin' job. I can't tell you the hours I've sat out by Granddaddy's farm sellin' corn out of the back of my truck to pay for my Brittany's lessons. She has her tap, gymnastics, ice-skating, and piano lessons. Then there's her orthodontist. Her daddy, we're divorced, lets her play Little League. But you and I both know there's no future in baseball for a girl unless she marries a major-leaguer.

"I've also taught Brittany the Bible. By the time she was ten she could recite all of the books. She wears a little Sunday-school medal around her neck for it." Belinda always carries a little photo album featuring Brittany, who indeed wears her gold cross along with a bit of rouge and mascara.

"She's so cute you'd just love to make her into a key ring, wouldn't you? There's nothing I wouldn't do to see her become Miss America," Belinda confides. In fact, she has made quite a study of the secrets of Miss America wanna-bes from Mississippi and Texas contestants. She shared some of their tips:

Miki's Melt-'n'-Your-Mouth Plumb-Good Cake

Baby food is a fact of life for every redneck mother. Cases of it are bought at Sam's Wholesale Club and then used as ingredients for adult recipes, as well.

1 cup Blue Plate mayonnaise
1 cup white sugar
1 cup brown sugar
3 large eggs
2 cups self-rising flour
1 teaspoon cinnamon
1 cup chopped pecans or walnuts
2 4-ounce jars plum baby food or strained apricot baby food with
 tapioca
1 tablespoon red food coloring

1. Preheat oven to 350°.
2. Grease and flour a tube pan or 2 loaf pans.
3. Beat mayonnaise and sugars until fluffy.
4. Add eggs, one at a time.
5. Combine dry ingredients and stir into sugar mixture.
6. Stir in jars of baby food and food coloring.
7. Bake for an hour, or until a broom straw comes out clean.
   The cake freezes well.

Glaze:

½ cup apricot nectar or orange-juice concentrate

2 cups confectioners' sugar

2 tablespoons oleo

1. Mix all ingredients in a saucepan.
2. Bring to a boil, stirring constantly.
3. Poke tiny holes in the cake with a toothpick.
4. Saturate cake while hot with glaze.
5. Decorate with candied red and green cherries.

Makes 12 to 18 slices

Mama's Eat-Your-Heart-Out Pink Ice Cream

Serve with Miki's Melt-'n-Your-Mouth Plumb-Good Cake.

30 ounces (2½ bottles) strawberry Shasta

2 cans Eagle condensed milk

2 cans Pet milk (you may need more to fill the ice-cream freezer to the line)

2 cups strawberries (may use frozen)

Red food coloring for desired pink tone

Mix ingredients and freeze in an ice-cream freezer according to the manufacturer's instructions.

Serves 6 to 8

Variation: Cream soda may be substituted for the strawberry Shasta to make bubble gum–flavored ice cream.

* To learn to glide down a runway, walk back and forth across a swimming pool in waist-high water while wearing skintight jeans.
* For a perfect smile, apply Vaseline to the front teeth.
* Truly glowing hair and skin can be achieved by drinking two tablespoons of fish oil every day.
* A little brown eye shadow applied to the cleavage and rolled-up nylon stockings in the lower cup of a Wonder Bra is the cheapest and safest method to achieve a better "rack."
* Never, ever let anyone take naked pictures of you.

A meeting of the Bull, Swine, and Shrimp queens.
KATHY RICHARD.

The redneck daddy is looked to for certain kinds of wisdom. . . .

Paul Prudhomme is one of America's most renowned chefs and the man who introduced blackened redfish to the world. He confirmed the role his father played in setting his moral compass. "My daddy was a sharecropper. Made forty-two crops in his life, too." Paul smiled as he flipped sautéed baby vegetables in a heavy black skillet. "By the time I was five, my twelve older brothers and sisters and I were working on the farm, alongside Daddy.

"Daddy taught us when you accepted a job you sold your time . . . not your soul. No matter if the job was something stupid like moving a pile of bricks ten feet and then moving 'em back. You had to do your best. But at the end of the day, you take your money and *git*!"

Dr. Deborah Adcock Bosley grew up in south Texas. "Daddy is the salt of the earth," says Deborah. "He was born on a dirt floor and rode a mule to school. Dad's career advice saved me in medical school, though: 'Believe half of what you read, a fourth of what you hear, and never get into a pissin' contest with a man.' "

Cara Ann, an auto mechanic, was raised with four older brothers. "I learned a lot about datin' from Daddy," she recalled. "He had all these animal husbandry sayings:

★ Cowboys come and go, but the bull hangs on.
★ You don't need to be scared of the bull, but you better watch out for the calf.
★ In real life it doesn't matter how many tries it takes you to land a steer, what counts is that he stays roped and tied!
★ Puppy love will lead to a dog's life."

There She Is,
Miss Peanut Butter and Jelly

—One of the titles held by the late actress Jayne Mansfield

This list of "nonvocal or unusual" acts performed by contestants in national beauty pageants to fulfill their talent requirement appeared in *101 Secrets to Winning Beauty Pageants,* by Ann-Marie Bivans. Bivans, a columnist for *Pageantry* magazine, cites the talents below to counter "the idea that only singers win."

Flower arranging

Horsemanship

Karate

Chinese sword dancing

Sketching

Mime

Chalkboard drawing

Fashion design exhibit

Marimba

Conducting pageant orchestra

Middle Eastern belly dancing

Roller-skating

Ventriloquism

Double ventriloquism

Archery

Upside-down tap dancing

Clogging

Trampoline

Stomping in broken glass

South Sea dance

Contortionist act

Hula dancing

Imitating Marilyn Monroe

Russian Cossack dance

Films of water ballet and high diving

Portraying Queen Elizabeth I in full costume

Portraying *Romeo & Juliet* in period costume

Furniture display

Driving a tractor

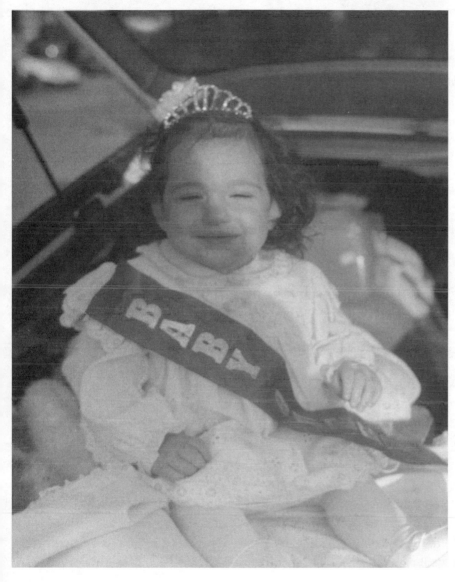

KATHY RICHARD

155   *I'm the Only Hell Mama Ever Raised*

MOTHER WIT

Unlike the Greeks, *Jews, and Romans, who made women responsible for man's unhappy lot, the Celts revered women for their "wisdom more than human" when it came to stealth, courage, secrecy, and resourcefulness. Publius Cornelius Tacitus (c. 55–117) remarked in* Germania, *volume 8, "tradition informs us that [Celtic culture] conceives that in women resides a certain, mysterious power of prophecy, and so as a result of this belief they consult women and take great stock in their replies."*

Most redneck moms don't trust Dr. Spock, who has two strikes against him—first, he's a man, and second, he took an antiwar stance during the Vietnam era. Besides, Dr. Spock doesn't tell you what you really need to know—hard-won woman-to-woman advice like this:

★ Don't waste your breath giving your children advice. No matter what you tell them, they will always follow your example.
★ If it don't fit, don't force it. When it breaks you can't take it back.
★ You ain't inheriting the world from your parents. You're borrowing it from your kids.

FOUL PLAY

Puppy love can also uproot an entire community. Consider the story of the Fighting Bobcats of Hempstead High, a school in a 3,500-inhabitant Texas ranching community. Of the school's fifteen cheerleaders, three became pregnant and were forced off the field by the local school board. Despite one Hempstead doctor's argument that cheerleading would be ideal exercise for a pregnant teen, and others who praised the girls for doing the right thing by not having abortions, the unwed pregnant teens still were benched, and the boys rumored to have gotten them pregnant

- ★ It doesn't matter what you do, as long as you can clean up the mess by yourself 'cause life has a 100 percent mortality rate no matter what.
- ★ Good judgment comes from experience, but the only way to get it is from bad judgment.
- ★ Never give excuses—your friends don't need 'em, and your enemies won't believe 'em.
- ★ Nobody knows everything. Nature and life will teach you everything worth knowing if you keep your eyes open. But beware of someone who preaches on their behalf.
- ★ Never tell anyone somethin' they're too lazy or stupid to figure out themselves unless they're related to you.
- ★ The only difference between a rhinestone and a diamond is what's inside.
- ★ Money isn't for keeping score; friends are.
- ★ There's no credit been invented that is as good as money.
- ★ If you do it well, it ain't showing off.
- ★ If bravery doesn't get you a raise, the job's not worth your life.
- ★ Old sins cast long shadows.

were allowed to continue playing. About that time, the Bobcats, once regional champs, began to experience massive losses. It was when the fourth pregnant cheerleader had an abortion and was allowed to continue cheering that the uproar really began.

In nearby La Grange, a rancher's wife and mother of three daughters shook her head in disgust. "Every girl is like a heifer on a rope. If you run off wild, you'll break your neck 'cause that rope's tied to God's tree."

Her husband, the rancher, scratched his head with the plastic filter of his cigar. "It seems to me the quickest way to stamp out the problem of

MOTHERHOOD:
IT'S MORE THAN A CAREER, IT'S AN ADVENTURE

—Bumper sticker

Bernice Turner has made a career in music as a performer, a bus driver, and the mother of a musician. She and her husband, Doyle, played with Audrey and Hank Williams Sr. in the 1940s. Then to support her family, Bernice became the first woman to customize and drive tour buses for entertainers.

Bernice got her career inspiration from Audrey Williams. "Now, Hank Sr. was a brilliant musician, but no one'd heard of him if it hadn't been for his wife. She pushed her husband to success. Without her he'da drowned in the bottle."

Bernice's Silver Eagle and Limousine Company has driven such diverse performers as the Commodores, Pat Benatar, and Robin Williams. But she might never have gotten into the transportation business twenty years ago if she hadn't been a worried mother. "Robby, he's my baby. He was tourin' with a gospel group by the time he was twelve. Ever heard of the Rambos?" Bernice grinned, tossing her cascade of raven hair with her perfectly manicured, cardinal-colored nails. "He looked full growed. You know, he was over six feet by the time he turned thirteen.

"That's when a 'well-known entertainer,' somebody we all know, asked me if I'd let Robby tour as his steel player." Bernice discovered that the entertainer was trying to kick a *bad* drinking

One of Bernice's prize possessions is the diamond ring Elvis gave to his stepmother, Dee. Dee gave it to Bernice in gratitude for taking her into her home after she left Elvis's father, Vernon Presley.
Syndey Byrd.

problem. So she made a deal with him. She'd agree to let Robby go on the road, but if she ever heard the entertainer had taken a drink, Robby was coming back home.

"But after Robby'd started workin' I discovered the entertainer smoked those funny cigarettes. It got me to thinkin': 'Bernice, how can you keep an eye on that child?' You know, without Robby bein' ashamed 'bout havin' his mama with him and all. Then I remembered somethin' the entertainer had told me 'bout his touring bus bein' repossessed. So that's how I got the inspiration to buy a bus. I learned to drive it. I customized it. And leased it back to Robby's boss. See, then they had to take me on the road with 'em as their bus driver."

Bernice slipped a cassette of the Highwaymen into the tape deck. "That's my son Robby on the steel guitar," she said proudly. "Didja see him on Jay Leno? He'd make his daddy, one of the greatest steel players that ever lived, and Hank Sr. and Audrey proud."

Doyle   Bernice   Bill   Hank   Audrey

unwed births is not to outlaw abortions, but to castrate the males who don't support the mother and child. I don't know how castration affects a boy's game of ball, but it sure as hell will put a curb chain on his off-the-field play."

IF YOU CAN'T TRUST ME TO MAKE A CHOICE, WHY WOULD YOU WANT TO TRUST ME WITH A CHILD

—*Bumper sticker on a maroon Pinto at Yellowstone National Park*
(it shared the bumper with a sticker for Rock City and
one expressing pro-gun sentiments)

Frank, a glass plant worker, carried a picket sign in a prochoice march. "I'll tell you what the antiabortion anti-choice thing is about: it's about men who can't control their women. These days, the women have the jobs, and the men are stuck at home. All alone with want ads, bawling brats, and soap operas. The only way a man can get his woman home—and get his wheels back—is for her to be pregnant.

"If you think this abortion thing is about protectin' life, you're nuts. These abortion clinic bombers also believe in the death penalty, and each one owns about six loaded guns. No, this is about getting women home. I feel like Deep Throat saying this, but I hear things at the bar at night. I have two sisters and two little girls. I'd kill any son of a bitch that did anything to hurt 'em. But I know I won't always be around. So the law has to do it." Then he yelled for the benefit of a television camera covering the demonstration, "Women's bodies ain't community property!"

While mule bonding can, of course, be witnessed at any sporting event, it's a peculiar stroke of fate that many a beautiful girl will inherit her daddy's drinking temper and passion for fast vehicles.
SUE ROSOFF.

Chips off the Old Block

The intensity of redneck parents' bond to their children is reflected in very public ways. Many redneck parents combine the child's father's and mother's names so that the world will always know who their daughter's folks were. A mother named Etta Mary and a dad named Paul gave their first-born the name Paul Etta. In actress Cybill Shepherd's case, her granddaddy was Cy, and her daddy is Bill, so she became Cybill. Victoria Principal was not named for the great British monarch, she's the daughter of Victor.

Other favorites:

Bertteen	Reg Gina	Delucey	Hualina
Ollene	Ken Jane	Homerlene	Doe Rae
Ray Mona	Johnette	Vernelle	Kate Don
Haroldana	Charlie Ruth	Dick Jane	Pollijon

YOU MADE A WANTED MAN OUT OF ME

— Ronnie McDowell hit

Politics and sex make strange bedfellows. Some rednecks even display a bumper sticker that reads HATE AIN'T A FAMILY VALUE.

Laura and *Marshall* had been engaged in college. "Breaking our engagement was a moment of truth," Marshall begins. "Laura's mother was Mama's best friend since they were kids. Our daddies owned horses together. But it wouldn't have been fair to Laura to marry me. Laura knew I was gay in high school. I couldn't ask her to live that kind of a lie. You know, bein' best friends is one thing; bein' married is another.

"Laura and I told our folks I was a homosexual after I got home from Vietnam. They thought it was a joke. I remember Mama's sayin', 'You can't be, that's ridiculous. You're a devout Christian. You're a football star. You ride a motorcycle. For God's sake, you were decorated for bravery in the marines.' But even as she was talking, I could see she'd known deep down I was tellin' her the truth.

"I know they didn't understand, but they didn't disown me," Marshall continued. "After a while they quit blamin' the military. I guess it took 'em longer to realize this wasn't a mental problem or the result of some childhood trauma. Jesus, did they pray a lot."

Marshall clarified his sexual orientation. "I don't dress in drag or pick up young boys. Never did. Never will. I'm just your garden-variety queer cowboy. Just another guy in the locker room checkin' out guys' butts. Thing was, I did somethin' about it. It started as a few experiences in high school. Drunk, horny guys foolin' around after we took our dates home. Let me tell you, it's a lot more fun than any deep mud or farm ani-

Despite *the fact that their wives are beautiful, the Celts have very little to do with them, but instead abandon themselves to a strange passion for other men. They usually sleep on the ground on skins of wild animals and tumble about with the bedfellow on either side. And what is strangest of all, without any thought for a natural sense of modesty, they carelessly surrender their virginity to other men. Far from finding anything shameful in all this, they feel insulted if anyone refuses the favors they offer.*

–Diodorus Siculus,
Historical Library,
book 5, c. 50 B.C.

mals. Of course, part of the redneck code is that guys contract amnesia under the sober glare of the sun.

"I've got a theory about why redneck men are so threatened by queers. Redneck men are by nature the horniest ethnic group on the planet," Marshall proposed. "Basically, we've been culturally endowed with dicks we can't control. It's like the joke the pastor told in church last Sunday: 'God says to Adam, "I got some good news and some bad news. The good news is you've got a brain and a penis. The bad news is you've only got enough blood to supply one at a time."'

"So, let's just say the opportunity exists for many a dyed-in-the-wool heterosexual redneck to 'look for love in all the most convenient places.' Look at their macho all-male, no-women career/recreational choices—the navy, cowboys, roughnecks, pro ball players. At the same time, being unmanly is considered far worse than rape."

Marshall's partner, *Hal,* is a handsome, prematurely silver-haired doctor, raised in Milan, Italy, and Princeton, New Jersey. He added his observations as a nonredneck living in the rural South. "What astounded me is that a gay redneck man or woman would come out and then remain within the most homophobic culture in the world," he said. "I went into what I thought was a honky-tonk in Atlanta. Then a cowboy came up and asked me to dance to a Randy Travis song. I thought he was putting me on.

"It's probably harder for gay rednecks to be in the closet than any other group of homosexuals," Hal suggested. "As you probably notice, rednecks don't have a filter between their brains and their tongues—if it's on their mind they'll come right out and say it."

Some of Marshall and Hal's compatriots have provided their kinsmen with local color. Mr. Boobie, a notorious female impersonator from the

1940s to 1960s, now lives quietly in his hometown in Arkansas. "Life out on the farm was borin'. We'd do most anythin' for fun. Granny used to dress me up in her old weddin' dress to lip-synch to the *Grand Ole Opry* on the radio. One summer I saved up my egg money to buy myself a lady's white swimsuit. Hell, I like to drowned myself in our pond doin' an underwater Esther Williams imitation for Mama's Stitch-'n'-Bitch Club.

"Me and the town whore tied for the title of class favorite in our graduatin' class of twelve. To celebrate, I wore a black strapless gown, slit to the hip, with black fishnet hose and a mop dyed black on my head to the prom. And what ole girl hasn't dreamed of being a drum majorette? Picture it, me in a stripped-down gold lamé gown, twirlin' two batons to 'Stars and Stripes Forever' at teacher's college." Mr. Boobie is positively gleeful.

"My first job after the navy was in a club in Dallas that Jack Ruby owned. You know the guy who killed Lee Harvey Oswald? Yep, I had me some great life. I just got sick of waxin' my legs and fixin' my hair. Nowadays, I'm just another retired navy Bubba with a bunch of chickens, an old yeller dog, and a pickup."

GETTIN' HITCHED

A child's choice of a life partner is an issue that causes redneck mothers' knuckles to turn white.

Beauty contest winner or not, a redneck girl has to be taught about her opposite number. One enthusiastic mentor is *Joy Kat,* a great-grandmother with ketchup-colored ringlets and lots of advice for young women. She's been married to the same man for forty-nine years. "We've had our share of problems," she admits, "but we sent our four kids to college. All of 'em have nice-payin' jobs and lovely families. After that, the two best things a woman can do for herself is keep lookin' good and joinin' AARP." Joy Kat's other good-wifery tips:

- ♥ Never forget: men are as fragile as hens' eggs. It's a wife's job to be sure life doesn't break him. The meaner they act, the more frightened they are. And, you better believe, the more they'll blame you.
- ♥ Cry in private. I'd slap my girls if they let a man see 'em cry. Most men are like buzzards when they spot weakness in you. Then you're really gonna need to hold you a pity party!
- ♥ Don't let your man drink too much. I know it's easier when he's not all over you. But I look at it this-a-ways: a sex maniac is a lot easier to keep outta trouble than an alcoholic!

While a few redneck women view sex with an acridness that would please Queen Victoria, others confess to having a sex drive "with no right foot." Outward appearances, however, don't betray which is which. One very prim Baptist churchgoer was overheard confiding to a friend over lunch at Shoney's that her marriage had lasted for more than fifty years because she got her husband to church every Sunday and "I've got a pussy as tight as a mouse's ear."

MOTHER-TO-DAUGHTER ADVICE

- ♥ A bachelor is a hunter that always misses.
- ♥ The horse with the best jockey wins the race.
- ♥ Don't start up the engine if you don't plan to drive it.
- ♥ There are few of life's problems that can't be tackled in a pair of rubber gloves, but the quickest way to climb the ladder of success is still in sling-back, pointed-toe stiletto heels.

The Era of Good Feeling

"When I was eleven I went to a slumber party and one of the girls had a *True Confessions* magazine," recalls Era. "We weren't even allowed to read the funny papers at our house. My sisters kept the box our sanitary napkins came in wrapped in a brown grocery bag and hidden behind the towels in the hall closet. So imagine, that magazine was like putting a time bomb in my brain. There were these two words that I remember that were used quite a bit to describe what certain girls did—bump and grind.

"After that slumber party I started stickin' out my two little 'mosquito bites' and rotating my hips when I walked down the hall at junior high. These stuck-up girls started calling me Jiggle Slut, and that's when their boyfriends started paying attention to me.

"In history class we studied something called the Era of Good Feeling. That's my name, Era. Once I had the reputation, well I just got asked out a lot, especially by the boys from the well-off families. Honey, that's when I learned what bumpin' and grindin' meant.

"When I was in high school the National Guard came to my hometown to stop the race riots. That's how I found out about the Era of Good Feeling. After that time, I guess I really was a full-blown slut. My sisters would tell on me, but it didn't matter, I'd just sneak out. I never hurt nobody with my bumpin' and grindin'.

"I'd kill my little granddaughters if I ever caught one of them even thinkin' about, you know. There are just too many diseases and weird things going on nowadays to have plain innocent sex."

When *I hear women talk
about their jobs, all they say
is him, him, him, and honey,
this ain't church.*

—Patsy Cline

♥ Never tell anyone you can type, prepare a tax return, make coffee, or iron.

♥ There are two kinds of girls in the world: those who believe what men say and those who know better.

♥ Always know who's at the end of the tow rope. The only difference between a bow and noose is the knot it's tied with.

♥ When somebody tries to treat you like a whore, raise up your head and make them pamper you like a call girl.

♥ Sometimes you've got to sleep with the devil to save your children from hell. Only do it once (unless you plan to turn professional).

♥ If you marry for money, you'll earn every penny of it.

A Good Catch

Choosing a life partner is clearly the most crucial decision for a redneck, man or woman. If they've been raised right, redneck women seem far more interested in men for their genes than for their bank accounts. As one woman said, "Honey, a woman's job is to keep the species goin', so marry you the one with the finest tilt to his kilt."

On the other hand, the most confusing message redneck men get from their parents is about what to look for in a spouse. Sometimes that message sort of evolves, as in the case of a mud-bog racer from Florida: "Granddaddy was part Indian, part black Irish," he said. "My cousins and I moved out to the country with him when we hit sixteen. After our Saturday chores, the old man gave us each twenty bucks and the keys to his '67 Chevy truck. He'd tell us: 'Make hay while the sun shines, boys. When you git to be my age you're too wored out to kiss a gal's belly button!'

Wedding in the deepest coal mine in North America.
Dennis Hall.

I'm the Only Hell Mama Ever Raised

"But after about three years that truck got to lookin' real trashy. I'd been writin' the girls' names I'd picked up on gum wrappers," the grandson conceded. "On my nineteenth birthday Granddaddy liked to broke my heart. He threw out all the garbage under the seat. That's when he sat us down. 'Boys,' he said, 'pickin' a wife's like figurin' which cow to put the bell on. You don't want no renegade or no fence trampler. You want the one with the best character. A wife's gotta set the example for the family. Any gal whose name is on these here gum wrappers ain't no lead-cow material.' "

There's no shortage of advice on this aspect of life. In a Kansas diner, a dapper, thirty-year-old UPS deliveryman summed up his idea of the perfect mate: "Granny tells me to look for a good sturdy woman who can lead the choir on Sunday, then drive the combine and make a healthy supper. Mama's picky, picky. I better not bring home no girl with chewing gum or a cigarette in her mouth. And no gal with a tattoo or an ankle bracelet. Now Daddy wants my wife to hunt and fish like Mama and my sisters. And you know he's right. It's nice to see a family enjoy stuff together. But me, all I know is that my wife better have a big set of hooters. And I wouldn't pass up one who can suck a golf ball through a garden hose."

Once the match has been made, it's best to pay heed to the realities of life. In the words of former president Lyndon Johnson, "There are two secrets to a happy marriage. The first is to let your wife think she's right. The second is to know in your heart that she is."

I'm a W-O-M-A-N

—*Song made popular by Maria Muldaur*

Nicholas Lemann of the *Atlantic Monthly* brought up the vexing contradictions of stereotypical portraits of redneck gender. "I imagine in some respects, redneck men are role models for all men. No matter what class or ethnic background," Nick speculated while adjusting his bow tie. "There comes a point in every man's life when he fantasizes about telling someone off, hopping on a horse or a Harley, and riding off into the sunset. As men move up the sociointellectual scale, they curb their brute impulses. But standing side by side with a construction worker in a urinal, you can't help envying his masculinity.

"But the conventional redneck wife . . . now that's a hard one. They seem to fly in the face of femininity and feminism," he added.

Redneck wives have long been viewed by outsiders with confusion and chagrin. Even before the American Revolution, visitors to the back-country, mostly from England or New England, observed that the Scotch-Irish frontierswomen engaged in heavy labor such as clearing forests, killing and hacking apart large swine with axes—all the tasks "too mean" for their husbands. Still, life was even harder for those women of Celtic extraction who stayed behind in the Old World. According to the 1884 journal of Charles Rogers, "The wives of Scots fishermen followed the peculiar age-old custom of carrying their husbands on their backs to and from their boats, which were anchored offshore, to keep their men's feet dry." On the other hand, unlike the Greeks and Romans, Celtic women could own property and even lead tribes in battle.

Tradition *informs us that women reversed defeat during battles, praying and baring their breasts [before their warriors] so that their men understood the women would not accept captivity.*

—Tacitus, c. A.D. 55–117

Till Death Do Us Part

The loyalty of a redneck wife often extends to defending him—literally, if need be. For this characteristic, too, there is historical precedent. Ammianus Marcellinus (c. A.D. 360) warned that an army had no hope against the Gauls (Celts) if a man called his wife to his aid, "Swelling her neck, gnashing her teeth and brandishing her sallow arms to enormous size, she begins to strike blows mingled with kicks as if they were so many missiles sent from the string of a catapult."

Tammy Wynette's "Stand by Your Man" is a reminder to many of how the singer went to Alabama to help the paralyzed George Wallace win reelection as governor of Alabama. That was the year the black vote won the day for the reformed racist. But Wynette's song also brings back the heroism shown by Wallace's wife during his bid for the presidency. As the assassin showered Wallace with bullets in Laurel, Maryland, in 1972, Cornelia Wallace ran across the stage to throw herself on top of her husband. "Stand

BEHIND EVERY GREAT MAN . . .

Women in the culture know their own power, yet will readily use it to empower their men to fulfill the role of protector. "Redneck women are the knot that will hold our culture together," said Janey, a proud redneck and computer graphic artist, referring to the ancient decorative motif of interlocking knots known as the Celtic knot. "We are far more complex and a lot stronger when we have men to hold together. Men would be nothing without us."

It is this concept of the power of women in Celtic/redneck culture that brings to mind both Boudicae (*Boo-dik-a*), the warrior queen, and Mother Jones, the crusader for fair labor practices. One redneck receptionist offered the same effective solution to get government under control that Aristophanes (445–386 B.C.) presented for ending the war with Sparta in *Lysistrata*. When the American government closed down in 1995 over the debate on a balanced budget, she expressed frustration that her kinswomen didn't unite. "All women need to do is go on a nookie strike. Refuse to have sex with one politician, newsman, or corporate executive until all the government workers go back to work! How long you think Newt could hold the line against other whining white men?"

by Your Man" could also serve as a title for a biography of a lady named Loreta, who, under the name of Harry Buford, had her own Confederate regiment and fought alongside her man at Bull Run.

IF A WOMAN'S PLACE IS IN THE HOME, WHAT AM I DOING DRIVING THIS TRUCK

—Bumper sticker spotted in Darien, Connecticut

Other women, however, seek careers that will give them freedom from men. *Sister Marta*, for example, is a rancher's daughter raised during the Depression. "When I was growing up in *Podunk*, Oklahoma, a redneck gal was supposed to stay on the ranch. You know, until she married a rancher and started having kids and all. Freedom only came when they planted you six feet under.

"Sometime after World War II, cowboys got the idea that the granddaughters of the women who'd fought Indians and survived drought and starvation needed a man to do their thinking for them," Marta said. "Maybe other gals had the fight bred out of 'em, but not me. I saw the life on the ranch like a long stretch of dirt road full of potholes leading straight to nowhere.

"My daddy liked to died when I told him I was leavin' home to go to a convent school in California. It was a scandal in our Baptist church. Old Lu Lu got her freedom from the rule of men. And that's when Sister Marta was born." She has worked for years as a teacher in Latin America.

Over the years, a few enterprising American businessmen have caught on to the fact that redneck women like Sister Marta make no-nonsense, loyal, brave, honest employees. In fact, sometimes women are so good at their jobs that they cause their bosses to reevaluate their own approach to business. That's what happened to *Melvin*. Abandoning the big-city business life, he moved back to the hollow and opened a large sporting goods–manufacturing company. "There are maybe five men who work for me at the factory. All the rest are redneck women. That's the strength of my business," said Mel. "Recently I hired a manager from California. He was a New Age type who wore these hot-pink tights and rode his bike through town. It didn't go over too well with the good ole boys." Mel related how his plant manager fired one of the women workers because she'd missed too much work. Her daddy and her husband, *Chester* and *Lester*, whom Melvin characterized as PWT (poor white trash), showed up drunk at the plant and pulled a gun on the manager. "My redneck secretary saw what was going on," said Mel. "And she knew that the manager from California couldn't handle it. So she walks right up to the guy with the gun. Damn, pulled it straight out of his hand, barrel first. She keeps it in her desk to this day!"

Redneck women receive high praise in traditional male jobs, too, such as coal mining. "Ladies're used to lookin' out for their husbands and their sons," says Sam Wright, the miner from Tuscaloosa. "There's less accidents with 'em around. You know how it is. They keep their 'mama's radar' on."

The redneck woman seems to be made of a special combination of loyalty, femininity, and sheer drive, as in this story told by writer Andrea June Hanson. "I was doing an article for *Ms.* magazine about a successful professional lady bronc rider. When I asked her if she was related to the world-renowned rodeo star with the same last name, she replied, 'Sure as

Gulf Shores, Alabama, barber: "I'm sorry to hear about your mama dying."
Gulf Shores, Alabama, barbershop customer: "Yeah. We sure are gonna miss her at the sawmill. She was the best damn worker we had!"

Working Girl

Del is a brilliant redheaded attorney from a small Virginia town. On her first day as an associate with a large Wall Street firm, one of the senior partners ogled her legs as he asked, "So, dear, I thought maybe you could work directly under me. Do you type?"

To which she replied, "Yes, and I fuck too, but never professionally."

---

shootin', that's my ex-husband! One night I got fed up with being the wife of a rodeo cowboy—being scared he'd break his neck or run off with a buckle bunny. I said, "Baby, it's me or the rodeo."

"'That's how I got started in the rodeo. You see, he admitted he'd rather ride a bronc for eight seconds than have sex with me. Shit, I figured if it was that good, I'd better try it myself! After that first ride I turned into a little witch. You know, all a little witch needs to keep her happy is lots of adventure and a big ole broom every now and then!'"

HE'S MY MAN

Despite the desire of some modern redneck women to be free of responsibility, there are many contemporary examples of those who still choose to live happily ever after, like Johnny Richard's wife, Kathy. During the year he'd been in federal prison on conspiracy-to-commit-piracy charges for smuggling marijuana, his wife had missed visiting him on only two weekends. When Kathy wasn't driving the six hours each way to the prison in Texarkana, she'd run Johnny's feed and cattle business. That was when she wasn't putting in a forty-hour week as the manager of the toy, stationery, and gun section at the Real Superstore.

Johnny and his wife live in a sharecropper's shack as cozy as the cabin of a sailboat. The front yard is dominated by Johnny's "cajun-uzi," a homemade Jacuzzi fashioned from a vintage chest freezer. The water is heated by the sun and kept circulating by a trolling motor. Inside on the old door used as a coffee table is a galvanized tin jug of wildflowers.

Kathy tells how she met her husband: "Johnny and Daddy worked together at the State Department of Agriculture. I guess we'd known each other for a few years. The problem was Daddy figured Johnny was as wild as Monday is long. But, you know, it didn't take me but one date to find out Daddy was wrong! Johnny took me to the Catahoula dog trials. Watchin' those dogs herd cattle is the coolest thing I ever saw.

"We were together for several years before we got married. Then things went all to hell. One night Johnny and I were in bed and the sheriff came, guns and all. He arrested my husband. To this day, when I see soldiers go off to war I cry, thinkin' about how hard it is being separated from the man you love. That's why I changed jobs after Johnny got his pardon."

Kathy's new job involves alligators. To get supplies for her jewelry-making business, she goes to the source. She parks Johnny's truck beside a large metal barn. The stench of ammonia, musk, and rancid fish assaults the eyes like pepper spray, but neither Kathy nor the throng of men inside seems to notice it. The stainless slabs and the concrete floor of the skinners are covered in alligator blood and guts. Kathy points out barrels and vats containing various salable pieces of the four- to twelve-foot alligators—the skin will eventually end up in shoes and bags made in Italy or France, the internal organs go to medical labs for experiments, the meat will go to seafood brokers, the alligator's penis will go to Japan for the aphrodisiac trade, and the teeth and bones will go to Kathy.

Kathy and Johnny create their own style of dressing that combines the Old West and the finest formal wear the Salvation Army can provide.

FROM THE COLLECTION OF KATHY RICHARD.

I'm the Only Hell Mama Ever Raised

"The men skin all night," Kathy explained. "I only want the fresh heads and the armor-plated solar panels along the back strap for my jewelry." With that, Kathy began hurling a pile of primordial alligator heads and bones into the bed of Johnny's truck.

Kathy talks of her career choice with exuberance. "I got the idea for makin' jewelry out of 'swamp ivory' when I was poor. I couldn't afford to buy Christmas presents for my family. All I had was some old alligator teeth. I had to improvise. Then they told me people were buyin' the pieces of jewelry right off their ears. So I thought: 'Kathy, maybe you could make a livin' stayin' home with Johnny and designin' jewelry.'

"You see while Johnny was in prison I realized somethin'—you can punch somebody else's time clock your whole life. By the time you earn financial security you've lost your health. Usually the person you wanted to share it with, too. Or to put it another way, some people spend their whole lives kissin' the ass that feeds 'em. Guess they shouldn't wonder why they end up eatin' shit.

"But I am the luckiest woman alive," beamed Kathy, wiggling her head to the beat of the Sammy Kershaw song on the radio, "Queen of My Double-Wide Trailer." "My husband wakes me up at dawn with a kiss and a cup of coffee. You can't beat that! And Johnny's mother even cooks for us."

Back at home, Kathy unloads the seventy-five alligator skulls and bones into a quarter-acre mud pit about a hundred yards from her house. In a few days the skulls will be overrun with black ants and Buick-sized flies who do the hard work of devouring the alligator flesh down to white bone. "Now all we have to do is pray for a north wind to blow the stink away from us and down to the neighbors. Since we don't have air-conditioning, I coat my bandanna in perfume and stick it in the window fan so we get a whiff of Blue Grass before the alligator-corpse aroma creeps into bed with us."

CHAPTER SIX

Rednecks, White Socks, and Blue Ribbon Beer

"'The love of drinking, which is . . . a prevailing passion with [the Celts], may readily be ascribed to. . . a natural fondness of excitement, to convivial feelings, or the extravagant notions too generally encouraged by universal hospitality,' commented an Englishman in the 19th century."

—Grady McWhiney, Cracker Culture

ONE THING IS FOR SURE ABOUT HONKY-TONKS: NO matter where they're located—North, South, East, or West, town or country—the territory doesn't change. The atmosphere has the testosterone charge of a chain-saw movie. The combination of liquor and country music entices, enhances, and incites. A few hours in a honky-tonk seems to work like a psychological high colonic on most of the male patrons, whether they happen to be called Marion, Gale, and June, or 'Moose,' 'Hammer,' or 'Mule Skinner.'

Today's rednecks seem to congregate at the honky-tonk for the same reason their kinsmen frequented taverns in the 1500s: "games, songs, gambling, blasphemy and disorder—that was usually at odds with official culture" (James C. Scott, *Domination and the Arts of Resistance*). These men appear to need the sort of social lube job that only whiskey's fire and the freedom from the domination of their wives can supply. As one redneck woman explains, "In the honky-tonks, men are men, and we're damn glad of it."

THE WORKER SPEAKS

The honky-tonk is a welcoming place for men to unwind at the end of a tough day at work. Here, they can gather and swig down a beer as they bemoan their bosses, criticize their coworkers, and joke about their jobs—in their own uniquely redneck words, of course.

* Alligator: To drag tail or work lazily; e.g., "It's so hot I'm just gonna alligator today."
* Asbestos: A person who is fireproof; e.g., the boss's son-in-law.
* Bork: To kill politically or to cause to be fired.
* Bull: Maine redneck term for grunt work done in an inefficient manner that produces sweat.
* College faggots: Fraternity boys who sign on to do manual labor in the summer.
* Few sandwiches too short of a picnic: Unreliable and stupid.
* Gator tail: A long drawn-out excuse, especially as it applies to an absence from work.
* JSB (jock-sniffing bastard): Anyone who tries to get above himself.
* Mexican raise: A better title without more pay.
* Pickle hearts: Big-city folks who wear suits to work.
* Presbyterian down: To get the better of someone in a business deal; e.g., "Junior sure Presbyterianed ole Ernie down on that Weed Eater."
* Sandbaggers: People who hold back on the work effort.
* See-through: Construction workers' term for a high-rise built by speculators that has no tenants.
* Straw-hat boss: Lazy superior at work who merely gives orders and grief.

Photo on page 179 by Syndey Byrd.

* Third basers: People who were born on third base, act like they batted a triple to get there, and haven't got a clue as to how to get to home plate unless someone bats them in.
* Woods yuppies: Folks in Maine who have to do business with city folks, so they bring a fax machine and an answering machine into their log cabin or trailer and live as far away from civilization as they can get.

Miners emerge after an eight-hour shift in the deepest vertical coal-mine shaft in North America, 2,140 feet. DENNIS HALL.

Indeed, it may sound odd that a woman would choose to venture into the intensely male atmosphere of the honky-tonk. But what better place for her to enjoy redneck men in their truest form, learn their secrets, and try to figure out what makes them tick.

After forty-five years tending bar and listening to men's problems at Deuce, Jean, the Den Mother, is considered by many to be the Wichita Falls, Texas, answer to Dr. Ruth—at least when it comes to male redneck behavior. "My customers are like my brothers," she says with a sentiment bordering on true sisterly affection. "We're really a family. When we're together, I guess you could say every one of us feels like we know we're part of a family," she says, pointing to the wall of pictures of the regulars who've passed away. Located in a converted filling station in the heart of downtown Wichita Falls, Deuce was originally P-2's, a dive *Texas Monthly* once referred to as the place where "the elite meet to cheat." The atmosphere inside recalls another era—a cement floor, beer signs, and cowboys playing cards. There's no jukebox, and hard liquor isn't served. Actually the guys don't drink much of anything except Bud, the brand of beer favored by the clientele out of deference to the local distributor. Yet Deuce is the undisputed seat of financial power in West Texas. Some of its customers are oil barons, others are unemployed, and all of them look like the cast of *The Unforgiven*.

The Den Mother has been there since the early days in the 1940s, when P-2's was a stag bar noted for having the coldest beer in Wichita Falls. As Jean recalls, "After World War II, when my husband got out of the service, we moved to Wichita Falls to work for Southwestern Bell. Neither of us were bringin' home thirty dollars a week. The lady next door bragged she made between fifty and a hundred dollars a night working as a carhop down at P-2's. My husband didn't like it one bit. But we wanted to buy a home. That's why I went to work with her."

"Hud," "3xMoore" (the undertaker), and K.R. (grandson of famed female trick-rider Tad Lucas) in front of Moore's Pepto-Bismol-pink Cadillac at 2 A.M. in Las Vegas during the National Finals Rodeo. SUE ROSOFF.

Beer Recipes

In the attempt to lure her man home from a honky-tonk, a redneck wife might be moved to continue the alcoholic beverage theme in her kitchen.

Beer is a readily available ingredient in nonteetotaling homes. Besides being added to barbecue sauce and chili, it's also handy for baking.

PBR (Pabst Blue Ribbon Beer) Biscuits

3 cups Bisquick
1 cup PBR, at room temperature
2 tablespoons sugar

1. Preheat oven to 450°.
2. Combine ingredients and mix until dough forms a ball.
3. Turn dough onto a floured surface. (If the dough is too gooey, chill for half an hour.)
4. Using a floured rolling pin, roll the dough ½ inch thick, then using a 2½-inch biscuit cutter (or an empty small Vienna-sausage can), cut out the biscuits.
5. Place on ungreased cookie sheet, 1 inch apart, and bake for 10 minutes.
6. Butter while hot.

Makes 1 dozen 2½-inch biscuits

Variations: The dough is ideal as a top crust for cobbler or, without the sugar, for a deep-dish potpie.

PBR Black-Out Cake

⅔ cup cocoa powder, plus ⅓ cup for dusting
1 cup Blue Plate mayonnaise
1 large package instant chocolate pudding mix
1 cup Pabst Blue Ribbon beer
2 cups sugar
Pinch of salt
3 large eggs
¾ cup sour cream
2 cups all-purpose flour
1 teaspoon Calumet baking powder

1. Preheat oven to 350°.
2. Grease 2 8-inch springform pans and dust with $1/3$ cup cocoa powder.
3. Cream mayonnaise, pudding mix, beer, sugar, salt, and $2/3$ cup cocoa powder.
4. Beat in eggs, one at a time.
5. Mix in sour cream.
6. Sift flour and baking powder and add into the creamed mixture, beating after each addition.
7. Pour batter into the layer pans and bake for 30 minutes, or until a broom straw comes out clean.
8. Cool on wire racks for 15 minutes.
9. Remove sides of pan and cool thoroughly.

Makes 10 to 12 servings

Jean pats her rich crude oil–colored hair into shape as she confesses that "sexual harassment" has always been just a part of the landscape for her. "When I started out I was in my twenties. Had me some big boobs, too. You know, I got propositioned a lot! But I cut those guys down with my big mouth. If a guy used vulgar language, I'd laugh and say, 'Go on, Sugah, say whatever you want. I know you're not allowed to open that mouth of yours at home!'

"Now, I respect their wives," says Jean. "I might love these guys, but I wouldn't want to be married to 'em for *anything* in the world! It's amazin'—men want their freedom. Then I noticed they spend most of their free time checkin' on their wives. But the real problem in most marriages is the women. They try to make their husbands into what they want them to be. Husbands can't be themselves with their wives. That's why they need to hang out here," Jean suggests.

"But, it's interestin'—I've noticed the guys who lay back here till it's dinnertime at home are the ones that stay married," Jean observes. "The ones who never go home cheat. Their wives divorce 'em. Then they're so miserable it's like they died. Men just don't get it—women are their power source. They're only happy when they're connected to a steady supply!"

DON'T ASK, DON'T TELL

At a honky-tonk near O'Hare Airport in Chicago, a particularly irascible-looking bartender (her name tag reads DOE NASK) pauses for a break during the midweek midafternoon lull. Behind the bar is a sign written in black marker: IF YOU CAME IN HERE TO BITCH, YOU JUST WASTED 98% OF YOUR TIME. USE THE LAST 2% TO GET YOUR ASS OUT THE DOOR. She swabs the bar while adroitly balancing an unfiltered cigarette on her lower highly glossed, iridescent, pontiff-purple lip.

"It's like me dear ole Irish mum, a former precinct captain for the Daley machine, used to say, 'A woman'll never have any problems if she stays away from anything with a carburetor or an asshole!'" says Doe with a slap of her wet dishrag against her bulging thigh. "I wish I'd listened to her . . . been married three times." After she pours herself a Kahlua and cream, she offers some personal observations. "I figure it like this . . . men are like dogs chasin' cars—once they catch you, all they want to do is bite the tires. Every once in a while one of 'em gets run over. But that doesn't teach 'em shit. They keep right on barkin' and runnin' in the road."

She squeezes her well-padded rump into a booth by the window. "I can't tell you how many elbows and hands this here pair of tits has had on 'em. The second I feel a jab, I just raise my arms right up over my head like this here," she says, revealing breasts the size of watermelons. "I tell 'em, 'You got ten seconds to grab whatever you want. Then I've gotta get back to work!' "

Doe admits she's reached an age when it's easier to date her ex-husbands. "The first one loved me the most. But he was young, immature, and real jealous. Now he's gotten over bein' young," she states with a hard squint. "My second, the cop, looked tougher than a beatin' by ten convicts. Shit, the man couldn'ta outrun Marlon Brando! Claimed he had a bad back and asthma. What a useless use of sex appeal! The third and me used to screw around a little while I was married to number two. I'll admit he ain't much to look at. My daughter said he looked uglier than my mother's big toe. He's rich, though. Trouble was, O'Hare wasn't big enough to hold that ego of his . . . turned out that was his favorite body part, if you get my drift," she concludes, fiddling with her many rings.

Over the jukebox at Doe's honky-tonk there are a couple of neon tequila signs and some ratty sombreros. On closer inspection it turns out they cover bullet holes—a perfectly executed USA done in sheetrock from behind the bar with Doe's .45.

After a few more drinks and cigarettes, Doe glides into a more elegiac mode. "Guys come in lookin' for the perfect woman—a combination of Mother Teresa and Madonna. If I give 'em lip they'll whine, 'You got a bad attitude. What makes you so mean?' I tell them I'm sufferin' with PMS. Then they'll back off. But I seen somethin' on *Oprah*. It made me realize all those guys thought I suffered from a health problem. No sir, the kind of PMS I've got is the result of *putting up with men's shit*. Come to think about it, maybe that *is* a health problem, a mental one.

"But I figure it this way," she concedes, "all men need to dump their shit somewhere. It might as well be on me rather than some other poor gal what don't care like I do."

LOOKIN' FOR LOVE
IN ALL THE WRONG PLACES

—Country song

In the honky-tonks, the male libido is on the prowl, and its prey must take heed. However, some women choose to treat overt expressions of lust as a dare rather than an affront. At the Pony Express on Staten Island, New York, a youthful woman with silver hair stands her ground as a pimple-faced cowboy with a straggly mustache tries to delight her with his mutt-grin. "Looks like a weasel from a Peter Lorre movie to me," she warns another woman in the bathroom. "If he bothers you, jus' tell him you're with me." Later, she brushes off his increasingly vulgar nuances with a sassy wink.

Writing on the Wall

Honky-tonk bathroom graffiti are ubiquitous and plentiful. Often really good graffiti selections make their way onto the hand-printed signs redneck proprietors hang behind the bar to scare off college kids, the politically correct, the humor impaired, and habitual losers.

HONKY-TONKS ARE LIKE WRANGLER JEANS—THERE AIN'T NO BALL ROOM.

—*Sign spotted in a Florida honky-tonk frequented by air force pilots*

Carved with a knife into the linoleum of a bar: WHY DO KENNEDY MEN WEEP WHEN THEY MAKE LOVE?
After lots of guesses scribbled in everything from felt-tip markers to crayon, the author supplied the correct answer: MACE.

— *From Alabama*

DADDY CAN'T FLY HIS KITE 'CAUSE MAMA WON'T GIVE HIM NO TAIL.

—*Sign above a bar in Austin, Texas*

BE WARNED: WE DON'T SERVE NO UGLY GIRLS HERE.
THEY JUST LOOK THAT WAY IN THE DAYLIGHT.

—*Sign in a Los Angeles honky-tonk*

In ballpoint: I FUCKED YOUR MAMA.
Written underneath, in black felt-tip: GO HOME, DADDY, YOU'RE DRUNK.

—*From Tennessee*

NO MATTER HOW CUTE YOU THINK SHE IS, SOMEONE, SOMEWHERE, HATES HER SHIT.

—*From Pennsylvania*

Biker couple at a motorcycle swap meet.
STEPHEN COLLECTOR.

"Most of us gals here tonight only got room for one asshole in our jeans!"

Many honky-tonk women seem victorious in the undeclared ideological guerrilla war between the sexes. *Twanette,* a Mississippi bartender, appears gift wrapped in a well-filled halter top made from two Confederate-flag bandannas. She makes a valiant effort to ignore a guy making lewd tongue and hand gestures. "Aw, Twanette, it'd sure be right nice to fuck your brains out," he pleads longingly.

"What a shame, *Voyd,*" she replies good-naturedly. "I'm clean out of brains!" Twanette offers her insights into male behavior. "I realized men're a lot more limited-like than women. Most of 'em ain't nothin' but *hypothetical* liars. And they can only operate five gears: if they can't eat it, drive it, fix it, or fuck it, they've gotta kill it! And you better believe, a woman's gotta be in that driver's seat to keep 'em from slippin' into that fifth gear."

Twanette's views are echoed by two women at a honky-tonk in Denver. As one put it, "I'm married to a very passionate man. I got a healthy respect for his warrior instincts, though. There's not a day I don't realize those same hands that'll kill for me could kill me."

The other woman, a redhead with big blue eyes and a short black skirt, says, "To each his own. . . . But at fifty I'm proud to say I've never been with one man for longer than Desert Storm. I like my men young, blond, handsome, strong, dumb, and with a short attention span. If you need protection and companionship, buy a 30.06 rifle with a scope and a collie! I tell you, if you can't meet a cute boy at a honky-tonk, try NAPA Auto Parts. They aren't lyin' when they say 'All the right parts in all the right places.' "

Several redneck-male-loving women weren't in the least doubtful about their anticipated victory in the battle of the sexes. The gorgeous wife of a country music sex symbol was overheard talking to one of her friends. When her friend offered sympathy over the couple's long separations while he was touring, the wife's mouth formed an O of displeasure.

"I gotta admit most of the time I only miss about eight inches of 'im!" she teased.

Her friend wondered out loud about the rumors that the country star occasionally had affairs. "Occasionally?" the wife said in mock surprise. "Try in every city! But what can I do? As the sayin' goes, 'A stiff staff ain't got no conscience.'

"Hell, when we were first datin' I asked him if there was anythin' he'd like to change about my body. We were in that dancin'-on-clouds phase. I expected him to say 'Nothing, angel, you're perfect.' You wanna know what the bastard said? Right outta the chute, he tells me I'd have the perfect body if I just didn't have a head!"

Her friend replied, "You oughta write a song—'Sometimes the best ass sure is the biggest!' " They clinked Coke cans together in a toast.

"But lovin' him is my job." The wife sighed. "I figure there're two kindsa men—those that have a midlife crisis and run away for good and those that'll sow their wild oats and then come home to settle in the pasture. I'm a patient woman. I don't plan to spend my golden years out in that pasture alone."

"I'LL WALK BEFORE I'LL CRAWL"

—A Janie Fricke strong-woman song

Other women are not as forgiving when it comes to their husbands' philandering. These fiery redneck wives seek vengeance to put their men back in their places, and concoct schemes that seem to work miracles in the behavior modification department.

One woman got her straying man home by writing on the side of their barn in spray paint CLEM ISN'T HOME, HE'S WITH BARB!!! As the barn could be seen from the highway, Clem heard about it by the time the paint was dry. He's since repainted the barn, and his wife has had no need to issue new bulletins to the community.

Other redneck women employ a time-honored preventive technique to keep their men out of trouble. Every time her man comes home drunk, a woman will take the opportunity to smear lipstick all over his underwear and douse his shirt in women's perfume. The woman then waits until her man awakens, finds his soiled clothes, and tries to hide the "evidence." Then she ambushes him. The poor guy swears he has no idea how the lipstick got on his underwear. All hell breaks loose. If he confesses, he's sunk; if he pleads amnesia, it gets worse. He spends a week treading on lightbulbs before she grants him parole. But it stays on his record.

"RED NECKIN' LOVE MAKIN' NIGHT"

—Conway Twitty song

Donnie Ray, a married L.A. film production electrician, explained the man's point of view concerning adultery in the theme parks of the libido. "In the world of the honky-tonk, cheatin' ain't cheatin' if you stick to the rules," he said as he stirred his Jack Daniel's and Coke with his screwdriver. "You aren't breakin' your vows if you do it outside of the zip codes where your friends or family live, or if you don't take your clothes off. Now, if the chick furnishes the condom or bumpin' uglies was her idea, well, you're safe there, too. But even if your wife catches you in the act, you never admit a thing. No sirreee, if there ever was a time for lying, that's it. Just look your lady right smack in the eye and tell her you were thinkin' about her the entire time. If that doesn't work, tell her you borrowed the dick you're doin' it with! And remember, in the time-honored tradition of man, never leave an angry woman in possession of a gun, a knife, or the last word.

"But seriously," Donnie Ray advised, "I'm straighter than a Kansas interstate these days. I've learned my lesson. You know, if you're gonna stand on your dick all night, you can't stand on your feet all day."

"SHE KEEPS THE HOME FIRES BURNING"

— Ronnie Milsap ode to the perfect wife

I'm supposed to have had more men than most people change their underwear.

—Tanya Tucker

Although men may seem to be the dominant force within the sexual arena of the honky-tonk, women are certainly not innocent bystanders. In fact, sometimes they're even the instigators.

Tiger ran a honky-tonk for years. In her view, it's not the male behavior but the predatory instincts of other women that's the usual culprit in sexual liaisons. "I was married at fifteen—had two kids by the time I was seventeen. My husband was the prince of the recliner. He still used his free time to run around on me and all. Here I was, this gorgeous woman, and he's cheatin' on me. Well, I showed him where he could stick it! I left his ass on my nineteenth birthday. That's how I got to be a barmaid.

"Back when I was tending bar, the guys who came in, the majority of 'em—I'd say seventy percent of 'em—were decent, churchgoing, God-fearing people," Tiger explained. "If a guy got outta line, he'd apologize. You

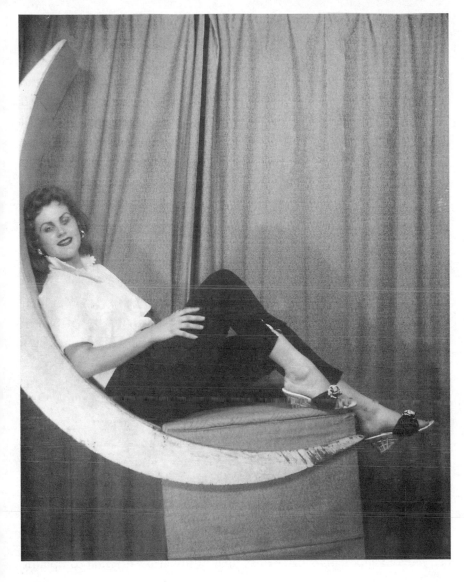

know, after they sobered up. But the thing I hate's a chippy. Now, a whore is a professional. A chippy just screws somebody else's man for the fun of it."

Indeed, inside the honky-tonk, women's behavior often rivals men's. They can be just as sexually voracious, just as loud, just as wild, and just as vulgar. There is a famous quote about country music legend Patsy Cline: "Patsy was the first woman in country who made you feel like cryin' outta one eye and winkin' with the other." To which singer Faron Young is said to have added, "You couldn't get ahead of Patsy. If somebody farted in her direction, she'd raise her ass and fart right back."

Strong-willed honky-tonk women might just be carrying on the traditions of their ancient kinswomen. Historians noted that Celtic women followed a different code of social conduct than their Greek or Roman counterparts. According to the laws of the Druids, Celtic men, and occasionally Celtic women, were granted permission to have more than one mate. Cassius Dio, a Roman Senator and writer, recounted an altercation he'd witnessed in the early third century A.D. between a Roman matron and a Celtic wife whom she'd charged with promiscuity. The Celtic wife jeered, "We fulfill the demands of nature in a much better way than do you Roman women. We consort openly with the best men, whereas you let yourselves be debauched in secret by the vilest."

Centuries later, on American shores, Rachel Donelson Robards, a willful female of Celtic descent, flaunted convention. She was the wife of Lewis Robards when she began carrying on an affair with Andrew Jackson. When confronted by the husband, Jackson threatened "to cut the ears out of his head." Jackson was arrested, but before the case came to court, Jackson went after Rachel's husband with a butcher knife. The husband fled into a canebrake. Fearing for his life, Rachel's husband neglected to appear in court. Consequently, Robards's original complaint against Jackson was dropped. This left Rachel free to marry Jackson, claiming she'd been abandoned by her spouse.

Victorian folklorists were scandalized by the lewd behavior of many of the backcountry women of Celtic descent. One reported that "young women would get upon a Tableboard and then gather-up their knees and their coates as high as they can, then they wobble to and fro with their buttocks, singing 'Up with your heels, down with your head, that is the way to make cockeldy bread.'"

There are over 100 different western dances. Some men admit to dancing six to seven hours a night. Sometimes they change shirts hourly.
SYNDEY BYRD.

I WOULDN'T TAKE YOU TO A DOGFIGHT, EVEN IF I THOUGHT YOU COULD WIN

—Country song

The language in a honky-tonk goes beyond colorful. Here one can hear "fuck" in one form or another used as a verb, a noun, an adjective, and a gerund—all in the same sentence. This isn't a new linguistic phenomenon, however. Travelers from England and New England characterized the language heard in backcountry drinking establishments as gratifying the patrons' basest passions—licentious, filled with filthy jests and scurrility. In eighteenth-century Lunenburg County, Virginia, two streams were originally named Fucking Creek and Tickle Cunt Branch.

Redneck Man Talk

* Bobbit: To cut off (end) anything from a relationship to a car's engine.
* Bow: Bitch on wheels.
* Bryn Mawr girls: New England term for loose rich girls who shoplift.
* Buckle bunnies: Rodeo groupies.
* Bunker: New England fisherman's term for girls at the low end of the desirability scale. (During the bleak winter months, bunkers automatically move up a category.)
* Bushwhacking: To harass people making out in cars.
* Coyote arm: When you open your eyes in the morning and realize the woman sleeping on your arm is so ugly you'd chew your arm off to get away before she wakes up.

* DLGs (daddy's little girls): Sorority and/or yuppie girls.

* Firin' up Joycelyn: To masturbate (a reference to the stated reason for the firing of Surgeon General Dr. Joycelyn Elders, which was her suggestion that masturbation could be an alternative to premarital sex for teens).

* Factory titties: Silicone breast implants.

* Fourteen(er) twenty: A fourteen-year-old girl will get you twenty years in jail; jailbait.

* Funch: A sexual liaison during the lunch hour.

* Fuzzy taco: Female sex organ.

* Hand sandwich: To hold hands.

* Hard bellies: New England term for sweet young things.

* Herring: A fisherman's classification for middle-of-the-road girls, usually those who are slightly overweight but who are lookers.

* Hide, wool, or split tail: Generic Western term for women.

* Hole in one: To get a girl pregnant after one sexual encounter.

* Holy mackerel: Top-of-the-line classification for women in New England.

* Husk: To undress.

* I-mond: When it grows up it wants to be a diamond.

* Kinky justices: Pubic hair (after Supreme Court Justice Clarence Thomas's alleged pubic-hair-on-the-Coke-can incident).

* Kitchen pass: Permission from a wife for her husband to go out at night.

* Lawn mower: A sheep used as a sexual partner.

* Little rock: An unwanted engagement ring.

* Lot lizard: Hooker in a truck stop.

* Necker's knob: A protrusion on the steering wheel so that the driver needs only one hand to hold the wheel.
* NI (pronounced "nye"): A feminist, literally "nookie impaired."
* Nigger defense or to O.J.: To commit a dastardly deed that you regret to the point you feel entitled to forgiveness.
* Nuclear submarine or one-eyed wonder worm: The male sex organ.
* Pet clam: Cape Cod man's ideal wife—passive and wet.
* Pit lizards: Race-car-driver groupies.
* Pit popsies: Drag-racing groupies.
* Ring worm: A boxing groupie.
* Rodeo love doll: An inflatable sheep with tubing for hot water.
* Run leg or trawl for wool: To look for girls.
* Shit in the nest or Turd in the punch bowl: To embarrass one's family and friends.
* Smoke the hog: To perform oral sex on a male.
* Snee na noonie: The sex act.
* Spanish mack: New England fisherman's term for the next-to-the-top grade of woman.
* Sport flirt: The setup for a one-night stand.
* Unzip: To break down defenses.
* Wet weekend: Woman's period.
* Whale tail: New England fisherman's term for bottom-of-the-line women.
* Wifebeater: A sleeveless white undershirt.
* Winter mack: Cape Cod term used to describe the status of girls who begin to look better and better the more desolate the weather gets.

IF YOU TREAT HER LIKE A THOROUGHBRED, SHE WON'T ACT LIKE A NAG

—Bumper sticker on a palomino-colored Mustang

The honky-tonk dance floor is the favorite hunting and courting ground for redneck men. Here the contradictions in the breed become as sharp as the edges of a broken beer bottle. On the dance floor even oafish-looking redneck guys assume the courtly grace of Fred Astaire. The couples, young or old, dance with the precision of the upper and lower jaws of a wolf. At new honky-tonks, dancers will test the surface of a dance floor. If they don't like it, they'll leave, taking those bystanders who come to watch with them.

In many rural areas, dances are held early Saturday morning or on

JUST WHEN YOU THINK LIFE IS A BITCH, IT HAS PUPPIES

—Kathy Richard's favorite button

Country music chronicles many human stories and offers a window into the tender heart of the redneck. Perhaps the most telling songs are those that center on a breakup. It's often hard to explain just how or why a relationship goes wrong, but then there's country music, with the uncanny ability of its songwriters to pour volumes into just one line. Former Dallas Cowboy and chewing-tobacco spokesman Walt Garrison likes to collect prosaic turns of phrase.

Walt Garrison's List of On-the-Rocks Songs

* "I've Got Tears in My Ears from Lyin' on My Back in Bed While I Cry Over You"
* "I've Been in Jail and I've Been in Love and I'd Rather Be in Jail"
* "The More I Think of You, the Less I Think of Me"
* "You're Driving Me out of Your Mind"
* "She'll Love You to Pieces, but She Won't Put You Together Again"
* "If Someone That Loves Me Could Hurt Me This Bad, Just Think What a Stranger Could Do"
* "I Don't Love You Any More, Trouble Is, I Don't Love You Any Less"
* "If the Phone Don't Ring, Baby, You'll Know It's Me"
* "I Gave Her a Ring and She Gave Me the Finger"
* "I Don't Know Whether to Kill Myself or Go Bowling"
* "My Wife Ran Off with My Best Friend and I Miss Him"
* "I May Fall Again, but I'll Never Get Up This Slow"
* "She's Just a Name-Dropper, and Now She's Dropping Mine"

- ✶ "I Bought the Shoes That Walked Out on Me"
- ✶ "Did I Fall Out of Favor Because the Only Ring I Ever Gave Her Was the One She Scrubbed Out of the Tub?"
- ✶ "It Takes Me All Night Long to Do What I Used to Do All Night Long"
- ✶ "Just in Time to Be Too Late"
- ✶ "Our Marriage Was a Failure, but Our Divorce Ain't Working Either"
- ✶ "My Pride's Not Hard to Swallow, Once You Chew It Long Enough"

Sunday afternoon to accommodate older people. In the old-time bars they'll request that grits or cornmeal be spread on the floor for glide. It is not unusual to see a gray-haired lady drive her mother to a dance, help the older lady hobble into the VFW hall with her walker, and then come back two hours later to take her home. But once at the dance, the crippled mother will dance every dance like a spry teenager.

Many men not only take their mates dancing weekly, but they dress in coordinated outfits. One couple dressed in this fashion wore identical black-and-white satin cowboy shirts with silver fringe, white cowboy hats, and suede boots, he in white jeans, she in a matching full white denim skirt. As they two-stepped closer, you could see that the man was about twenty-five and the lady had to be eighty. On another occasion, the crowd was impressed by the passion and virtuosity with which an elderly couple, dressed in coordinated cherry-and-lime cowboy outfits, were dancing. As they both wore wedding bands, a visitor commented, "You and your wife are the best couple on the floor." They ignored the compliment. Later the "wife" took the visitor aside and confided, "We *are* married, but not to each other."

"I CAN WALK THE LINE (IF IT AIN'T TOO STRAIGHT)"

—Country song by Joe Diffie

There probably would be no honky-tonk dancing if not for its necessary fuel: the good, honest tunes. Country music has been called everything from a cultural supermarket to jukebox philosophy. Either way, it provides the wink and glimmer—not to mention socioeconomic commentary—to the honky-tonk. Dr. Cecelia Tichi, a professor of

English at Vanderbilt University, thinks country music is not only linked to the nation's literature and art, but it addresses the same serious topics Thomas Jefferson addressed—love, class struggle, and loneliness. "If you think those songs are easy to write, write one," she challenges (Rheta Grimsley, Johnson, *Atlanta Journal Constitution*, Sunday, January 7, 1996).

Although country music may try to unify all people and welcome all races, it's far harder to participate if the musician happens not to be a redneck. As Charlie Pride is often quoted, "Only a white guy can get away with sounding black in country. I can't."

For African American performers, the honky-tonk is not always a welcoming place. "I swear we were prayin' for chicken wire that night in Pasadena, Texas," laugh Essie and Al Morris, Mr. and Mrs. Country Soul. "This was in the mid-1980s. We'd been playin' at a honky-tonk on Spencer Highway near Gilley's in Houston. This guy comes up and says, 'Man, you wanna make one hundred dollars just showin' up at a country jam session? Here's the first fifty dollars now.'"

Essie and Al stand out wherever they go—a six-foot-plus black couple decked out in twenty pounds of Navajo jewelry. Al, born in Temple, Texas (thirty-five miles south of Waco), in 1938, moved back to his Texas roots after playing R-and-B guitar during his nineteen-year career in L.A. touring with Marvin Gaye, Etta James, and James Brown. "They never let me sing, though," Al remembers. "Sometimes I'd slip in a country lick. They'd say, 'Shut up that cowboy noise!'

"Country music is my heritage. In my part of Texas, you know, there were only two kinds of music on the radio—gospel and country. My inspiration was B. M. Daily and the Hot Brown Boys. Ever hear of them? They played all over central Texas. Being black, you couldn't go into any country bars unless you were in the band. But when you took an intermission, you knew you'd better stay on that dang stage."

Essie jumps in to describe her background. "I'm a native hillbilly from Harris, North Carolina, who can pick peaches, plow with a mule, and chop cotton. My father had his Ph.D., you know. I'm still working on mine, but it's sort of on hold. I'm following my dream—to be the black Patsy Cline!"

Essie continues Al's story: ". . . so we're drivin' on down Spencer Highway, and Al says, 'That man last night sure had a fine sense of humor. Did you see that?' We had to turn the car around and stop to take our picture by a sign the size of an eighteen-wheeler, WELCOME TO PASADENA, TEXAS, HOME OF THE KU KLUX KLAN."

Al and Essie were not deterred. They couldn't wait to see what "a bunch of honky-tonkin' Ku Klux Klanners were gonna say when they saw us! Those rednecks-to-the-bone were shuckin', jivin', and puffin' on their beers up until we hit that doorway. The plug was pulled on that jukebox. We heard scufflin' of chairs, and about six hundred pairs of eyes aimed at us.

"With extreme sarcasm there came this mocking voice from the back . . . 'I think we done bees loss,' but Al ignored him as he walked up to the bartender to ask what time the jam session started," recalls Essie.

" 'Whenever you set up,' sneered the bartender," continues Al. "But you coulda heard a cotton ball drop the whole time we were totin' in our equipment! As I said, we were prayin' for chicken wire! But since there wasn't any, we knew the next best thing was to go for the jugular of country."

Essie takes over again: "You can't cut any deeper than Ernest Tubb, George Jones, Hank Sr., and Tammy Wynette. That's what we did—one song after the other without a pause for applause. After a while, the audience started coming round. By the tenth song the bartender hired us to play for the rest of the night."

Coca-Cola Christmas tree.
GERARD SELLERS.

Al adds, "To me the nicest part was when we'd finished playing. This big old cowboy came up to shake hands. 'I want to apologize,' he said. We told him he hadn't done anything to us he needed to apologize for. But he insisted. 'It wasn't anythin' I *did* I want to apologize for. It's for what I wuz thinkin'. From now on anybody wants ta mess with you's gotta get through me first!'"

THINGS GO BETTER WITH COKE . . .

Many rednecks are vehement teetotalers. Soft drinks become the backbone of their social life. Coca-Cola (pronounced "Co-Cola") is to the Southern redneck what tea is to the British. In 1886, John Pemberton, an Atlanta druggist seeking a remedy for headaches, combined coca leaves, cola nuts, sugar, and cocaine to create Coca-Cola. In the old days, preachers were able to buy Coke at a special discount. Nowadays, old-timers grumble that vending machines treat the clergy as they would anyone else.

Among many Southern rednecks Coke is the universal name for all soft drinks, in much the same way that the term "soda" is used in the North. "What kind of Coke you gals want? Mountain Dew or Dr Pepper?" At many a small neighborhood soda fountain, the syrup can still be bought over the counter as the top remedy for curing stomachaches and diarrhea. However, many youngsters report they've been warned not to mix Coke with aspirin. According to folklore it could turn into a serious mind-altering drug, a Mickey.

CHAPTER SEVEN

Drop-Kick Me, Jesus, through the Goalposts of Life

All the Galata [Celts] believe in the soul's immortality, so they have no fear of death and go out to embrace danger.

—Iamblichus, *Life of Pythagoras*, book 30, c. A.D. 300

IF IT'S THE BIGGEST HELL-RAISERS WHO BECOME THE MOST rock-ribbed believers, then the high number of born-again Christians among rednecks is not surprising. To those whose souls have been lost and rescued, God is as much a part of daily life as death and taxes. And "In God We Trust" (the phrase that has appeared on American money since 1864) is a value worth protecting.

Country roads are dotted with advertisements for Jesus and fire-works on the same flashing billboard. There are food outlets like the Thank You Jesus Hot Dog Stand and Jo-Bob's Full Service Texaco and Full Gospel House of Prayer next to a neon sign for COLD BEER TO GO. And there are more than thirty truck-stop congregations—Truckstop Ministries of America.

The power of guidance received from such sacred roadside attractions can be considerable. On May 21, 1991, Atlanta journalists Lillian Guevara-Castro and Lawrence Viele reported that "dozens of motorists" said they had seen the face of Jesus in an oversize spoonful of pasta and tomato sauce depicted on a billboard for Pizza Hut restaurants. Joyce Simpson insisted, in fact, that the sighting had changed her life: While leaving a Texaco station positioned in the shadow of the billboard, Simpson explained, she had been debating whether to continue singing in her church choir or pursue a professional music career. At that moment, Simpson felt "compelled" to look up. "I saw Christ's face," Simpson told a reporter. Inspired by her vision, Simpson stuck with the choir.

PHOTO ON OPPOSITE PAGE BY BOB SCHATZ.

REDNECKS ON THE ISSUES

B.K. (short for Black Kat) is a Southern Baptist high school teacher in West Virginia. "From what I can tell, the religious *wrong* has about the same respect for freedom as the Red Chinese. You gotta think there's something like fifteen hundred different religions in this country 'cause most of us can't agree on anything but that we need the freedom to disagree.

"When the Patsies (Robertson and Buchanan) start claiming their political agenda is religion—that's when I want to say to them, 'Refresh my memory on God's opinion on guns?' I'll bet if you ask them to explain God's will in regard to Baptism or Holy Communion you'd see a religious riot that'll make Northern Ireland look like the *Wheel of Fortune!*"

Drop Kick Me, Jesus

LOUIS SAHUC

Redneck Heaven   212

These public proclamations of Protestant chauvinism are only one mani-
festation of the bravado with which many rednecks worship. As early as
1848 many freethinking Americans had begun to create their own homegrown religions. They established doctrines short on compassion and
high on retribution, where the Ten Commandments didn't come with a
Bill of Rights. And there were inevitable splits. Fundamentalists believe
that the Bible, "the sword of the Lord," is all that is needed, while the full-
gospel Pentecostals also communicate with God outside of the Bible
through dreams and visions.

Today high-test evangelical Christianity is far more popular with
churchgoing rednecks than the grace-based backbone religions. Many
favor Christian academies for their kids, schools where "Onward,
Christian Soldiers" is played as a football fight song by a lockstep march-
ing band accompanied by sparsely clad bump-and-grind fire-baton-
twirling majorettes.

One self-proclaimed redneck trucker who's Catholic told of the
time he got stuck in a traffic jam in a small South Carolina town. "There
was this young Fundamentalist candidate running for the local school
board. He had that rally whipped in a frenzy over the sin of wasting
money to teach kids foreign languages and the history and literature of
foreign cultures. I'll never forget it. After he finished reminiscing about
World War *Eleven*, he added, 'And if English was good enough for Jesus,
it's good enough for the children of South Carolina!' "

Another popular development in the redneck religious community
has been the rise of the evangelical preacher. Wildly waving their Bibles
and praising the Almighty, these flamboyant messengers of the Word

Signs From God

In a culture that depends on bumper stickers and T-shirts to function as its official newspaper and archive, exhibiting religious messages assumes great import.

GOD, GUNS & GUTS: MADE THE USA GREAT

CHRISTIANS AREN'T PERFECT—JUST FORGIVEN

ACTS 2:38

WE NEED A BREATH OF FRESH PRAYER

A COINCIDENCE IS GOD'S WAY OF STAYING ANONYMOUS

LET ME TELL YOU ABOUT MY BOSS

GO TO CHURCH: DON'T WAIT FOR THE HEARSE TO TAKE YOU

JESUS WOULD HAVE RIDDEN A HARLEY

IN CASE OF RAPTURE, THIS VEHICLE WILL GO OUT OF CONTROL

PLEASE LORD: LET ME PROVE THAT WINNING THE LOTTERY WON'T TURN ME INTO A DEVIL

GOD IS LIKE SCOTCH TAPE: YOU CAN'T SEE HIM YOU JUST KNOW HE'S THERE

EVANGELISTS DO MORE THAN LAY PEOPLE

THE WAGES OF SIN ARE DEATH, BUT THE HOURS AIN'T BAD

Spreading the message of God to others is a full-time job. Turning a vehicle into a moving billboard for the Lord is an efficient method of proselytizing.
SYNDEY BYRD.

often come complete with state-of-the-art sound systems, Armani suits, and corporate lawyers to aid them in their holy work. In fact, their tidings have changed very little since the early frontier days. Back then, preachers were heard to warn, "Repent ye, ye brethren, of your sins. Fer if ye don't the Lord'll grab yer by the seats of yer pants and hold yer over the fire till ye holler like a coon!"

The Reverend Skipp Porteous, a writer and lecturer from western Massachusetts, was a Fundamentalist preacher for more than twelve years. Although he received his formal training at LIFE (Lighthouse of International Foursquare Evangelism), the seminary founded by Aimee Semple McPherson in Los Angeles in 1944, it was watching Billy Graham that taught him how to rub words together to make sparks.

"I borrowed Billy Graham's tried-and-true technique," said Skipp, paying homage to the elder statesman of evangelists, the former Fuller brush salesman who has brought the word of God to more than a billion people. "It's based on the dynamics of group hypnosis and crowd motivation. All evangelists do this. You preach a rousing sermon. You blame specific sins for causing the trouble in people's lives and in the world. With the popular ones like drinking, lust, and adultery, you hit the bull's-eye with every shot. At the conclusion, you warn people things'll get worse if they don't accept God's forgiveness.

"The sermon leads into a prayer. You just condense the list of sins. Then you follow up with the consequences and a plea for forgiveness. The evangelist will ask the folks to raise their hands for a special prayer. Once the worshipers become participants, you got 'em snared. You reel them in with the altar call. You get those in back to come up first. Volunteers herd the uncertain ones forward."

If money is to be earned from earthly pleasures, it might as well be used for God's work.
BETHANY BULTMAN.

God Will Provide

One resourceful salesman from God offers incentive gifts. Bill Beeny, one of the 1970s' more extravagant Christian broadcasters, promised his contributors a self-defense package including a stove, five fuel cans, a rescue gun, a radio, and the Defender—a dye gun useful for marking attackers—making them easy targets for police.

For a modest ten-dollar gift, Beeny offered contibutors a blue-steel, pearl-handled tear-gas pistol, plus "the informative and inspirational Truth-Pac 4." An alternative selection—Beeny's own album of eighteen songs about heaven, accompanied by the Paralyzer, a product of "the famous Mace Company."

I HAVE SEEN THE LIGHT

Evangelism transforms religious worship into a flashy affair, a highly effective approach to turning ordinary folk into fiercely faithful, Bible-wielding believers. *Dixie*, a widow with a copious swirl of meringue-colored hair, and her widowed ex–cabdriver boyfriend, *Alvin,* are members of the Assembly of God, but admit they haven't been back to church since the mid-1980s. Their lapse in attendance coincided with the defrocking of their pastor, televangelist Marvin Gorman, due to adultery, money troubles, and a $90 million defamation suit against Jimmy Swaggart. Nevertheless, they were curious to see if Gorman and his new Temple of Praise ministry still had the "gift." They tracked Gorman down to his new ministry, temporarily housed in a converted swimming-pool-

Doin' *my best to piss off the Religious Right.*

—Bumper sticker spotted on a truck at the First Baptist Church in Gadsden, Alabama.

Baptism, usually by total immersion, is often a requirement for salvation. During the "Invitation Song," altar call, or "Hour of Decision," the preacher invites the sin stained and suffering into the baptismal pool. CHARLES DAVIS.

supply warehouse. It smelled more like a public swimming pool than a church. Gorman's affiliation with the small nondenominational World Bible Fellowship, headquartered in Irving, Texas, afforded him the credentials to continue his ministry, but not many followers. Alvin was appalled; he whispered, "This is what the polecat deserves. You ever seen such a bunch of losers? Probably ashamed to show up at a regular church."

But once Gorman had the mike in his hands, he was transformed. The man who looked like a granite-haired IRS auditor took on a Mount Rushmore presence. He lashed out against Satan with a voice that snapped like a bullwhip. He gesticulated against sinners with one hand while holding out the other in supplication. The audience was on its feet, arms waving, eyes closed. Working the barn of a room, Gorman cast out demons, spoke in tongues, and calmed a couple of screaming babies. Dixie moved forward like a sleepwalker to receive Gorman's blessing. She let out a whimper and fell over backward, her eyes glistening like pond water in the moonlight. And in that exuberant moment, she was born again. Alvin grumbled that bingo was a lot cheaper and a whole lot more exciting.

It may take a true act of God to awaken skeptics to the joy of rebirth. Journalist Don Lee Keith pointed to the night that Cheryl Prewitt of Chester, Mississippi, glided down the Atlantic City runway as Miss America in 1979 as a miracle. When Cheryl (pronounced "Churl") was eleven years old, she was badly crippled in an automobile accident. But one day, God led her to a revival meeting in Jackson, Mississippi. When she returned home from the meeting, she prayed, and that night her injured leg grew two inches. Cheryl credits her glorious rhinestone crown to those two inches.

"I figure ten thousand people become born again every week," continues Skipp. According to him, Jesus is the antidote to fear, guilt, and human sexuality for many people. "To be born again is to leave problems behind. Remember how John De Lorean became born again when he was busted for cocaine? And Nixon's hatchet man, Charles Colson, became an evangelist in prison? You know Jeffrey Dahmer, who'd murdered and cannibalized seventeen people, was a born-again preacher when he was

American luxury cars serve a
dual purpose to some redneck
Christians—an advertisement
for the God-given superiority of
the American automotive
industry and an example of the
special economic blessings that
God has showered on the driver.
KATHY RICHARD.

murdered by another prisoner in November 1994. Well, another example is Pat Robertson. He and his wife attended the Word of Life Camp during one of the summers I'd been there. Robertson had just graduated from Yale Law School. But he flunked the bar exam. He turned to Jesus for solace. Now he's an ordained Baptist minister."

Buddy Killen is a country music mogul. His early memories of religion also bring shame to mind. "When I was a little kid I believed if I didn't go to church, I'd go to hell," Buddy recalled. "But hell, I cried all the way to church because I was so humiliated after a rat ate the seat out of my poor little suit. In the country you got beaten down all week by poverty. Then the preacher used religion as a stick to beat you some more. I finally figured it out—people who let that kind of abuse control their lives aren't using the gift God gave them—a brain."

THE LAYING ON
OF HANDS

Religious fervor brought *Vallerae*, a Habitat for Humanity volunteer, to a different conclusion from Skipp's. "When my brother and I were in high school, we were so wild Mama was at her wit's end. There was this famous evangelist on television who came to our town to hold a tent revival. This was in a small town in Indiana in the late 1960s, and we'd do just about anythin' for entertainment, so we all went. Besides seein' a TV star, there was a chance somebody we knew might testify to some big sin," Vallerae recalled.

"When the preacher read the gospel the congregation was so quiet you coulda heard a pocket handkerchief drop. That night even my hell-raisin' greaser brother got born again. The high emotion of that preacher

If *you've been a broad-based heathen, honey, you're gonna make a broad-based Christian.*

—Louise Mohr, evangelist

Drop Kick Me, Jesus

had a whole other kind of effect on me, though," she said, lowering her voice to a conspiratorial whisper.

"The preacher asked Mama if he could take me to supper. She musta thought he was givin' me special attention. You know, with my miniskirt, bleached hair, and white lipstick and all, he was helpin' a heathen, like.

"I got filled with the spirit of the Lord, all right! I'd never got fucked like that in my life! Let me tell you he put all those high-school boys to shame. You know what's the real shame, though. The second it was over he pulled me out of that bed. Both of us stark naked. Made me kneel down at the foot of the bed and pray, 'O Lord forgive me for I was overpowered by the sins of the flesh.' But I added under my breath, 'And, next time I find a guy that's this great in bed, please don't let him be a preacher!' "

Despite being born again, twice, Skipp became disaffected with the church's teachings and preachings. He left both his ministry and Fundamentalism in 1977. Since 1984, he has served as president and national director of the Institute for First Amendment Studies, Inc., a nonprofit educational and research organization that defends the separation of church and state. He also publishes *Freedom Writer* magazine, which monitors the religious right.

"After studying two thousand years of history I'll tell you one thing," he concluded. "True Christianity is about self-sacrifice. It has nothing to do with self-aggrandizement through un-Christian acts."

RELIGIOUS TALK:
FROM YOUR LIPS TO GOD'S EAR

Nuke Gay Whales for Jesus
—Bumper sticker

Amen: Exclamation to add emphasis, i.e., "I love that ole gal. Amen!"

Christers: New England term for Protestants

Churched: To be expelled from church

Glory hole: Part of a creek or pond used for baptisms or a special fishing spot

Glossalalia: The spiritual gift of speaking in tongues

Holy laughter or the Toronto Blessing: Contagious, uncontrollable laughter that spreads during services in Pentecostal churches

Jasper: A religious person

Jerusalem slim: Jesus

Kid top: Revival tent

Kluckster or klucker: Derogatory term for a Klansperson

Knee bender: A religious person

Lose your religion: To get so mad that nothing holds you back, or to go out of one's mind

Pine coat: Coffin

Prayer bones: Knees

Sal: The Salvation Army

Sunday pitch: A great show

Swallow the Bible: To lie

Whiskeypalian: An Episcopalian

Pat Robertson Quiz

—From Skipp Porteous's Freedom Writer magazine

1. Pat Robertson usually wears:
   a. *L. L. Bean boots*
   b. *penny loafers*
   c. *Western boots*
   d. *sandals*

2. Pat Robertson raises:
   a. *Arabian horses*
   b. *poodles*
   c. *alligators*
   d. *tropical fish*

3. Robertson prophesied that the former Soviet Union would invade:
   a. *the United States*
   b. *China*
   c. *Israel*
   d. *Saudi Arabia*

4. What popular pair formerly had an act on *The 700 Club*?
   a. *Siegfried and Roy*
   b. *Jim and Tammy*
   c. *Amos and Andy*
   d. *Click and Clack*

5. What historical event does Pat Robertson hope to televise?
   a. *the Second Coming*
   b. *the big California quake*
   c. *the first manned landing on Mars*
   d. *O.J.'s civil trial*

6. According to Robertson, Mormon religious beliefs are:
   a. *confusing*
   b. *wrong*
   c. *scandalous*
   d. *sound*

7. According to Robertson, Jehovah's Witnesses are:
   a. *lazy*
   b. *obnoxious*
   c. *highly spiritual*
   d. *not Christians*

8. In Robertson's ideal taxation system, proceeds from a flat 10 percent tax would go toward:
   a. *paying off the national debt*
   b. *feeding the poor*
   c. *building highways and bridges*
   d. *religious instruction*

9. Robertson thinks oral sex is:
   a. *disgusting*
   b. *against nature*
   c. *unsatisfying*
   d. *exciting*

Answers: (1) c, (2) a, (3) c, (4) b, (5) a, (6) b, (7) d, (8) d, (9) b

A particularly flamboyant display of faith takes its cue from literal interpretations of Scripture, especially the Book of Mark 16, 17, and 18 in the King James Version: "And these signs shall follow them that believe: In my name shall they cast out devils; they shall speak with tongues; they will take up serpents; and if they drink any deadly thing, it shall not hurt them; they shall lay hands on the sick, and they shall recover."

Although most theological seminaries teach that those particular passages of Mark were scribed later, that hasn't dampened the enthusiasm of snake handlers. The practice was begun in Appalachia after World War I by George Went Hensley, a man obsessed with these biblical passages. Hensley left Ooltewah, Tennessee, hiking up White Oak Mountain in a prayerful search for a sign from God. That's when a rattlesnake appeared to him, and he carried this sign from God down the mountain to his followers. Hensley continued to spread his spiritual ecstasy through "anointing" until his death from a snakebite in 1955.

The story of Albert Teaster, another snake-handling minister, is known by many. Gary Carden and Nina Anderson penned a written account that supplies the details in *Belled Buzzards, Hucksters, and Grieving Specters: Appalachian Tales: Strange, True, and Legendary.* (Asheboro, N.C.: Down Home Press, 1994). In the mountains of North Carolina in 1934, Albert Teaster, a self-ordained minister of the Cullowhee Mountain Church of God, decided to take up a diamondback as part of his sermon on these pages of Mark. By dim lamplight Teaster grabbed the five-foot snake by its middle. The viper aimed its flat head at the preacher and struck, spurting poison into Teaster's right hand between his index finger and thumb. But the preacher kept a hold on the venomous creature. He wanted to give God every opportunity to save him. By the time the serpent had bitten him twice more, pain got the better of him. The two dozen or so worshipers had already fled the tiny log sanctuary when the snake hit the floorboards.

For days the preacher suffered every imaginable agony, refusing all medical or alcoholic solace, insisting he was in the hands of the greatest doctor of them all, Jesus Christ. The story might have ended there, but for the intervention of the press. A young reporter, John Parris, gave the story to the Asheville paper. Even though Teaster's arm was "swollen to the size of a stovepipe," he crawled out of bed so a photo could be taken to accompany the story. Before long the wire services had flashed the story all over the world. And the public loved it!

A week later Teaster was back preaching from the porch of the home of one of his parishioners. Only this time God had provided him with the means to spread the word of Jesus Christ to the world. Pathe News was there to film Teaster and his Holiness flock's rituals: speaking in tongues, dancing and chanting "Commoco, commoco, commoco, commoco" and "Ioeeeeee" as they kissed the fang marks on their preacher's misshapen arm.

A star was born, and the Reverend Albert Teaster left the mountain to tour the country with revivalists. A poem printed in the *Asheville Journal* at the time of his departure reflected the home folks' growing skepticism:

Saw Albert Teaster in a store, preparing to go to Akron
Buyin' a pair of suspenders.
Laughed myself sick awonderin' why he should need 'em.
Faith strong enough to cure a snake bite
    sure should hold up trousers.

Many states outlawed serpent handling in the 1940s. Yet from

Twang!

Twang is a lot like Lik-M-Aid, the powdered tart candy that kids lick out of their palms. The original flavor is pickle, though it is also available in lemon-lime. Its ads say, "It'll pep up popcorn, fuel those French fries, and soup up soup." This is the ultimate convenience food for those who want the lip-puckering thrill of a dill pickle sold in condom-sized packages. "Twang in beer is my idea of goooooood," says *Dale*, a trucker from New Mexico. "You pretty much get it at any Diamond Shamrock mini-market in the South and in the West."

Bride's Day-Glo Jell-O Twang Cake
(aka Sunshine Cake)

This wedding cake is found most frequently in Arkansas and Tennessee at receptions hosted in rural church halls. The groom's cake is often attached to the bride's cake by a plastic bridge, with each cake having a pair of brides and grooms.

1 large box lime Jell-O
¼ cup water or lemonade
1 box Duncan Hines Lemon Supreme cake mix
1¼ cups Blue Plate mayonnaise
1 box instant lemon pudding mix
4 large eggs
1 12-ounce can Mountain Dew or 7-Up
Green and yellow food coloring (for Day-Glo effect)

1. Preheat oven to 350°.
2. Grease and flour a tube pan.
3. Dissolve Jell-O in either ¼ cup of water or lemonade.
4. Blend into cake mix.
5. Bake at 350° for 1 hour.
6. Ice when cool.

Twang Icing:

1 box confectioners' sugar
3 small packs Lemon/Lime Twang
1 medium can crushed pineapple, drained
1 large package cream cheese

Mix everything together.

Variation: Garnish with plastic daisies.

Makes 10 to 12 servings

Indiana and Michigan to Florida and California an estimated three thousand Pentecostal Holiness faithful flirt with martyrdom to test their devotion to God. They join the wailing semicircles who fondle writhing rattlers and copperheads and drink strychnine and battery acid. Dewey Chapin of West Virginia, an assistant pastor, has been bitten 118 times since 1960 and lived. Since the turn of the century, however, 75 other worshipers haven't been so fortunate.

JESUS IS BETTER THAN TIDE, HE REMOVES ALL TRACE OF SIN

—Fundamentalist bumper sticker and water-bottle slogan

In small communities the church functions as a social club. Nowhere can this be seen better than at a wedding. Lionel Bevan, a Texas-longhorn breeder, rocked back in his chair in a Fort Worth cocktail lounge that doubles as his in-town office. "Nothing can match a Fundamentalist Texas cowboy wedding for style. I was just at one over in Mineral Springs. The happy couple was fresh out of high school. The grandmothers were wearing matching dresses in different pastel shades. The great-grandmothers had on medic-alert lockets. The service was finished in less than five minutes. I think the preacher had to head out to the country to do a funeral.

"They followed family tradition, though," Lionel recalled as he waved his empty highball glass at the waitress for a refill. "The wedding party toasted each other with Mountain Dew in champagne glasses. I swear it looked like Day-Glo urine.

"At about three o'clock in the afternoon they got in the truck we'd decorated. She was still in her wedding dress. He changed back to his

Gospel Cake (aka The Good Book Cake)

The true test of a Christian's knowledge of the Bible comes in the preparation of this cake. (For those who don't have their concordance handy, the ingredients include flour, butter, sugar, raisins, figs, almonds, honey, salt, eggs, milk, baking powder, cinnamon, allspice, nutmeg.)

4 1/2 cups	1 Kings 4:22
1 cup	Judges 5:25, last clause
2 cups	Jeremiah 6:20
2 cups	1 Samuel 30:12
2 cups	Nahum 3
2 cups	Numbers 17:18
2 tablespoons	1 Samuel 14:13
Dot	Leviticus 2:13
6	Jeremiah 17:11
1/2 cup	Judges 4:19, last clause
2 tablespoons	Amos 4:15
Dot	2 Chronicles 9:9

1. Preheat oven to 350°.
2. Grease and flour a Bundt pan.
3. Mix everything together, and bake for 1 hour.
4. Nonteetotalers will poke holes in the cake with a broom straw and drizzle Wild Turkey over it.

Makes 10 to 12 servings

Waco Orange-Jell-O Cookies

A Baptist preacher's wife claims, "You'll end up addicted and beggin' for forgiveness!"

1½ cups I Can't Believe It's Not Butter
2 3-ounce packages orange Jell-O (reserve 1 tablespoon for garnish)
1 cup sugar
1 large egg
1 tablespoon orange-juice concentrate
4 cups sifted all-purpose flour
1 teaspoon double-acting baking powder
Pinch of salt
Pinch of nutmeg

1. Preheat oven to 400°.
2. Cream the I Can't Believe It's Not Butter, and gradually add all but 1 tablespoon of the Jell-O and all the sugar, alternating 1 tablespoon at a time. Add egg and orange-juice concentrate.
3. In separate bowl, sift flour, baking powder, salt, and nutmeg twice.
4. Gradually mix dry ingredients into Jell-O mixture, mixing well after each addition.
5. Either chill, roll out on floured surface, and cut with cookie cutters, or force dough through a cookie press. Use ungreased baking sheets.
6. Bake for 10 to 15 minutes, or until golden around the edges.
7. Garnish with the reserved 1 tablespoon Jell-O while still hot.

Variations: Use lemon Jell-O and frozen lemonade concentrate in place of the orange-juice concentrate, or lime Jell-O and frozen limeade concentrate. Garnish with Twang instead of Jell-O.

Makes 5 to 6 dozen cookies

jeans. They raced back and forth through town draggin' cans and blowin' their horn. All us were chasin' 'em in our trucks."

LOVE THY NEIGHBOR

When redneck Christians encounter strangers, questions as to their religious affiliation often take precedence over those about the new-comers' hometown or occupation, or the classic Southern polite question: "Who are your people?" An Arkansas businessman who exhibits an exuberant display of lights in celebration of Jesus's birthday remarked: "I grew up Baptist in Fort Smith in the 1950s. Even our parakeet followed the faith. He'd greet our guests by saying, 'I'm a Baptist, what are you?' "

But other rednecks, like Dixie, don't have much respect for other faiths. "Why don't Baptists have sex standing up?" she joked. The answer is that someone will think they're dancing. "Everybody knows that after Catholics, Baptists are the worst sex fiends in America," explained Dixie.

Redneck religion has broken off into various factions and sects, each with its own customs, style, and interpretation of the Bible. While some churches enforce plainness and modesty, others have fostered a culture of gospel glamour in the Tammy Faye Bakker mode. Many participate in enormous celebrations involving hundreds of friends singing hymns from two- and three-story human Christmas trees or on cross-shaped platforms. Others take turns standing outside at night on their lawns in front of their homes in a living nativity scene. There are congregations that eschew music altogether. Others offer a radiant knee-slapping fusion of street-corner Salvation Army, Brother Al

*Cowboys for Christ (CFC) was founded in 1970 by world-
famous bulldogger Ted Pressley. He traded rodeo life for the
Southwestern Baptist Theological Seminary in Fort Worth. After
that, he began lassoing the devil as the self-appointed chaplain
for the Professional Rodeo Cowboys Association, which has three
hundred rodeo preachers in twenty countries and a worldwide
congregation of sixty-eight thousand.*

   Philosophy: After everything else fails to save you, try Christ.

   *Bottom line: CFC publishes a newspaper and sells souvenirs,
such as a belt buckle the size of a license plate that bears the
CFC logo.*

SUE ROSOFF.

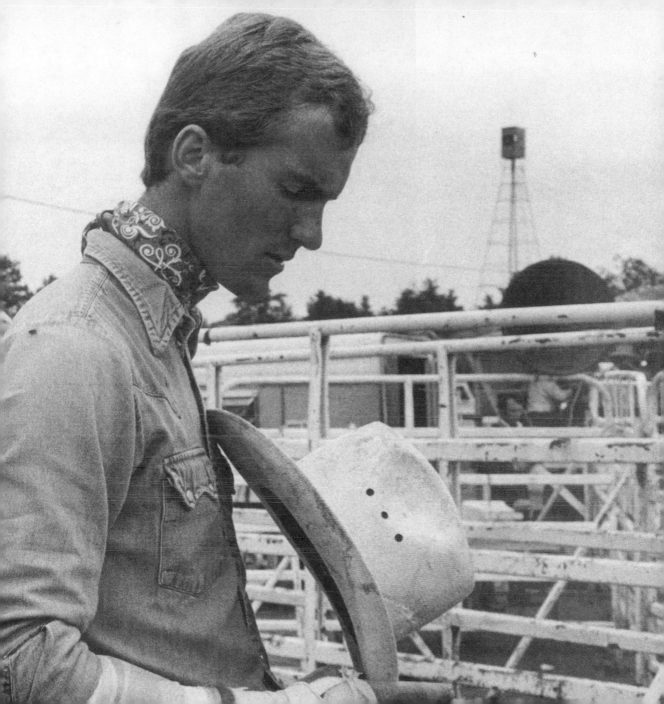

Green, and Jerry Lee Lewis, accompanied by devotional bands with electric guitars, drums, and tambourines.

WHO'S WHO IN THE CHURCH

Disgust over sin pales in comparison to redneck distrust of competing faiths. Here's an overview of the main divisions of Fundamentalist Protestantism from which the 800 or so sects descend. While the typical Protestant congregation draws between seventy-five to eighty-five people, here are some of the biggest groups.

Pentecostal

Founded: The year 1866 marks the formation of the oldest Pentecostal denomination in America. However, it was not until 1901 when followers of Charles Parham began spreading the practice of speaking in tongues (glossolalia). They embrace the spiritual gifts cited in Corinthians 12–14 and stress the name of Jesus.

Beliefs: According to the revised articles of faith written in 1993 by the United Pentecostal Church, "We wholeheartedly disapprove of our people indulging in any activities which are not conducive to good Christianity and Godly living."

- ★ No dancing, no mixed bathing
- ★ Women cannot cut their hair, wear makeup, or wear clothing that exposes the body (no skirts shorter than twelve inches from the floor, and sleeves must cover the wrist bone).
- ★ No worldly sports or amusements
- ★ No theater, no unwholesome radio programs or music, no television

★ Sects include the Assemblies of God, the Pentecostal Holiness Church, and several brands of Churches of God.

Bottom line: Ten million followers

Noted practitioners: Oral Roberts, Jimmy Swaggart, Jim and Tammy Faye Bakker (Tammy Faye, now Messner, reemerged with a talk show with gay actor Jim J. Bullock in 1996)

Baptist

Founded: In 1639, Welsh Puritan Roger Williams, recently banished from Massachusetts, established the first Baptist church in America in Providence, Rhode Island. The Southern Baptist Convention (SBC) was established in 1845 due to a falling-out with Baptists in the North over slavery.

Beliefs: This faith focuses on sin and local church autonomy. Sexuality and spiritual control over the body are prevalent themes. (In January 1996 Baptist Baylor University loosened its regulations to allow dancing.) On every Halloween, the Two Rivers Baptist Church featured a haunted house called Judgment House. It scared the bejesus out of about ten thousand teens by showing them the official Baptist vision of what hell is like through skits on suicide, drugs, and premarital sex.

★ Subdenominations include Primitive, Southern, Full Gospel, Missionary.

Bottom line: Largest Protestant group, with more than 15 million followers in over 50,000 congregations

Noted practitioners: Billy Graham, President Bill Clinton, and former President Jimmy Carter

LDS—Church of Jesus Christ of Latter-Day Saints (Mormons)

Founded: In 1827, Joseph Smith found a set of "golden tablets" in a field near Palmyra, New York, and started the LDS Church. Smith and his brother were lynched by an anti-Mormon mob in Illinois in 1844. Brigham Young led the Mormons to Utah in 1847. Today more than three quarters of the citizens of Utah belong to the LDS. One minority T-shirt in Utah reads, "Eat, drink, and be merry. Tomorrow you might move to Utah!"

Beliefs:

- ★ Uphold conservative family values.
- ★ Tithing is expected: members must donate 10 percent of their income to the church.
- ★ Abstain from coffee, tea, tobacco, alcohol, and drugs. (A few hard-liners believe in the baptizing of the dead, prohibit the use of birth control, and practice polygamy.)
- ★ Wear a spiritually significant white undergarment day and night.
- ★ Although they are Christians, Mormons prefer not to be referred to as Protestants.

Bottom line: Fastest-growing faith in the world with 9 million paying members in 130 countries

Noted practitioners: Osmond family, U.S. Senator Orrin Hatch, and Bill Marriott (founder of Marriott Hotel chain)

Jehovah's Witness

Founded: In 1871 Charles Taze Russell split with the Baptists and started this sect in Rhode Island.

Beliefs:

- ★ A literal interpretation of the Bible
- ★ Theocratic rule of God
- ★ The sinfulness of organized religions
- ★ An imminent millennium
- ★ Keep the original Sabbath on Saturday
- ★ No celebration of Christian holidays like Christmas or Easter, since these are pagan festivals that Emperor Constantine incorporated into his Holy Roman Empire in A.D. 313.
- ★ Separation of church and state (most Jehovah's Witnesses won't even vote). In a case brought by Jehovah's Witnesses in 1943, the United States Supreme Court ruled that children need not salute the American flag at school if it is against their religion.
- ★ Pacifism

Bottom line: Almost 5 million practitioners worldwide

Noted practitioners: Jackson family—La Toya, Janet, and Michael were raised in the faith

Nondenominational

Founded: Since before the American Revolution there have been autonomous congregations. However, the single most well-attended church in the United States is the nondenominational Willow Creek Community Church outside of Chicago, created in the 1970s as the result of a poll of nonchurchers in the area. It now consists of a network of eight hundred churches, called by competitors McChristianity.

Beliefs:

✶ Self-sacrifice and theology are boring

Bottom line: With an annual budget of $13 million, this religious corporation provides worship, a food court, and a sports complex. Fifteen thousand worshipers relax in theater seating as they watch a staff of actor/ministers performing secular morality plays.

My Boss Is a Jewish Carpenter

—Christian bumper sticker

A note of anti-Semitism also seems to have become a common characteristic in many homegrown American Protestant faiths. A lot of the splinter groups insist that Jesus wasn't really a Jew and that God didn't actually designate the Jews as his chosen people. As with racism, however, anti-Semitism is not universally practiced by all rednecks. Bob Marcus is the coauthor of *The Good Book Cookbook,* a modern version of the recipes cited in the Old Testament. "My mother told me a story I'll never forget," Bob said. "In the late 1970s, when Jimmy Carter was president, there was this well-publicized relocation of the Soviet Jews to the United States. One of the places they went was within a few miles of the Texas, Louisiana, and Arkansas borders. You know, the ringworm belt, where cotton and Christ are king.

"Two rabbis, all of the other religious and community leaders, and every politician in the county were at the airport when the Russian Jews landed. Everyone pulled together to get the Jews settled.

"Our local Jews did their best. But being a Jew in my part of the world, I'm afraid, is more of a gastrointestinal experience. Every social consideration was extended: they were invited to play golf; dinner parties with lox and bagels were hosted. The problem, as my mother tells it, was that the Russian Jews were simple people with devout beliefs.

"The Jews arrived in the spring. By the time fall rolled around, the media got the idea of covering the Soviet Jews' first New Year, their first Rosh Hashanah, in the land of freedom. So the national and local media assembled at the temple.

"But no Russian Jews show up. The rabbi got worried, so he makes a phone call," Bob reported.

"According to my mother, the rabbi was horrified to discover that the reason the Soviet Jews didn't want to be members of his congregation was that they wanted to join the First Baptist Church!

"It seems they'd become quite friendly with the good Baptist church ladies. They had a lot in common. You see, they were both devout people. They liked to talk about biblical history, the wrath of God, the Old Testament, and Yahweh.

"Realizing the potential embarrassment, the rabbi called up the pastor of the Baptist church, who was an old pal. 'What are you trying to do to me?' The minister told him he'd like to get the Jews to convert. But he saw the potential headlines like—'Soviet Jews Come to America and Forsake Their Religion!'

"After much negotiating it turned out that, sure, the Soviets liked talking to the nice Baptist women. But what the Jews really liked was the Baptists' bowling alley. So a deal was struck: if the Jews would agree to worship as part of the Jewish congregation, the Baptists would keep a lane reserved for them."

MANY ARE CALLED . . . BUT FEW ARE CHOSEN

The intolerance apparent between the varying sects and subsects of Christianity is not surprising considering the particularly turbulent waters flowing between political agendas and spirituality.

Evidence of the strength of the Three Rs—rednecks, religion, and racism—is still prevalent today. Indeed most Klan officials are not only harbingers of racial hatred but also ordained Christian ministers. However, there seems to be a change in the once-strident quasi-Protestant message of the Klan. Some liberal chapters have actually welcomed Catholics into the fold. A teenage girl selling Baptist raffle tickets at a Klan-sponsored rodeo had a novel pitch: "Will you buy a chance for a wide-screen surround-sound color TV? Our church youth group is raisin' money to see 'the three Kings' in Memphis over Christmas break."

The three Kings turned out to be not a nativity play but her slang for the events the church group would be attending in Memphis—a Southern Baptist Sunday-school service to celebrate Christ's birth, a visit to the Martin Luther King shrine, and a tour of Graceland.

Admittedly, rednecks are clannish, but the subject of the Klan is touchy. While Klan membership in the 1960s might have been considered honorable by some rednecks, those who claim this stripe today are the object of most rednecks' slurs—"sheets for brains," "klans of worms," "pointy-headed spooks." Many proud rednecks express anger when the media allows "them ass-wipe kluckers," whom they consider a ragtag bunch of white trash vigilantes, to be the spokesmen for their culture. Some rednecks even find sport in spraying the backs of their white robes with Mountain Dew from a water pistol. "Looks just like the chicken-shit bully peed his pants," said one anti-Klan prankster.

Other rednecks like to ridicule those who hide in bed linen. Back in 1993 the Grand Dragon of the KKK in Waco, Texas, had to get an ACLU attorney, an African American, to defend his right not to reveal the names of his members. In 1996 in Lauren, South Carolina, an irate white man crashed his van through the window of The Redneck Shop on purpose. Then he climbed on top of the vehicle and beat the store's sign with a stick. The sign read "The World's Only Klan Museum." Some rednecks say he wasn't thrilled about the Klan trying to identify with rednecks.

So despite rivalry between religious factions, the appeal of the religious right in tough economic times, and the effects of the three-R trinity, left to their own devices, most redneck Christians are far more spiritual than they are political. As Dixie, the born-again former Gorman follower, says, "All I can figure is God gives everybody a soul. You gotta watch out for it. And you'd better keep an eye peeled for false prophets. On Judgment Day if you tell him 'I practiced racism' or 'I killed a doctor because my pastor told me to,' God'll tell you you was a fool for breakin' his commandments! Then you'll go to hell right along with the preacher you put before God. "

Deliverance

A stunning copper-skinned opera singer grew up as a privileged Creole of color, the daughter of a prominent physician and a university professor. She will never forget the first time she experienced redneck culture. "I was driving through the mountains of North Carolina one cold winter night en route to give my first operatic performance in Washington, D.C. I had a rented car. About two A.M. I noticed that the oil light had come on. I was on this narrow deserted mountain road, so I prayed it was just a fluke. Then the brake light came on. The next thing I knew the car was filled with the smell of burning rubber.

"As I sat shivering by the side of the road, cold and scared, I saw the lights of a car coming toward me. My heart sank when I saw it was a pickup truck with a gun rack. As the truck pulled off the road next to me, I contemplated jumping off the side of the mountain. Up close, I could see that the driver and the passengers were all dressed in camouflage. They had toothpicks clamped in their snaggled teeth.

"Before I knew what was happening, these rednecks had opened the hood of my car and were peering inside. I heard one of them say, 'Looks like you've got a heap of trouble. We'll get *Joe Tom* out here with his wrecker, but you're gonna have to spend the night.'

"I figured I didn't have much choice, so I crammed myself into the truck with the three rednecks. No one said a word. They just kept looking back and forth at each other. About half an hour later they stopped in front of a very modest motel. The lady behind the front desk said, 'What are you boys up to? You know we don't serve niggers.' My good Samaritans were looking pretty angry by the time they loaded me back in the truck. The one named *Clarence* took me to his house and told me to sleep on the sofa. The next morning I woke up to find that I was sleeping under a Confederate flag in a room with five recliners in it.

"It turned out Clarence had gone back with the wrecker and had stayed with my car all through the night while it was being fixed. By seven o'clock my car was parked outside, tanked up with gas, and with the heater running. Clarence wouldn't hear of my paying him a penny. 'Mail me a check, if you think 'bout it' was all he said. As I was pulling out of his yard, before I could get my window rolled up, this pretty little blond child in Woody Woodpecker pajamas ran around from the back of the house. He was yelling at the top of his lungs, 'Mama, Mama, Granddaddy done brought him a nigger girl home from the Klan meetin'.' I guess I was lucky those good old boys were Christians first and Klansmen second."

CHECKING UNDER THE HOOD

Despite recurring acts of violence and dwindling support, the KKK has taken to portraying themselves as civil whites. Here's information from a KKK membership solicitation pamphlet recently handed out at a Senior Citizens' Crafts Fair in Missouri:

1. The white race: The irreplaceable hub of our nation, our Christian faith, and the high levels of Western culture and technology
2. America first: First before any foreign or alien influence or interest
3. The Constitution: As originally written and intended; the finest system of government ever conceived by man
4. Free enterprise: Private property and ownership of business but an end to high-finance exploitation
5. Positive Christianity: The right of the American people to practice their faith—including prayers in schools

THE FIERY CROSS

The blazing spirit of Western Christian civilization. It must be said that the fiery cross was used in Scottish history as a signal of opposition to tyranny and obedience to God.

HERITAGE GARMENT WORKS

P. O. Box 5672
Columbia, S. C. 29202

Name _____

Address _____

City_____ State _____

Klanslady _____ ☐   Granddragon_____ ☐

Klansman _____ ☐   King Kleagle_____ ☐

Kleagle_____ ☐   Grand Officer_____ ☐

Titan_____ ☐   Exalted Cylops_____ ☐

Fury_____ ☐   Kludd_____ ☐

Satin ☐ Price $35.00

Kiavern Officer_____ ☐

Knight Hawk_____ ☐

Mask   Yes____No____ $2.00

ROBE MEASURE

Please follow measurement instructions carefully.

Drop Kick Me, Jesus

CHAPTER EIGHT

Trigger

Brake *for Moose, It Could*
Save Your Life

—Bumper sticker provided
by the New Hampshire Fish
and Game Commission

I've *got more guns than I*
need and less guns than I
want.

—Republican Phil Gramm to
the NRA

THERE'S NO WAY TO EXPLORE THE REDNECK CULTURE without becoming intimate with its most coveted tool: the gun. From defending oneself against an abusive mate to keeping a pack of wild dogs at bay, a gun is the essential symbol of redneck power.

Rednecks also wield guns to fulfill their traditional roles as hunters. To hear the men and women buying guns tell it, hunting for meat is the most important domestic chore that the foreman of the food chain needs to perform. Geoffrey Norman, a novelist and sportswriter, explained, "Up in Vermont, where I come from, deer season only lasts for two weeks. It starts on Veterans Day, when forty to fifty thousand men fill up the woods. For the next two weeks, you can just forget getting a roof repaired or a toilet fixed. All the rednecks are in the woods."

Hunters love to describe the rituals they follow—the preseason trips to get the deer stand or duck blind constructed, the gear roundup. Rural convenience stores in hunting country lay in a supply of high-season necessities—hunting licenses, bullets, and gas generators to power color TV sets so the hunters don't miss their football games.

The frontier philosophy of hardship building character gets set aside during this crucial time. Kids are even allowed to miss school for such monumental occasions. A man will actually agree to wear serious underwear, wool socks, and even earmuffs on a trip to the woods to procure meat. Tiny thermometers are attached to zippers inside and outside the hunter's jacket to keep him at an ideal temperature. Women insist their men wear bright orange vests over their camouflage so as not to be bagged by another hunter. Some hunters go so far as to take a bath and wash their clothes in Camo soap and rinse their mouths with Camo mouthwash to remove all human scent. Then they dip rags in the urine of a doe or Jersey cow in heat and drag it behind them from their base to their deer stand in a tree.

The pupils [of Celtic descent] are, mostly, rude—real young hunters, who handle the long rifle with more ease and dexterity than the goosequill, and who are incomparably more at home in 'twisting rabbit,' or 'treeing a possum,' than in conjugating a verb.

—Philip Henry Gosse, Letters from Alabama (1859)

PHOTO ON OPPOSITE PAGE BY DAN GRAHAM.

REDNECKS ON THE ISSUES

A pair of well-armed Hell's Angels expressed their views on guns. "I bet you think rednecks are just itching to put a fascist dictator in power, right? Well, you're dead wrong. There's never been a dictator in history that wanted an armed populace. Say some power-hungry loony toon gets in office. Who you gonna call to take him out?" they asked, patting their sidearms in unison.

The thrill of hunting doesn't have to end even at death. Jay "Canuck" Knudsen Sr. of Des Moines, Iowa, has a company called Canuck Sportsman's Memorial, Inc., which loads a departed hunter's cremains into shotgun shells or fishing lures. When one member of a six-man duck-and-goose-hunting party passed away, each of the five remaining men was given a hand-carved duck decoy containing a portion of their hunting buddy's cremains.

Gun-Activist Bumper Stickers

TEDDY KENNEDY KILLED MORE PEOPLE WITH HIS CAR THAN I KILLED WITH MY GUN

BUY A GUN: PISS OFF A LIBERAL

FEAR THE GOVERNMENT THAT FEARS YOUR GUN

THIS GUN AIN'T ILLEGAL. I GOT IT FROM OLLIE

I'D RATHER BE TRIED BY TWELVE THAN CARRIED BY SIX

THE WEST WASN'T WON WITH A REGISTERED GUN

CAUTION: NOTHING IN THIS VEHICLE IS WORTH YOUR LIFE

STOP FOREST FIRES, REGISTER MATCHES

GOD CREATED ALL MEN & COLT MADE THEM EQUAL

IF THEY OUTLAW GUNS, I BECOME AN OUTLAW

IF YOU LOVE SOMETHING, LET IT GO: IF IT DOESN'T COME BACK, HUNT IT DOWN AND KILL IT

YOU CAN HAVE MY GUN WHEN YOU PRY IT FROM MY COLD DEAD FINGERS

THE THRILL OF THE CHASE

Part of the pleasure of hunting involves adding an element of risk by evading the federal hunting laws. Raising fields of millet to attract birds and spotting deer are not seen as violations of environmental protections, since it is superseded by the redneck code which allows man to procure nature's free food. A cashier in a hunting supply store in Tallahassee, Florida, tells a joke about a poor old farmer who was arrested for killing a pelican. After giving him a stern lecture about breaking the law and killing a bird on the endangered species list, the judge took pity on the man and gave him a suspended sentence. That judge's curiosity got the best of him, though, and when he ran into the farmer on the street, the judge asked him, "So *Brady,* what did that pelican taste like?" The farmer thought for a minute, then he looked at the judge and said, "Gee, Your Honor, I don't know— bald eagle, I guess."

Otherwise law-abiding citizens "swallow the Bible" when it comes to poaching or illegal hunting. This story comes from *Noveena,* the wife of a small-town politician. "When I was about nine, there was a man here in town who'd posed as the Tom's Peanut Man," she said. "It turned out he was a federal game warden out to catch the men in town sellin' the game they were killin'.

"Well, one morning he took the school bus to arrest all the men. Daddy's a hunter, but thank you, Jesus, he'd only bartered his ducks. When I showed up at school there were just two of us in the entire class. The rest of the kids were too ashamed to show up.

"It wasn't two weeks later that our pastor asked Daddy to get enough game to feed everybody at a special dedication. Ya better bleeeeeve Daddy set out a ton of sweet potatoes in the field to attract the animals," she said.

"Well, the federal game wardens called up to come hunt with Daddy on our farm. Mama woke up in the middle of the night and said, 'Get up, get up, we got all those rotten sweet potatoes. That's against the law.' So Mama and Daddy got all five of us kids out of bed. All night long we were freezin' and pickin' up all of those putrid potatoes and buryin' 'em in pits in the woods."

Noveena says the minute the wardens finished hunting, her family went back into the woods, dug up the potatoes, scattered them around, waited until dawn, and started shooting. In two days they had enough meat to feed 150 people. "That Sunday, the preacher congratulated Daddy in public. And, don't you know, the local game wardens came up and shook his hand."

There are times, however, when redneck cleverness is outdone by that of an animal. "There's one guy I knew who always bragged about how well trained his dog was," said Johnny Richard, a working cowboy who seems to enjoy the ironies of life. "The dog could open the refrigerator and get him a beer. Not just any beer, but it had to be a PBR (Pabst Blue Ribbon). This one time, the guy and a bunch of his buddies had been out hunting at night. As they were coming along a dirt road they noticed the glow of a cigarette way up ahead. So the guy just quietly rolls out of the truck bed and hides in the bushes while his buddies get busted by the game warden. But, as the warden unloaded all the guys' ducks, my friend's dog started getting his ducks out of the pile and carried them up the road to where his master was hiding. He got busted, big time, and it was all his dog's fault."

GOING TO THE DOGS

To *Curtis Lee,* one of a long line of hunting-dog breeders in Georgia, "a dawg's not a pet. It's a workin' animal. A really good hunting dawg goes for about five to six grand. Even though they may be fenced into a backyard, our dawgs're trained to hunt, track, protect, and be cooled out enough to be used as a footrest. They're not s'posed to chase Frisbees or look cute on the backseat of a Range Rover. The dawg doesn't have to have papers. He doesn't even have to be trained to go on the papers. He just has to hunt, know what a coon's ass smells like, be gentle with children, and know who the boss is.

"Some guys I know who work at the Garland, Texas, airport still dine out on the story of the time a Cessna landed and a sort of rangy-looking guy got out with his seven hunting dawgs," Curtis recalled. "The next thing anybody knew, the dawgs were out behind one of the hangars takin' a leak. Before too long, the guy and the dawgs came back across the runway, climbed onto the plane, and took off.

"Have you ever smelled huntin' dawg breath?" Curtis asked, switching the match to the other side of his mouth. "The guys say the plane smelled worse than the inside of my truck! But you want to know who that old boy was? It was the late Sam Walton, the richest man in America. They've been Wal-Mart shoppers ever since.

"Look at it this way: you can judge a man by how he treats his dawgs. A person who has to hire folks to take care of his dawgs might as well be hirin' somebody to sleep with his wife. That Sam he loved them dawgs. Yes, sir."

Hunting in Red River Parish, Louisiana, with "The Ole Man."

Dan Graham, from the collection of Dr. Houston Bosely.

YOU MAY BEAT OUR PRICES, BUT YOU CAN'T BEAT OUR MEAT

—Advertising slogan for Doe's Steakhouse

Just as it's always been the hunter's job to slay the bacon, cooking it outdoors for kith and kin remains his task. In the back field at motorcycle rallies and Little League games the air grows pungent with woodsy smoke billowing up from huge open-air pits. Sometimes they're great yawning ditches dug in the earth; on other occasions they're huge, split-open oil drums. As the cook rotates the slabs of meat over the flames, the juices crack and sizzle, and the redneck man becomes, once again, the hunter and provider, recounting his glory days.

"That's the one I shot with *Stump, Mertis,* and 'em up on Mount Airy," he'll boast, slathering sauce over a side of venison. "He 'uz a ten-point buck. Shit, I took him down in one shot clean between the eyes. I swear we liked to froze to death up there. And old Bucky broke his leg in six places haulin' it down in the dark."

The word "barbecue" may have come from the West Indian word *berbekot* (referring to the metal grill used for outdoor cooking), which began to be used in 1665. By 1773 George Washington was hosting barbecues, according to his diary. One of the biggest barbecues on record fed more than 100,000 people in 1923 to celebrate the inauguration of the governor of Oklahoma. The revelers ate buffalo, bear, reindeer, beef, antelope, squirrel, mutton, possum, coon, pork, rabbit, and goose, all cooked in a series of open pits that stretched out over a mile.

The one universally accepted truth about barbecuing is that it takes a long time, so that the outside meat gets crispy, while the inside meat stays so tender it melts. Some of the techniques have been around for

K. D. Kilpatrick, a burial insurance salesman and avid hunter, remembers, "The most remarkable gun story I ever heard came from this old guy I met up in Wyoming. He said he had actually seen it. It's an A. C. Smith on a L. C. Smith frame. It'll shoot three times before you cock it and nine times before you can stop it. The hole in the barrel weighs two pounds, and it don't have a caliber on the barrel. It just says BIG GUN."

generations. Stonewall Jackson was reputed to have been a legendary rib cook. Jackson argued, contrary to popular belief, that ribs done to perfection had to be slow simmered in a covered pot for hours.

Among redneck chefs, however, everything is up for debate; even at the table, the battle lines are clearly drawn between the Dippy Sauce and the Dry Meater camps. Individual taste decrees a specific mix of woods, a particular depth of pit, an heirloom smoker; regional prejudice declares the choice of meat: Cowboys go for the rib eye, while Californians favor tri-tips. Adaptable midwesterners might be content with either beef or pork. But to a Southern redneck, there is only one meat—*pig,* the meat traditionally favored by the Celts.

ANSWERING THE CALL TO ARMS

Polybius noted in 140 B.C. that when Celts' shields failed to protect them from a storm of javelins and arrows, they "rushed at their adversaries like wild beasts, full of rage and temperament, with no reasoning at all; they were chopped down with axes and swords, but the blind fury never left them while there was breath in their bodies; even with arrows and javelins sticking through them they were carried on by sheer spirit while their life lasted. Some of them even pulled the spears they were hit by out of their wounds and threw them or stabbed the soldiers who had thrown them."

While Greek and Roman soldiers fought as disciplined battle units, their Celtic opponents engaged in mob dynamics combining elements of *Animal House* and the valiance of the heroic defenders of the Alamo. By all accounts, the macho bravado of the Celts came close to scaring the Romans to death before the first thrust of a sword. Imagine how soldiers trained in the classical rules of warfare must have viewed intoxicated naked warriors covered only in blue paint and gold jewelry who blew shrill horns and taunted them with fearsome cries. And once the battle had begun, Celts sought out the enemy of highest rank so they could cut

Coca-Cola Cuisine

"My three little boys'll come in from a hunting trip with that damn tough old moose or buffalo meat," a Montana wife confided. "There's no way you can break their precious little hearts by saying those animals are just too tough to eat. But you take a couple of bottles of Coke and soak a roast for two days in the refrigerator, and it'll be nice and tender. You slow cook it like a pot roast. Don't go forgetting the meat in the Coke, though. After a week the meat won't have a licka texture."

Ranch-Style Coca-Cola Roast

Either pork, venison, moose or beef roast
Garlic cloves, slivered
2 12-ounce cans Coca-Cola (it may be flat)
$^{1}/_{2}$ cup brown sugar
2 onions, sliced
2 cups ketchup
Carrots
Celery

off his head, the ancient Celtic equivalent of home movies.

When it comes to fighting contemporary wars, no one has ever questioned America's reliance on redneck courage, resourcefulness, and loyalty. The code of honor, the unconventional bravery, and the independent streak that sometimes veers into insubordination can also make a redneck an ideal hero. He's the wily Swamp Fox, the cunning Old

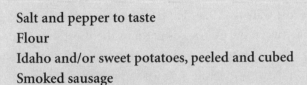

Salt and pepper to taste
Flour
Idaho and/or sweet potatoes, peeled and cubed
Smoked sausage

1. Poke holes in roast and insert slivers of garlic.
2. Mix together Coke, brown sugar, onions, and ketchup, and marinate roast.
3. Place in the refrigerator in a Zip Loc bag for 2 days.
4. Preheat oven to 450°.
5. Make a rack of peeled carrots and stalks of celery in a Dutch oven.
6. Dredge roast in mixture of salt and pepper and flour.
7. Place in oven for 15 minutes. Lower heat to 325°, cover, and cook until done.
8. An hour before the roast is done, add the Idaho and/or sweet potatoes and smoked sausage.

Variation: Serve with creamed potatoes made with cream cheese.

Makes 10 to 12 servings

Hickory, the fearless Jeb Stuart, the gutsy Patton, the arrogant MacArthur, and the list goes on and on. With some rednecks, the daredevil in them can cut short a promising career in the military. One World War II vet from the hills of Tennessee tells of two buddies who lost their lives on a training flight. They thought it would be fun to fly under the Mississippi River bridge at Vicksburg. "They just missed it by a hair, though," he boasted.

War stories and military lore play a significant role in redneck culture. Of course, it's the lost wars that have left permanent scars on the redneck psyche. The War Between the States was perhaps the most damaging assault on the dignity of the white working class, for it pitted such men against one another. On the Confederate side was an army of volunteers, with no munitions plants, no industry, and no training. On the Union side was a well-supplied standing army and an endless supply of immigrants to draft. On both sides, history has sanctified the men who fought as characters in a legend that evokes the same reverence as the Book of Genesis. Each soldier who died gave his life for the vision he believed to be that of the founding fathers; each soldier has contributed to the story of the war, which by now has grown into an epic worthy of Homer or Virgil.

True to form, the Southern rednecks have their own phraseology for the Civil War—the War to Suppress Yankee Arrogance, the Late Friction, or simply Round One. Defeat is not easily forgotten. As one frustrated wife put it, "I wouldn't mind so much that my husband didn't remember our anniversary, if he forgot other stuff, too. But that's not the case. He can tell you the date of every battle of the Civil War down to the casualty figures."

Vietnam, three generations later, remains the freshest assault on redneck pride, especially since so many volunteered to fight. "It took me about ten seconds to decide to trade in my high-school diploma for a dog tag," recalled *Dozer,* a veteran in a VFW hall near Pensacola, Florida, with a well-developed torso and a missing leg. "You couldn'ta found a more gung ho soldier in Vietnam. 'Kill a Commie for Christ' is something I believe, 'cept in a few years who'll remember what a Commie was?"

But the best war of all was the last one, according to Phil "Wire Dawg" Cobb (below, left), who was David Allan Coe's road manager for five years. "Desert Storm was the ultimate redneck war—it was short, there was lots of shooting, and we won big. A bunch of my biker buddies had a war party that lasted from the first shot to the homecomin'."

Phil "Wire Dawg" Cobb and his buddy, Neil, are lifelong bikers.
BRANDI DOWNS, FROM THE COLLECTION OF PHILIP "WIRE DAWG" COBB.

Wire Dawg's Red-Hot Redneck Ham-It-Up

1 fully cooked ham
24 whole cloves

Glaze:

1 cup brown sugar
6 ounces orange-juice concentrate
6 ounces root beer
2 tablespoons Colman's dry mustard prepared with Wild Turkey
Hot sauce to taste (⅓ cup is good and spicy)
¼ cup Wild Turkey

1. Preheat oven to 425°.
2. Score the ham in a checkerboard pattern, and stud with cloves.
3. For the glaze, mix together the brown sugar, orange-juice concentrate, root beer, mustard, hot sauce, and Wild Turkey.
4. Coat the outside of the ham with several ladles of the glaze.
5. Turn down oven to 325°.
6. Bake for about 20 minutes per pound until the ham registers 140° to 160° on a meat thermometer. Baste often with a mixture of the pan juices and the glaze.
7. Cool for an hour (cold ham slices easier) and slice thin. Drizzle the spicy glaze from the bottom of the pan over the slices on the platter.

Variations: Substitute hot pepper jelly for the hot sauce and orange juice, and/or substitute ½ cup red-hot candies for half of the brown sugar.

Makes 10 to 12 servings

Wild Turkey Gobbler Sweet Potato Mash

Serve with ham.

6 medium sweet potatoes, baked and peeled, or 3 1-pound cans
   sweet potatoes
½ cup Eagle condensed milk
¼ cup mayonnaise
¼ cup orange-juice concentrate
¼ cup brown sugar
1 cup chopped roasted pecans
2 tablespoons or so Wild Turkey
Pinch of ground cinnamon
Pinch of ground nutmeg
Pinch of ground allspice
Pinch of salt
Marshmallows

1. Preheat oven to 350°.
2. Mash the sweet potatoes with the milk, mayonnaise, orange-juice concentrate, brown sugar, pecans, Wild Turkey, cinnamon, nutmeg, allspice, and salt.
3. Pour the mixture into a buttered 2-quart casserole.
4. Top with the marshmallows.
5. Bake uncovered for 45 minutes.

Makes 10 to 12 ½-cup servings

LAYING DOWN THE LAW

It may be the combined predilection for weapons and warrior instincts that has led so many rednecks into law enforcement. Perhaps the contradictions of bravery and bravado are most evident in events sponsored by redneck lawmen—groups like the Sons of Custer and the Good Ole Boy Round-Up. *Bayne* is a small-town deputy sheriff from northern California who's one of the four hundred lawmen who has attended the annual Good Ole Boy Round-Up on the second weekend in May in Ocoee, Tennessee, for the past three years. (Ocoee is where the 1996 Olympic kayaking event took place.) Bayne was horrified that the press labeled it as a racist event. "Shit, rednecks make fun of everybody, most of all themselves," he explained, his blue eyes twinkling. "I know personally of six black guys who attended and had a helluva fine time there, too. If there was a 'nigger checkpoint' I must have missed it. Hell, it's nothing but a raunchy five-day beer bust where you can let your hair down amongst your brother officers. A retired cop from around Knoxville won the title of Good Ole Boy of the Year one year by publicly attempting to get a blow job from a sheep. The Secret Service blew away the competition in the beer truck push at the last one. It was awesome, they'd been drinking for five days. The rest of us were ass deep in mud, but they brought these six-foot-nine-inch guys who literally picked up the truck and carried it one hundred yards up a steep grade to win. Our president is guarded by the best."

GANG BANG

To receive a thorough armaments education, the best place to visit is a redneck gun show. One popular show is located in a sprawling entertainment complex in a Houston suburb. From booth to booth, the array of weapons is staggering. While it's perfectly acceptable for browsing shoppers to swagger around with large rifles dangling from buckled leather shoulder straps, live ammunition has to be checked at the door. Visitors absentmindedly empty their pockets and weapon chambers into Styrofoam cups as they enter the gun lover's nirvana.

    In a booth sandwiched between the ammo-check desk and a rotating display rack stocked with buck grunters, fawn meows, and doe-in-heat bleaters, a freckled ten-year-old boy sells brass knuckles. The booth

They [the Celts] held comradeship in highest esteem, since the most feared and powerful among them were those who were thought to have the most attendants and retainers.

—Polybius, Histories, book 2, c. 140 B.C.

Dent "Wildman" Meyers.
KIRK MARTIN.

belongs to the boy's father, and since it's illegal to sell brass knuckles for the purpose of inflicting injury, the child sells them as paperweights. "They come in two sizes—six dollars and ninety-five cents and nine dollars and ninety-five cents. Your paper won't never get back up with the nine-dollar-ninety-five-cent one," the boy says, looking up from his copy of *Sweet Revenge: A Serious Guide to Retribution.* His younger sister combs the sleek lavender nylon mane of her My Little Pony doll. The child's flaxen pigtails jiggle underneath a black baseball cap with the message GUN CONTROL MEANS USING BOTH HANDS.

Gun enthusiasts eagerly shop through rows of rifles, revolvers, pistols, and state-of-the-art weaponry, perhaps pausing to pick up a pair of earrings made from gold-dipped bullets. In addition to the impressive array of merchandise, the gun show also offers a large selection of literature, featuring titles such as: *Detonating, How to Disappear Completely and Never Be Found, The Manual of Fighting in the Street,* and *Paranoia.* These works reveal a curious ecumenical tone, as though Allen Ginsberg, M. Scott Peck, and Charles Manson had drafted a manifesto with Ross Perot and Ollie North on a weekend retreat at Timothy Leary's house.

The gun show is also a political opportunity for fringe groups. Dozens of pamphlets from organizations such as the Soldiers for a Tax-Free America and SWAT for Jesus are on display. Militia groups use these publications, along with the deep cover of talk radio and computer software, to reach out to others, enlist them in the fight against their enemies, and spread their odd patchwork of conspiracy theories. The gun show is one of the few places they appear in public. The level of their armed paranoia makes racist rhetoric and McCarthyism seem almost benign. Instead of the horrors of communism, they speak with authority about elaborate plots within our government.

Using a BB gun in the summer to shoot blackbirds is good training for the duck season in the winter, when a steady aim with a more serious gun is critical.

KATHY RICHARD.

Trigger

Don Lusk is a Cold Springs, New York, sanitation worker. Don shows his gun collection to his daughter.
LOWELL HANDLER.

Redneck Heaven

The World According to the Militia

★ AIDS, the Kennedy assassination, the death of the pope and Elvis, and My Lai were CIA plots. Ross Perot has proof, and so does Dan Rather.

★ Microchips are being employed by ultra-secret agencies to spy on every citizen. As long as you don't have a driver's license, a phone, credit cards, bank accounts, a computer, visit a hospital, pay taxes, or vote you're invisible and safe.

★ There are extraterrestrials among us. Many high government officials are the product of unions between aliens and humans that happened in the wake of the bomb in Hiroshima. (It's easy to pick out these nonhumans because they don't have auras.) The Pentagon has proof.

★ Every war and revolution, including the Gulf War, was plotted by a coalition of Freemasons and Zionists. Pat Robertson has the proof. Just watch *The 700 Club*.

★ President Kennedy isn't really dead and neither is his wife, but Rose Kennedy has actually been dead for ten years. Lyndon Johnson knew.

★ Jesus wasn't a Jew. The Holocaust never happened. Read the books by William M. Grimstad and the biblical research Bryan de la Beckwith did while he was in prison.

★ Bob Dole and Newt Gingrich are liberal pawns. Dwight Eisenhower was a Communist agent. Their voting records prove it. Pat Buchanan and the John Birch Society can tell you.

* Feminism is an anti-Christian/antidemocratic movement that destroys the family unit by encouraging lesbianism, murder of children (abortion), and the practice of witchcraft. Jimmy Carter is an unwitting tool of the United Nations, which is a satanic front. Operation Rescue has the evidence.

* Hillary Clinton and Janet Reno, in addition to all of the other women in politics and journalism, are lesbians. Jesus won't come back to restore order in the world until all homosexuals have been stoned to death in accordance with biblical instruction. It's in the Bible.

* Man has never been to outer space. The Communist threat was a lie, too. They were elaborate corporate marketing strategies designed by the Templars in the twelfth century. Just ask Pat Robertson.

* Procter and Gamble is a satanic corporate cult that can be defeated only by the positive energies of Amway and Mary Kay products.

* The public-school system is the vehicle for the "Clintonistas" and Satan. It discourages prayer and promotes premarital sex. Studies of African and Native American cultures are thinly veiled attempts to introduce paganism and witchcraft. Home schooling is the only answer. William Bennett has the evidence.

* The environmental movement is a plot by Jewish bankers to get control of the farmland (and food source) of America. Rush knows.

★ The Fifth Order of the Klan is so secret it never holds meetings. Many high-ranking Pentagon, police, and CIA officials, prominent doctors and nurses, and entertainers are members. They're always at the ready "to take over" when the revolution starts. It is hoped that they're guys of the caliber of Ollie North and G. Gordon Liddy. Tune in to talk radio and the Internet for details.

FEMMES FATALES

Legend has it that the reason the Romans never attempted to conquer Ireland was that as they approached its shores they saw a tribe of glaring six-foot Celtic women. If this was the size and temperament of the women, the Romans reasoned, they didn't want to encounter the men.

One of the most noted Celtic warriors was Boudicae, queen of the Iceni of East Anglia (Norfolk), who "avenged the lost freedom of the Celts." Before she and her army of male Celts capitulated in A.D. 61, they'd massacred more than seventy thousand Roman invaders and burned three major Roman towns, including London. Boudicae's terrified opponents described her as having red hair to her knees, blazing eyes, and a harsh voice. She rallied the Celtic tribes with her cry to arms: "If you weigh well the strength of armies, and the causes of war, you will see that in battle you must conquer or die. This is a woman's resolve; as for men, they may live and be slaves" (*Annals of Tacitus*, book 14, c. A. D. 56–c. 120).

Annabelle Cope, the sheriff's daughter, was a well-rounded frontier gal who could shoot as well as she did needlework.

Just as some of the great Celtic warriors were women, so are many redneck gun owners. It is estimated that more than 20 million women in America own guns, no doubt a large percentage of these being rednecks. In 1996, a Florida grandmother became the president of the NRA (National Rifle Association).

Judge Steve Noles, an attorney from Fort Payne, Alabama, is the grandson of the late famed sheriff of DeKalb County, "Doodles" Noles (see page 92). He tells one of his grandfather's favorite stories from the 1940s.

"You've got to realize, up until recently there was a sign on the outskirts of my hometown—THE UNITED KLANS OF AMERICA WELCOME YOU TO

FORT PAYNE. It's particularly interesting, since DeKalb County has such a tiny African American population.

"There was this Klansman who was having a land dispute with his redneck neighbor up on Sand Mountain," Steve remembered. "The thing the Klansman didn't realize was the redneck was out of town. The man's wife and a handful of little kids were up there alone. Anyway, the Klansman sets off a bunch of dynamite on their land. Well, that lady was petrified. She called up Granddaddy, the sheriff, and was sobbin' so hard she could barely talk."

Steve's grandfather looked all around her property, but he couldn't find any evidence to pin the damage on the Klansman. As he drove home he worried about the poor woman's safety, since she lived in such a remote area.

"A few nights later, Granddaddy was awakened in the middle of the night by a weeping child on the telephone: 'Mama says to hurry—them kluckers is back!' Even goin' full steam with the siren blaring, it took Granddaddy twenty minutes to get up to her place. As he lit up there, he was imaginin' what those vicious Klansmen were up to with the poor woman—that the children had been hanged, that the house was in flames.

"He brought the police car to a screeching halt behind a line of pickup trucks. He drew his gun and started makin' his way up to the house. But once he saw what was going on, it took him ten minutes to stop laughing.

"You see, there were ten Klansmen, shakin' in their sheets. Their pointy hoods were all pulled back. They had their hands up in the air. There was also a twelve-foot cross soaked in kerosene. Hell, that was one mad little redneck mother! And she had a shotgun pointed at the men.

She yelled to Granddaddy, 'Sheriff, I done told these bastards I'd blow the ass off the first one of 'em what put a match to that there cross.' "

Bonnie without Clyde

It's the power of strength over adversity that attracts some unlikely candidates to gun ownership. *Clarice,* a lanky grandmother with a tight white permanent and strident antiabortion sentiments, was shopping for a "persuader" at the Lock, Stock and Barrel Gun Shop in a small town on the outskirts of Greensboro, North Carolina. She and her friends in her Holiness Quilting Club had been saving up for a pastel Lady Smith, the .38 Special Smith & Wesson, to keep in the glove compartment of their church's Chevy van.

Clarice, a former schoolteacher, had a gun tale to fit any occasion. "One afternoon this old gal came home from work in the middle of the day. She planned to surprise her husband, who worked the night shift down at the plant," Clarice began. "Well, sir, she surprised him all right! He was in bed with her best friend. Yessirrreeeee, she pulls his hog-leg .38 out of the bedside table. Backed him up to the corner with the barrel aimed below his waist. So he pleads, 'Oh, baby, come on and give me a sportin' chance.'

"You know what she did? She backed away a few yards and said, 'Sugah, you get 'em swingin' and I'll see which one I hit!' "

At the conclusion of her story, Clarice pulled out a red snakeskin coin purse, the group's kitty, and began counting neatly rolled twenties and fifties.

After the transaction to purchase the .38 was completed, her friend in the pink gingham housedress grabbed the gun and pointed it at the wall. "Just call me Dirty Harriet." She chuckled, pink terry-cloth slippers planted two feet apart on the cracked linoleum.

Life Is Like a Dog Sled— If You Ain't the Lead Dog, the Scenery Never Changes

The Roman observer Publius Cornelius Tacitus (A.D. 55–117) wrote of the noble Celts, "We Romans desolated all western Europe and called it peace. We killed truly admirable people."

IF YOU HAVE THE URGE TO VISIT REDNECK HEAVEN, DO IT fast—sadly, as the subtitle of this book suggests, it's a vanishing state of grace. Forces from both within and beyond are doing to the redneck what our forefathers did with guns to the red man and the buffalo. This time the rednecks have the guns but not the right weapon: rectangular scraps of green paper featuring the images of dead presidents. Rednecks may have one hell of a prodigious will and be ferociously clinging to their independence, dignity, and the values of their Celtic ancestors, but success takes a fierce optimism and a steady income.

THE ONLY THING I CAN COUNT ON IS MY FINGERS

—Country music lyric

If you've read this far, you must know that I believe redneck culture is worth saving, but I have no idea if rednecks are willing to set aside their punitive instincts and take stock of their resources. Certainly they have enormous power both in the voting booth and at the cash register. After all, whose product loyalty helped keep old Coke alive and banished new Coke from the marketplace? An executive at one of the Big Three automakers confided that his CEO panicked when he overheard a few rednecks say they thought their new 1996 truck was "a pussy piece of shit!" Rumor has it that the CEO ordered continued production of the 1995 models, just in case.

As Jerry Clower, the East Fork, Mississippi, farmer and entertainer, put it, "The redneck voter needs to ride herd over those who control the elected officials. Corporations may buy a politician, but that doesn't mean we have to buy either them or their products. Somebody ought to remind these guys we can vote often—once at the poll and lots of times at the cash register!"

For me the question is not so much how long redneck culture will last, but rather, in a world in which most corporate chiefs and media icons confuse the objectives of capitalism with the fairness of democracy, how long can our system of government survive *without* rednecks? In many ways rednecks are the last exemplars of the independent spirit of our founding fathers, with their live-free-or-die philosophy. The Celtic determination to be neither the slave nor the enslaver is one of the backbones of contemporary American democracy. It also puts rednecks at odds with corporate America.

PHOTO ON PAGE 275 BY SUE ROSOFF.

Today, ornery rednecks have in effect been told by the establishment—in the words of the popular honky-tonk sign—"Be Nice or Leave." (James I gave virtually the same choice to their Celtic ancestors: Assimilate into the mainstream or join the disenfranchised economic underclass of social outcasts.) In our celebrity-crazed world, where the rich and famous have the status of royalty, rednecks have a bizarre role. Clint Eastwood, Mel Gibson, and Bruce Willis make millions portraying rednecks as icons of independence. Yet the very word "redneck" earns sneers and snickers from those who view any attempts at cultural protection as racism. Redneck culture is in fact an alternative culture, and it strikes me as unfair that in the absence of a national redneck organization or an official advocate, the mainstream sees rednecks not as victims but as victimizers.

THE BEST THING YOU CAN DO FOR THE POOR IS NOT TO BE ONE OF 'EM

—Redneck aphorism

Traveling the backroads of America, I soon realized that as the grand-daughter and niece of farmers, I am part of a minority that's circling the drain. The bumper sticker TO HELL WITH WHALES, SAVE THE COWBOY (FISHER-MAN, FARMER) voices the frustration of those who feel powerless as both their economic viability and their communities are destroyed by the very free-enterprise system they helped to create. Today three-quarters of all Americans live in urban areas, a mere 2.5 percent of the nation's land mass. This sounds familiar; in ancient times the Romans tried to break the power of the Celts by forcing them off the land and into the cities, where they could be more easily controlled.

Lady Bird Johnson told me her husband, former President Lyndon Johnson, foresaw the loss of this ancient way of life. "When Lyndon gave five hundred acres of the LBJ ranch to the National Park Service," she explained, "he stipulated it had to continue to be maintained as a working ranch in perpetuity. Even when people get their food in pills, this ranch will operate so people in future centuries can see where their ancestors got their food."

The American farm population has declined from about 30 million in 1900 to 5 million today. According to the 1992 census, 1.65 million of the nation's 1.9 million farms are sole proprietorships. But these figures don't speculate on the consequences of losing our rural heartland.

The redneck farmer is the embodiment of three thousand years of Celtic agrarian prowess wed to the beloved land. It was at the Farm Aid concert that I began to understand the importance of this farming history and the true meaning of the redneck term of endearment "I love you better than dirt." *Curly*, a Michigan farmer, was one of the many farmers I met there who philosophized about his way of life. "Owning a farm isn't a job or an investment, it's my home. It's who I am. I'll tell you one thing, my brother is a G.M. executive who's lived all over the world. When he comes back home for a visit, he asks why we don't get bored watchin' the moon come up over the hayfields. He tells me I wasted my opportunity to go to college and all. I tell him I didn't waste one darn thing. After I saw the world, I'd still know our farm's the most beautiful place on the whole damn planet.

"Do I trust international corporations to control my food supply? Hell, no! And where do we go if we lose this place—to Detroit, into the paper-hat world of minimum-wage glaze or into the line of folks who suck on the government's tit? Why can't our government make certain we keep our farms so we can keep rural America productive and pay our taxes?"

FRIENDS IN LOW PLACES

Rednecks are essential. Corporations may think they can save money by cutting jobs, but who, I wonder, will be left to run the business? When Garth Brooks sings about "Friends in Low Places" and "Standing Outside the Fire," he's speaking another truth about rednecks—they are both loyal and unafraid of decision making. As in the movie *Nine to Five,* many corporations in America are run not by the CEO but by his redneck secretary. Miki, my own redneck assistant, has an uncanny ability not only to coax phone numbers out of complete strangers but to gain access to celebrities.

There's another side to this, too. In the words of a favorite redneck saying often needlepointed and framed for the office: "Beware of the toes you step on today. They may be attached to the ass you have to kiss tomorrow." I heard a midwestern trucker on a CB radio. He and his wife were huge Joan Collins fans who enlisted a few other CB chatters in support of the author-star. If her publisher succeeded in their recent lawsuit to retrieve a million-dollar book advance from his favorite TV star, the trucker agreed he and his wife would see that a few truckloads of the publisher's books ended up as "wallpaper." Fortunately for Random House, Miss Collins was victorious.

PR people might be paid to control entree to the stars. But it's the bus drivers, the make-up people, and the roadies who control their shows. And like the clan system of old, if you are friends with one redneck roadie, you can pretty much make contact with any performer in the country. I've learned that the best concert tickets don't come from my former college classmates—who are now producers and agents; they come from the redneck sister of a farmer I interviewed, who is the secretary to the president of the company that sells the tickets.

Catalog companies may produce some of their products cheaply in China, but their sales are only as good as their telephone sales force. Maybe that's why some of the most successful companies headquarter their sales departments in the mountains of Tennessee. And maybe that's why, after I made friends with one of these redneck women on the phone, her company sent me an impressive free gift "to brighten up redneck heaven."

As a tourist in redneck heaven, I began to speculate on just how much of the culture that the United States is renowned for was fostered in farming communities. It was in rural America that cross-cultural collaborations between black and redneck musicians, athletes, and entertainers were forged to create what the world perceives as American culture. I marvel at the diverse genius that percolated out of agrarian soil in my home state of Mississippi alone—Leontyne Price, Charlie Pride, John Lee Hooker, Robert Johnson, B. B. King, Muddy Waters, Howlin' Wolf, Jimmie Rodgers, Tammy Wynette, Glen Ballard (1995 Grammy-winning songwriter), Beverly Lowrey, Donna Tartt, Marty Stuart, Jim Henson, Thomas Harris (*Silence of the Lambs*), John Grisham, Turner Catledge (*The New York Times*), Jack Nelson (*Los Angeles Times*), William Raspberry (*The Washington Post*), Rae S. Hederman (publisher of the *New York Review of Books*), Hodding Carter, Will Campbell, Myrlie and Medgar Evers, Willie Morris, Beth Henley, Tennessee Williams, Richard Wright, Richard Ford, Eudora Welty, William Faulkner, Walker Percy, Ellen Gilchrist, Shelby Foote, Morgan Freeman, Diane Ladd, James Earl Jones, Oprah, and Elvis, to name but a few.

Farmers aren't the only independent wage earners to be edgy about losing their piece of redneck heaven. Between WWII and the early 1970s most blue-collar workers saw their income more than double. But since that time only those white-collar workers in the top 20 percent tax bracket continue to thrive. The bottom fifth on the economic scale have seen their livelihoods stagnate, no matter how hard they work. The *real* weekly earnings for the majority of blue-collar workers has dropped 5 percent since the early 1980s. At the same time the power of the unions has begun to decline. Membership in the Teamsters' Union, the nation's largest private-sector union (encompassing everyone from truckers to the munchkins who wave and prance at Disney World), has dropped by approximately a half million, to 1.5 million members. The longshoremen had 40,000 members in the 1950s; today they have just over 10,000 members.

EDUCATION IS A FOUR-LETTER WORD

— Redneck aphorism

If redneck culture is to be saved, perhaps the best place to start is by revamping the educational system so it does what Ben Franklin did with a kite and a key: harness the spark of the redneck brain. Yet as things stand now, the redneck culture is particularly self-defeating when it comes to education. Most rednecks of all socioeconomic levels are proud to flaunt their rebellion against the school system. Unfortunately for them, however, it's predicted that by the year 2000, 75 percent of all new jobs will require some college background or special training, yet only 50 percent of all U.S. workers graduate from high school. Research indicates that 30 percent of all U.S. students can't read at even the most basic level, while 75 percent of the population doesn't have the technical know-how to read a manual and program their VCR.

Dr. Tim Ryan, director of the Division of Business and Economic Research at the University of New Orleans, explains the primary reason for the rednecks' economic woes. "After the Second World War, while the rednecks' minority counterparts were investing in higher education to get a leg up into white-collar management, medicine, and law, rednecks were buying more farmland and machinery. Then, in the 1970s, many people left the farms to go into industry, where there were higher-paying jobs. Three or four years later the plants closed down. Manufacturing moved to countries where labor costs were fifty cents a day. This left the rednecks out of their jobs. Corporate America views these American workers as grunts, and grunts are redundant in the Information Age."

For some rednecks, public school is nothing more than an exercise in cultural gelding. Russell Hebert is an Archuleta County, Colorado, undersheriff and rancher. During his long career in law enforcement he was a Louisiana state trooper who held the line against the Klan in Bogaloosa and served as bodyguard to George Wallace and Hubert Humphrey. He also has firsthand experience with how education can be employed to destroy the values of a minority culture.

"My people are Cajuns," Russell said, describing the American branch of the Celts of Brittany. "We've been in the New World since long before the American Revolution. Americans forget that as French-speaking Catholics, we had to fight the Anglo-Saxon subjugators before they did. The British stole our land in Nova Scotia and made us suffer every degradation imaginable, from slavery to genocide.

"Then our people found a new 'safe' homeland in the remote swamps of Louisiana. We were free to speak our language, play our music, and practice our religion, up until World War II. That was till the WASP teachers came in and whipped us when we practiced our culture. When you saw Dick, Jane, and Sally in the reading book, you wondered who you were. Children were told their parents and grandparents were ignorant. They made us ashamed of who we were."

Beneath the redneck disrespect for academia, I found wise and creative people who express a mixture of shame and hatred for an education system that values pupils who have the ability to be quiet and take tests over those who exhibit true creativity.

Recording company executive and country singer John B. Wells was one redneck who grimaced at the thought of school. "Whip me, kick me, make me pray, but for God's sakes don't bore me. The mere thought of having to sit still and listen to someone lecture makes me want to climb the wall like spirea!" John is in good company. His kinsman Thomas Edison's parents were told by teachers that their son was not only unruly but mentally retarded. Elvis is another example of one at odds with schooling. Even after making three successful movies, he was asked at a press conference if he might want to take some acting lessons. The King replied with forthright politeness, "No sir, I prefer to learn by doin'. "

Most school systems have abandoned the method of beating the devil out of "spirited pupils." They now seem to prefer Ritalin, a prescription medication, and strict regimes of behavior modification to override the cultural inclination to daydream when faced with the grueling tedium of most overcrowded American classrooms. Curiously, many of these same bored students admit that a lust for knowledge leads them to prefer the Discovery Channel and TLC (The Learning Channel) over MTV.

Henry Ford biographer Carol Gelderman points out that the automotive pioneer shared the inborn redneck disrespect for formal education. "One time Ford was with several other corporate chiefs. When someone asked Ford where he'd gone to college he scoffed, 'Thank God, I barely finished school. I had to get to work to make jobs for poor college-educated guys like you.' "

Even in business, Ford always preferred the amateur to the expert. He once said, "Our opportunities at Ford are directed by men with no previous knowledge of the subject, and therefore haven't had a chance to get on really familiar terms with the impossible."

Dr. M. B. Rawlings grew up among redneck families in Pennsylvania and Ohio and now focuses her attention on creative teaching techniques for specialized learning styles. "It strikes me there is a strong correlation between redneck values—anything worth having is worth having now—and what Dr. David Kiersey [*Please Understand Me*] calls the Concrete Pragmatist. These are people who process information in a kinetic manner. In other words, brain impulses go directly to the muscles, so the tool becomes the immediate extension of the arm. The kids with this learning style can often become exceptional musicians, surgeons, pilots, athletes, and craftsmen."

The problem as Dr. Rawlings explains it is that 38 percent of the population fits into this learning style, as compared to only 4 percent of the teachers. They learn best in an environment of experiential education, a movement that so far hasn't had much effect on public schooling. But it seems as though creating an educational system for this type of learner might have benefits for all segments of our society. "We'll tell you one thing," said a husband-and-wife cab-driving team in Atlanta, "if a group of rednecks had built that there Hubble telescope, that sucker woulda worked," they bragged. "And when you're out stuck on a deserted road in the middle of the night with a broke engine, you ain't prayin' for fuckin' Alan Greenspan or Henry Kissinger to he'p you. No sir, you want one of us Ivory soap rednecks. You know, if Ivory is 100 percent pure, we're 900 million percent redneck to the last speck."

WHEN THE SHIP HITS THE SAND

—Country song

Charlie Daniels had been right five years ago when he told me I'd be a far different person after I experienced redneck America. It didn't take me long to realize that the fire of the ancient Celts still burned in my DNA.

Our Celtic ancestors may have proven the rednecks have the stuff it takes to survive, but as many historians surmised, some of us accomplished this by fine-honing some of our most dysfunctional social characteristics: clannishness, viewing all outsiders as enemies, and an inclination toward swift and violent retribution. All of this economic anger, frustration, and fear exacerbates my least favorite redneck characteristic—persecution of outsiders.

Even if we're not all racist in our beliefs, many rednecks most definitely talk the racist talk. Perhaps it's as one of the descendants of the McCoy clan suggested, "Some of us rednecks are forty-eight percent intolerant and fifty-two percent Christian, and others are fifty-two percent Christian and forty-eight percent intolerant. It's just that in redneck culture you have to observe that four percent real closely to learn which is which. But one thing is certain: You call one of our black friends a nigger in front of us and we'll kill you dead."

Nevertheless, within that bigoted four percent I heard the n-word constantly. At the same time I witnessed the close bond between rednecks and blacks among rodeo cowboys, factory and construction workers, teachers, coaches, and teammates. When the two groups were together, they acted like they belonged to the same clan. Ironically, in the presence of African Americans, the n-word was used, not by rednecks, but by the African Americans.

I have come to believe these contradictions exist within redneck culture because bigotry has its roots in cultural protection, whereas racism is an outgrowth of economic strife. A look at Southern history may provide an insight into the fierce intolerance of most rednecks. As Celtic people, their own experience of having suffered generations of cultural oppression and slavery made many of them disinclined to own slaves themselves. But pre–Civil War redneck farmers were forced to compete both economically and socially with the aristocratic plantation-owning cousins who amassed vast fortunes because of slave labor. Once freed, these former slaves did not threaten the livelihoods of their former owners, however. Rather, they were left to compete for scarce food with the redneck farmer. To any farmer, life is precarious enough without haggling over the same turf—the middle ground that exists between the status of the aristocrat and the degradation of white trash.

During better economic times, Dr. Martin Luther King Jr. (the great-grandson of an Irish woman) effectively presented the lack of civil rights for his people as an affront to Christian principles. While some of the economic elite *amen*ed racial equality, it was the redneck who was directly impacted by the doctrine of "goodwill toward men." When George Jefferson, the black dry cleaner on *All in the Family,* moved into a white neighborhood, he didn't end up next door to the Cleavers, the Brady Bunch, or Rob and Laura Petry. It was Archie Bunker who had to wake up to the reality that the neighborhood in which he'd invested his life savings had become the petri dish for the New Generation. And then hard times set in. It's sad but true that as rednecks lose their communities to economic blight, they also tend to lose their compassion.

BANG, BANG . . . YOU'RE DEAD

Another of the rednecks' questionable traits is their pathological urge to face down oppression, exploitation, and denigration with a good head of rage. Conservative commentators like Pat Buchanan exploit a murderous indignation about the loss of freedom and dignity when they remind their redneck audience of what the British soldiers looked for during the American Revolution—the colonists' guns. "Once they took away their guns, they could impose their will on them."

According to a National Academy of Sciences report, half of the households in the United States already have at least one gun. I can honestly say that doesn't apply to rednecks. In all the redneck homes I've visited over the past five years, I've been in only one home with one gun. In my experience, rednecks own guns by the dozens. And that doesn't take into account the at-home displays of flare guns, railway torpedoes, Claymore land mines, grenade launchers and live grenades, and automatic and semiautomatic weapons. From what I know of redneck firepower, it's three hundred years too late for Americans to debate gun ownership. Instead, it's crucial that our society address gun accountability.

I encountered a few rednecks who agreed. These folks didn't seem to fear gangs nearly as much as they feared the hair triggers of brother rednecks. Take for example the recent case of Gordon Reid Hale III, the licensed handgun owner from Grand Prairie, Texas, who fired his legally concealed .40-caliber pistol at Kenny Tavai, a delivery truck driver. Tavai began to punch Hale after Hale's truck clipped his delivery truck's mirror at a red light. Tavai took a bullet in the chest and later died in the hospital.

As a child, Joe Cook saw his family lose everything they'd worked for because of the redneck code of honor, alcohol and guns. Joe is the son of an Arkansas hog farmer whose father went to prison for shooting a neighbor in retribution for threatening his wife and children. As Joe told me, "You know, there are guns in the hands of some pretty unstable folks. Especially when you realize that half of the people killed by guns in this country are killed by family members or friends. When people say they don't want the government to control guns, you ask them who they'd call for help if the guy next door had a nuclear bomb?

"Wouldn't it seem that the estimated eighty million dollars a year the NRA spends to defeat gun-control measures could be better spent helping to cover the eighty-five percent of the three billion dollars' annual health costs of firearm injuries the taxpayers get stuck with?"

"None of the politicians will face the fact that the problem isn't guns, it's the violence in American society," explained Sheik Richardson, a former marine marksman who is now a professional photographer. "It came to me when I saw Nixon give a speech against anti-Vietnam protesters: right there on the presidential seal there's an olive branch with three arrows next to it. We say we want peace, but we use guns to enforce it.

"We've got more people locked up than any country in the world. It hasn't changed the fact that we've got the highest rate of violence of any industrialized nation," Sheik speculated. "It worries me that the more guns we have, the more violence, the more people get frightened, and the more willing they are to give up power to politicians."

Gloria grew up in a truck stop where she witnessed more than one gunfight. She has adopted her mother's stance on gun legislation. "Why can't we treat guns like automobiles instead of penis extensions? Make gun owners prove they can use them, and own insurance. Hell, make people show proof of liability insurance in order to buy ammunition. You know, sort of like the number on a prescription. All the tax money can cover the cost to society of gun ownership—medical costs, prisons, police benefits. And for those gun owners who don't have insurance— you go straight to jail and all of your property gets confiscated. You know, Mama always taught me freedom without responsibility is nothing but stealing."

WHEN A FELLER LOSES HIS ROOTS HE'D BETTER GROW HIM SOME LONG CLAWS TO HANG ON WITH

—Redneck aphorism

In large part, the rednecks' great strength and worst weakness are that we continue the three-thousand-year-old Celtic cultural tradition of being lone wolves. When we howl, we may howl the loudest and longest but never in unison. The noble Celts had their own values, mythology, and art forms, but we never managed to create a central government or a history of intracultural cooperation.

A lack of cohesive ethnicity is another factor that adds to the rednecks' economic disenfranchisement. If we don't join together to gain the power of self-representation, we can't effectively fight for ourselves. It's that old adage, "The only thing two rednecks ever agree on is how bad a third redneck is." The consequence is what one out-of-work construction worker in Vermont complained of: "Fellas like me're as helpless as a flea betwcen two nails."

As the redneck farmer and factory worker look down from the cheap seats high above the American sociopolitical field, the liberals' and conservatives' team colors look awfully similar. Both parties are vying for the estimated 25 to 40 million redneck votes, but neither one is speaking for the rednecks' real benefit— they just manipulate redneck fear to their advantage. "What the blue-collar folks think they want to hear a politician say is, 'I'll cut the budget,' " Dr. Ryan explained. "But what's getting cut are the very programs that directly benefit them. In truth, it was government handouts that gave many rednecks their spot in the middle class. What was the GI Bill but one of the largest handouts in the history

DON'T TREAD ON ME

—Revolutionary War flag slogan

The rattlesnake is an ideal symbol for rednecks. It is unique to North America. It has no eyelids, so it's always vigilant. It never provokes an attack or attacks without warning, but once engaged with an enemy, it will fight to victory or death. It never attacks its own kind. It might be attractive in youth, but it becomes magnificent with age. Each rattle is independent; singly the rattles can't make a sound, yet together they make a sound that strikes terror. The rattlesnake's weapons of attack may seem insignificant, yet they inflict wounds that are often fatal—but only if the snake chooses to discharge all of its venom. The American Indians viewed the rattler as a sacred link to the spirit world. If one was killed, they believed, dozens would take its place. For these and other reasons, Benjamin Franklin advocated adopting the image of a coiled rattler with the legend "Don't Tread on Me" for the American flag.

While the rattler did not become the nation's icon, it has remained important to rednecks. Perhaps the time has come for them to take it up as a symbol of their freedom, pride, and defiant dedication to their values in the face of adversity.

of democracy? And aren't Social Security and Medicare also government handouts?"

Unfortunately, in recent years it is by exploiting redneck rage that our politicians can get the redneck voter to put the muscle into punitive isolationist measures to reduce imports and immigration and kill health-care initiatives, health-care reform, and affirmative action. It is as if both parties have relied on rednecks to become unwitting accomplices in the dismantling of their values of life, liberty, and the pursuit of happiness.

So how can rednecks change their fate? To whom are rednecks going to turn for help? Do they join angry kinsmen like alleged Oklahoma City bomber Timothy McVeigh, who seems to be following in the footsteps of seventeenth-century rebel Guy Fawkes, who tried to halt repressive policies by blowing up James I and the British Parliament?

The more I hear politicians manipulate the rednecks' natural dislike of outsiders, the more I wonder why no one suggests the logical solution: that rednecks have themselves classified a minority and demand government support to help them realize their potential. "We the People" begins the doctrine of individual liberties for a multiracial nation founded in part on Celtic principles, especially protection from government authority. For a change in mainstream policy to occur, minorities must simply join together to fill the middle ground. Health care, jobs, education, and community supports that all minorities—rednecks included—desperately need would quickly be provided if our current politicians felt their *own* jobs were in jeopardy. To paraphrase the words of Malcolm X: "Apart, we have fingers; together we have a fist."

THE END

Bibliography

Allen, Frederick Lewis. *The Big Change 1900–1950*. New York: Bantam, 1952.

Ashmore, Harry S. *Arkansas, a History*. New York: Norton, 1978.

Ayers, Edward L. *The Promise of the South*. New York: Oxford Univ. Press, 1992.

Bauman, Zugmunt. *Socialism, the Active Utopia*. London: Holmes & Meier, 1976.

Bede. *A History of the English Church and People*. Trans. Leo Sherley-Price. London: Penguin, 1955.

Beeman, Richard R. *The Evolution of Southern Backcountry: A Case Study of Lunenburg County, Virginia, 1746–1832*. Philadelphia: 1984.

Bivans, Ann-Marie. *101 Secrets to Winning Beauty Pageants*. New York: Citadel Press, 1995.

Blackman, Marion Cyrenus. *Look Away! Dixie Land Remembered*. New York: McCall, 1971.

Boorstin, Daniel J. *An American Primer.* Chicago: Univ. of Chicago Press, 1966.

Booth, Mark. *American Popular Music.* Westport, Conn.: Greenwood, 1983.

Caesar, Julius. *The Gallic War.* Trans. H. J. Edwards. Cambridge, Mass.: Harvard Univ. Press, 1966.

Cahill, Thomas. *How the Irish Saved Civilization: The Untold Story of Ireland's Heroic Role from the Fall of Rome to the Rise of Medieval Europe.* New York: Anchor Books, Doubleday, 1995.

Campbell, Colin. *Toward a Sociology of Religion.* London: Macmillan, 1971.

Campbell, Will D. *Forty Acres and a Goat.* New York: Harper & Row, 1986.

Carden, Gary, and Nina Anderson. *Belled Buzzards, Hucksters, and Grieving Specters: Appalachian Tales: Strange, True, and Legendary.* Asheboro, N.C.: Down Home Press, 1994.

Cash, W. J. *The Mind of the South.* New York: Vintage, 1941.

Chadwick, Nora. *The Celts.* New York: Penguin, 1970.

Chandler, David Leon. *The Natural Superiority of Southern Politicians: A Revisionist History.* New York: Doubleday, 1977.

Chapman, Malcolm. *The Gaelic Vision in Scottish Culture.* Montreal: McGill-Queen's Univ. Press, 1978.

Chestnutt, Mary. *A Diary from Dixie.* Boston: Houghton Mifflin, 1949.

Chute, William J., ed. *The American Scene: 1600–1860.* New York: Bantam, 1964.

Claritas Corporation. *The Prizm Handbook for Marketers.* Alexandria, Va.: Claritas, 1991.

Clark, J. G. D. *Prehistoric Europe*. Stanford, Calif.: Stanford Univ. Press, 1952.

Cole, J. P. *Geography of World Affairs*. New York: Penguin, 1963.

Cunliffe, Barry. *The Celtic World*. New York: Crown, 1979.

Cunningham, Rodger. *Apples on the Flood: Minority Discourse and Appalachia*. Knoxville, Tenn.: Univ. of Tennessee Press, 1987.

De Tocqueville, Alexis. *Democracy in America*. New York: New American Library, 1956.

Dillon, Myles, and Nora Chadwick. *The Celtic Realms*. New York: New American Library, 1967.

Dionne, E. J., Jr. *Why Americans Hate Politics*. New York: Simon & Schuster, 1991.

Dollard, John. *Caste and Class in a Southern Town*. New Haven, Conn.: Yale Univ. Press, 1937.

Drew, Elizabeth. *On the Edge: The Clinton Presidency*. New York: Simon & Schuster, 1994.

Du Bois, W. E. B. *An A.B.C. of Color*. New York: Seven Seas, 1963.

Elliot, Thomas H., et al. *American Government*. New York: Dodd, Mead, 1965.

Eluère, Christine. *The Celts, Conquerors of Ancient Europe*. New York: Abrams, 1993.

Filip, Jan. *Celtic Civilization and Its Heritage*. New York: New Horizons, 1962.

Fisher, David Hackett. *Albion's Seed, Four British Folkways in America*. New York: Oxford Univ. Press, 1989.

Foxworthy, Jeff. *Hick Is Chic: A Guide to Etiquette for the Grossly Unsophisticated*. Marietta, Ga.: Longstreet, 1990.

Foxworthy, Jeff. *Red Ain't Dead: 150 More Ways to Tell If You're a Redneck.* Marietta, Ga.: Longstreet, 1991.

——. *You Might Be a Redneck If. . . .* Marietta, Ga.: Longstreet, 1989.

Fuller, J. F. C. *Julius Caesar: Man, Soldier, and Tyrant.* London: Eyre & Spottiswoode, 1965.

Fussell, Paul. *Class.* New York: Ballantine, 1983.

Garrison, Walt, and John Tullius. *Once a Cowboy.* New York: Random House, 1988.

Goldman, Eric F. *Rendezvous with Destiny.* New York: Vintage, 1952.

Gomme, Alice B. *The Traditional Games of England, Scotland, and Ireland (1894–95).* New York: Dover, 1964.

Goodrich, Norma Loree. *Merlin.* New York: Franklin Watts, 1987.

——. *Priestesses.* New York: Franklin Watts, 1989.

Graves, Robert. *The White Goddess.* New York: Farrar, Straus & Giroux, 1948.

Green, Miranda J. *Dictionary of Celts Myth and Legend.* New York: Thames & Hudson, 1992.

Grun, Bernard. *The Timetables of History, Based on Werner Stein's Kulturfahrplan.* New York: Simon & Schuster, Touchstone Books, 1963.

Guralnick, Peter. *Last Train to Memphis: The Rise of Elvis Presley.* Boston: Little, Brown, 1994.

Hallowell, Edward M., M.D., and John J. Ratey, M.D. *Driven to Distraction: Recognizing and Coping with Attention Deficit Disorder from Childhood through Adulthood.* New York: Pantheon Books, 1994.

Hartman, Thom. *Attention Deficit Disorder: A Different Perception.* Grass Valley, Calif.: Underwood Books, 1993.

Hatt, Jean-Jacques. *Celts and Gallo-Romans.* Geneva: Nagel, 1970.

Herodotus, 4 vols. *The History of Herodotus.* Trans. George Rawlinson. New York: Wilkinson, 1889.

Herter, George Leonard, and Berthe E. Bull. *Cook and Authentic Historical Recipes and Practices.* Waseca, Minn.: Herter's, 1960.

Hubert, Henri. *The Greatness and Decline of the Celts.* Boston: Benjamin Bloom, 1972.

Jacobs, Jane. *The Death and Life of Great American Cities.* New York: Vintage, 1961.

James, Simon. *The World of the Celts.* New York: Thames & Hudson, 1993.

Johnson, Haynes. *Sleepwalking through History.* Landover, Md.: Anchor, 1991.

Jones, George, with Tom Carter. *George Jones.* New York: Villard, 1996.

Keirsey, David, and Marilyn Bates. *Please Understand Me: Character and Temperament Types.* Del Mar, Calif.: Prometheus Nemesis, 1978.

Kennedy, Roger G. *Hidden Cities: The Discovery and Loss of Ancient North American Civilization.* New York: Free Press, 1994.

Kephart, Horace. *Our Southern Highlanders: A Narrative Adventure in the Southern Appalachians and a Study of Life Among the Mountaineers.* Knoxville, Tenn.: Univ. of Tennessee Press, 1976.

Kirwan, Albert. *Revolt of the Rednecks: Mississippi Politics 1876–1925.* Lexington: Univ. of Kentucky Press, 1951.

Kleppner, Paul. *The Third Party System, 1853–1892.* Chapel Hill: Univ. of North Carolina Press, 1985.

Krythe, Maymie R. *What So Proudly We Hail: All about Our American Flag, Monuments, and Symbols.* New York: Harper & Row, 1968.

Leyburn, James G. *The Scotch-Irish: A Social History.* Chapel Hill: Univ. of North Carolina Press, 1962.

Lynd, Helen Merrell. *On Shame and the Search for Identity.* New York: John Wiley & Sons, 1967.

MacCulloch, J. A. *The Religion of the Ancient Celts.* London: Constable, 1991.

McNeill, John T. *The Celtic Churches.* Chicago: Univ. of Chicago Press, 1974.

McWhiney, Grady. *Cracker Culture: Celtic Ways in the Old South.* Tuscaloosa, Ala.: Univ. of Alabama Press, 1988.

Mallory, Merrit, and Emerald Rose. *You're the Reason Ours Kids Are Ugly.* New York: Harper Perennial, 1995.

Montana, Gladiola. *Never Ask a Man the Size of His Spread.* Salt Lake City, Utah: Gibbs-Smith, 1993.

Morgan, Dan. *Rising in the West: The True Story of an "Okie" Family from the Great Depression through the Reagan Years.* New York: Knopf, 1994.

Napolitano, George. *Championship Wrestling.* New York: Brompton, 1991.

———. *The New Pictorial History of Wrestling.* New York: Gallery, 1990.

Nietzsche, Friedrich. *On the Genealogy of Morals.* Trans. Kaufman and Hollingsdale. New York: Vintage, 1969.

Nordenfalk, Carl. *Celtic and Anglo-Saxon Painting.* New York: George Braziller, 1977.

Peterson, Wallace G. *Silent Depression: The Fate of the American Dream.* New York: Norton, 1994.

Phillips, Kevin. *Arrogant Capital: Washington, Wall Street, and the Frustration of American Politics.* Boston: Little, Brown, 1994.

Piggot, Stuart. *The Druids.* New York: Thames & Hudson, 1975.

Polsby, Nelson, and Aaron Wildavasky. *Presidential Elections: Strategies of American Electoral Politics.* New York: Scribner's, 1968.

Raftery, Joseph, ed. *The Celts.* New York: Mercier, 1967.

Reddick, L. D. *Crusader without Violence: A Biography of Martin Luther King, Jr.* New York: Harper & Brothers, 1959.

Rees, Alwyn, and Brinkley Rees. *Celtic Heritage*. New York: Thames & Hudson, 1961.

———. *Celtic Heritage: Ancient Traditions in Ireland and Wales*. New York: Thames & Hudson, 1989.

Reid, Jan. *The Improbable Rise of Redneck Rock*. Austin, Tex.: Heidelberg, 1974.

Richmond, I. A. *Roman Britain*. London: Penguin Books, 1955.

Ross, Ann. *Everyday Life of the Pagan Celts*. London: Routledge & Kegan, 1970.

Roucek, Joseph S. *Contemporary Political Ideologies*. Savage, Md.: Littlefield, Adams, 1961.

Rourke, Byron P. *Nonverbal Learning Disabilities: The Syndrome and the Model*. New York: Guilford Press, 1989.

Rozwenc, Edwin C. *The Causes of the American Civil War*. Lexington, Mass.: D. C. Heath, 1961.

Rutherfurd, Edward. *Sarum: The Novel of England*. New York: Ballantine Books, 1987.

Schoenwald, Richard L. *Nineteenth-Century Thought: The Discovery of Change*. Englewood Cliffs, N.J.: Prentice-Hall, 1965.

Scott, James C. *Domination and the Arts of Resistance: Hidden Transcripts*. New Haven: Yale Univ. Press, 1990.

Sexton, Patricia Cayo. *The Feminized Male: Classrooms, White Collars, and the Decline of Manliness*. New York: Vintage, 1970.

Sherrill, Robert. *Gothic Politics in the Deep South: Stars of the New Confederacy*. New York: Ballantine, 1969.

Stark, R., and C. Y. Glock. *American Piety: The Nature of Religious Commitment*. Berkeley: Univ. of California Press, 1970.

Strabo. *The Geography of Strabo.* Trans. J. R. S. Sterrett and Leonard Jones. London: Jones, 1917–32.

Tacitus, Publius Cornelius. *Historae.* From The Histories. Trans. Kenneth Wellesley. London: Penguin Books Ltd., 1976.

Terkel, Studs. *Working.* New York: Ballantine, 1972.

Thompson, Hunter S. *Better Than Sex: Confessions of a Political Junkie, Trapped Like a Rat in Mr. Bill's Neighborhood.* New York: Random House, 1994.

Tierney, J. J. *The Celtic Ethnography of Posidonius.* Proceedings of the Royal Irish Academy, 1960.

———. *The Book of Kells.* Facsimile ed. New York: Abrams, 1991.

Tolstoy, Nikolai. *The Quest for Merlin.* Boston: Little, Brown, 1985.

Trimble, Vance H. *Sam Walton, Founder of Wal-Mart.* New York: Signet, 1990.

Virgil. *The Aeneid.* Trans. T. H. Delabère-May. New York: Bantam, 1961.

Vlahos, Olivia. *The Battle-Ax People.* New York: Viking, 1968.

Wald, Kenneth. *Religion and Politics in the United States.* New York: St. Martin's, 1987.

Weber, Max. *The Protestant Ethic and the Spirit of Capitalism.* New York: Scribner's, 1958.

Weiss, Michael J. *The Clustering of America.* New York: Harper & Row, 1988.

Whaley, Bo. *The Official Redneck Handbook.* Nashville, Tenn.: Rutledge Hill, 1987.

Wheeler, R. E. M. *Maiden Castle Dorset.* New York: Oxford Univ. Press, 1943.

Williams, Lycrecia, and Dale Vinicur. *A Daughter's True Story, Still in Love with You: The Story of Hank and Audrey Williams.* Nashville, Tenn.: Rutledge Hill, 1989.

Williams, T. Harry. *Romance and Realism in Southern Politics.* Athens, Ga.: Univ. of Georgia Press, 1961.

Wills, Garry. *Witches and Jesuits.* New York: The New York Public Library and Oxford Univ. Press, 1995.

Wilson, Charles Reagan, and William Ferris. *Encyclopedia of Southern Culture.* Chapel Hill: Univ. of North Carolina Press, 1989.

Wolfe, Tom. *The Kandy-Kolored Tangerine-Flake Streamline Baby.* New York: Farrar, Straus & Giroux, 1993.

Woodmason, Charles. *The Carolina Backcountry on the Eve of the Revolution: The Journal and Other Writings of Charles Woodmason, Anglican Inteneret.* Ed. Richard J. Hooker. Chapel Hill: Univ. of North Carolina Press, 1953.

Photographers

Syndey Byrd—A former Miss VFW of Hattiesburg, Mississippi, Ms. Byrd has devoted herself to documenting unique folk cultures the world over. A longtime protégée of the great photographic colorist Ernst Haas, Ms. Byrd was one of the eight photographers featured in the 1991 PBS documentary *Ten Thousand Eyes.* Her ethnographic photography has been published in *Geo, Americana,* and *Horizon.* She is currently working on a book on the street culture of Mardi Gras.

Stephen Collector—This Virginia native has made his home in the mountains of Colorado for more than twenty years. He has spent his career doing documentary portraits of the rugged life on the western ranch. His *Law of the Range, Portraits of the Old Brand Inspectors* was published in 1991 by Clark City Press in Montana.

Charles Davis—As a North Carolina herpetologist in the 1970s, Mr. Davis documented the lives of the backwoods Crusoe Islanders in the Green Swamp.

Lowell Handler—A native of upstate New York, Mr. Handler was the subject of a *P.O.V.* documentary titled, "Twitch and Shout," chronicling his life as a photographer with Tourette's syndrome. He is currently traveling across America working on a book by the same name.

Kathy Richard—From her home base in a cabin beside a bayou in the Louisiana swamps, Kathy Richard records the everyday lives of Cajun cowboys and their families. When she's not taking photographs, Ms. Richard makes jewelry from alligator bones.

Sue Rosoff—When internationally renowned photographer Ansel Adams saw his assistant Sue Rosoff's photographs of the rodeo, he insisted that she drop everything else to pursue this culture. Ms. Rosoff has spent the past twelve years photographing and producing small rodeos. She is currently working on a book on the rodeo from her studio in Red Bluff, California.

Louis Sahuc—An award-winning commercial photographer whose clientele includes NBC, Fox, CBS, and HBO, as well as various state tourist boards. Mr. Sahuc captures the essence of heartland America wherever he finds it.

Bob Schatz—A Nashville native who moonlights from his corporate assignments to record the essence of his favorite segment of American society—the redneck.

Gerard Sellers—A fifth-generation alligator hunter, Mr. Sellers is both a filmmaker and photographer who specializes in the culture of the Gulf oil rigs, trappers, and hunting camps.

The Redneck Heaven Hall of Fame

N THE BEGINNING THERE WAS A BLANK PAGE. *REDNECK Heaven* is a cultural portrait of this much-maligned culture that broke free of my misconceptions because of the acts of generosity and support of those who shared their philosophy, frustrations, passions, humor, anguish, and vision. Characters identified by full names are portrayed as accurately as the context, a vigilant legal department, and a word-weary editor would allow. Sometimes, however, to protect the innocent (and/or the guilty) I've disguised personalities, altered events, and changed geographic locations.

My heartfelt thanks to the guardian angel of rednecks for sending Miki de Jean, director of research, office manager, and friend, who treated the book as a crusade rather than a job. And for the incredible talents of the dedicated resident rednecks and colorful research staff—

Gerard Sellers, Kathy Richard, and Matthew Johnson. All treated their interviews as more than a job and people they interviewed as more than sources. We all wish to express our appreciation to Cherry and Beth, who painstakingly transcribed our numerous hours of interviews.

In sincere appreciation to those who have supported the beliefs that rednecks are "the army that fights for dignity" and have stayed with this book through all of its trials: my own private Inspector Morse and agent, John Ware; political advisers Beth Rickey, cofounder of the Coalition Against Nazism and Racism, and Leslie Korshak, former Louisiana director of the Congress of Racial Equality (CORE); spiritual adviser Brother Awest; and the brilliant lawyers who, in the words of one trucker, "knew how to crawl up the corporate ass like a fire ant and sting 'em where they can't scratch"—Elliott Hoffman, Sonja Keith, Jan McGrath, Temko and Temko, Lauren Field, and Jim Uschold.

This manuscript would have remained a hologram had not Fran McCullough stumbled over my threshold one cold afternoon for hot muffins. It is she who oversaw a process requiring the bullwhip of wisdom and the patience of Job. When an overabundance of voices and insights produced intellectual gridlock and a manuscript that could be transported only in a wheelbarrow, it was saved by the perseverance and sharp knives of several brilliant editors: Dean Albarelli, Alice Rosengard, and Lauren Janis. And then there was A. J. Verdelle, the ever-insightful voice who added verve to the verbs.

Big hugs to my old friends, without whose love and support this would have been another of those projects that simmer like yesterday's coffee—Henry Adams; Gregory Amenoff; Mildred Amer; Pamela Bardo; Sally Belk; Royce Bemis; Kell, Delia, and Dorain Bennett; Lionel Bevan; Margot and Charlie Blair; Marian Bogan-Bebeau; Brunhilde Bondo and

Lollipop; Jim Brousseau; Lucy Buffet; Loosie Anna Burnett; Judi and David Burrus; Syndey Byrd; Bill Carr; Bess Carrick of Queen of Hearts Productions; Philip Carter; Gayle Chitty; Beverly and Johnny Church; Jesse Core; Lucy Core; Ethel Crownover; Kent and Charlie Davis; Sharon Dodd; Kit Duane; Marigny Dupuy; Cathy and Bob Edmundson; Margaret and Karl Ewald; Judy and Tom Feagin; Nell, Fran, Ed, and Scott Fetzer; Pat Galloway and Peter Webb; Garden District Books; Carol Gelderman; Terry George; Beth Gill; Judy Girod; Judy and Gary Goldman; Elizabeth Green; Tania Grossinger; Foster and Wendy Guillory and "Old Betsy"; Taylor Hackford; Herbert Halpern; Andrea Hanson; Budd Hopkins; Jed Horn; Beth Houston; Lucile and Ray Hume; Mitzi and K. D. Kilpatrick; Chris King; K-9 Kornhauser; Dr. Alfred Lemann of the Historic New Orleans Collection; Doris and Bill Leopard; Del Long; Steve Lorant; Candace Loving; Bob and Susie Marcus; Helen Mirren; Irene Morrah; Melinda Muse; Vance Muse; Peggy and Dr. Craig Nielson; Nancy Novgorod; Kathleen Nowell; David Oestricher; Marguerite Oestricher; Carl Palazzolo; Mary Ellen Parker; Laura and Bobbie Peery; Dr. Muriel Pollia; Iler Pope; Alice Randall; Simone Rathle; David Rawle; Dr. Mary Belle Rawlings; Mary Frances Ready; Bryce Reveley; Barbara Rhodes; Cayetano Ribas; Betty Richards; the Reverend Hill and Macon Riddle; Jim Roberts; Dr. Sue Rosenfeld; Rita Rosenkranz; Grady Ross; Chuck Sanders; Terry Sistrunk; Julie Smith; Tobias Steed; Dr. Fred Stielow; Lena Tabori; Emma Tanner; Billy Tully; Gracie Tune; Jan and Roger Tutton; Cynthia Ware; Mel Wathen; Victoria and John B. "Stormy" Wells; Marybeth Weston; Ann Wilkinson; Lynn Wilson; Chris Wiltz; and Francis Wright.

Many people had divergent things to say about my argument in its oral and written form that improved my powers of observation and determination. In particular John Bridges, Austin Brook, Connie Clausen, Don Lee Keith, Diane Reverand, and Ron Ridenhour.

The great gift of any project is the special friendships that spring from it and those that are nurtured by it—photographer Rosemary Carol Butler, Stephanie Bennett and Jim Mervis, Sally and "Wire Dawg" Cobb, Stephanie and Janie at Colorpix, the Computer Shoppe, Manuel Cuevas, Sandi Ellis, Dr. Aaron Fox, Walt Garrison, Dennis Hall of Jim Walter Resources, Lance Hill of the Coalition Against Racism and Nazism, Hoot, Emyl Jenkins, Dan Katz, Dr. Ron King, Anne Leone, Beverly Lowry, Albert McGrigor, Tim Meaghen, Flo Milsted, Essie and Al Morris, Chef Paul Prudhomme, Dr. Douglas Rose, Sue Rosoff, J. C. Shardo, Gene Sizemore, Jane Smoot, Liz Theils of Network Ink, Bernice Turner, Jean Woodley, Bobbie Westerfelt and Joe Sanford of Pelican Pictures, Deb Wehmeyer and Glen Yago.

Many thanks to all of those who have shared their expertise and advice: Ace Hardware, especially Jessica Krauser and John Cameron; Geraldine and Curtis Alleman; the American Telemarketing Association; Herb Anderson; Erby Aucion; Trish Avila; Robert Baier; Ralph Baldwin of the *Houston Post;* Morris Bart; Alvin Bartlett; Karen Nussbaum; Chris Bell; Richard Belous; Berea College; Leigh Ann Betters of the Produce Marketing Association; Dr. James Blackwell; Roy Blount; Gene Blum; Mr. Boobie; Byron Burton; Dr. Bill Bertrand; Tom Buckholtz; Mayor Jane Rule Burdine of Taylor, Mississippi; Hodding Carter of Main Street Productions; Kim Carson and Steve Miller of WNOE; Hiro Clark of Welcome, Inc.; Dr. Jack Clark of the Newport Ramp Festival; Newcomb College Department of Classics; Claritas Communications; Stephen Collector; Council for Tobacco Research; Country Music Hall of Fame; Cowgirl Hall of Fame in New York; Dollywood, especially Barbara Headla and Ray Sanderson; John

Duab of the Health Science Center at the University of Utah; Eagle Productions; Betty Ann Eaves of the National Association of Catahoulas; Roger Ebert; Arlene Evans; Dave Exnacious; Fat Possum Productions; Peter Franklin; GLOW (Gorgeous Ladies of Wrestling); George Galloway; Peggy Gershany; the Good Ole Boy Round-Up guys; Mark Graff of Graff Pay Per View; Jon Graubarth; Merle Grimm of the Combine Harvester Demolition Derby; Lisa Groves of Acme boots; Jack Gyben; Jim Hammond, David Boul, and Alice McGehee of *Oprah;* Lowell Handler; Buzz Harper; Bunky Healey; Charlie Hickson; Donna Hilley of SONY/Tree; Joe Hineman; Dr. Arnold Hirsch; Home Team, especially Mary and Tague Richardson and Gene Brown for the fried-turkey advice; Walt Johnson of the National Retail Hardware Association; Karen Johnston of Hunt Wesson Foods; Jo Ann Jones; Beverly Kaplan; Jon Kardon; Donna Dayton Kelly; Dr. Lewis Killan; Aprill Kingsley; Dr. Fred Koenig; Bill Lancaster of *Geraldo;* Jay Leon of Camelot Entertainment Sales; Anna Lifsey; Sam Lovullo of Gaylord Entertainment; Lumberjack World Championships, especially Anita; Macho Man Randy Savage; Bill and Bobby Malone; Archie Manning; Ed Martin of Custom Chrome; Larry E. McPherson; Bert Medley; Glen Mennard of the Texas Motor Plex; Steve Miller; Bill Mikulewicz; Joy Moe; Mohair Council of America; Abe Morris; Jerry Moss; NAAWP (National Association for the Advancement of White People); National American Sociological Association, especially Bill Martino; National Hot Rod Association; The Daughters of Charity; National Peanut Council; Bill Nassis of the Perlis truck stop; Jon Newlin; Randy Newman; Sandy Nivens; Geoffrey Norman; Nancy Ott of the U.S. Championship Tractor Pull in Bowling Green; Chris Owens; Virginia Parks; Will Peneguy of the Louisiana Superdome; Reverend Skipp Porteous; Mike Posey and "Cassidy"; Pro Rodeo Hall of Fame, especially Steve Fleming and Sherry Compton; Ellen

Jones Pryor; Bob Rafelson; Kelly Reily of Just Justin; Harold J. "Dusty" Rhodes; Sheik Richardson; Tandy Rice; Dr. Tim Ryan; Charlie Sampson; Rick Shay of VA Affairs; Danny Scheter; Kip Sonderman; Gene Siskel; SKOAL; Smith Bucklin and Associates, especially Lisa Levy; Lowery Sims of the Metropolitan Museum of Art; Southern Poverty Law Center; Mayor Lester Stillinger; Jennifer Stuart; Congressman Gerry Studds; Bob Summer; Professor Fred Suppe of the Department of History, Ball State University; Arne Svenson; T L Enterprises; Roxanne Taft of Circus Hotel; Elizabeth Taylor of Planned Parenthood; Shawn Taylor of Handgun Control, Inc.; the Texas Longhorn Breeders Association; the Texas State Diamond Hunters, especially Steve Raines; Lisa Thomas of Gang, Tyre, Ramer and Brown; the Tobacco Institute; Deane Trompeter; the International Council of Shopping Centers; Theresa Underdown of Wrangler; United Mine Workers Union; Dale Vinicur, Rob Wait, Booth Waltenine of the Utah Farm Bureau; Mike Webber of SRO Pace; Dr. Peter Wells of the University of Minnesota; Kay West; Jaston Williams; Lawrie Williams; Mat Williams; Molly and Lula Williams of the Frog Jumping Festival; Ulysses Williams; Curtis and Ann Wilke; Babs Wilson; Woody's Bar-B-Que; Charles Wyatt of the *Cherokee Chronicle;* Mary Yancy of the Alabama Rattlesnake Company; Robin Yates of Turner Broadcasting; Dr. Milton Yinger; Glenda Yoder of FARM AID; John Yow of Longstreet Press; Leonard Zeskind of the Center for Democratic Renewal. And a special thanks to those who have done their best to save me, I hope, from lamentable blunders in regard to the genesis of the rattlesnake on the American flag: George Bryant, Newport Historical Society, Naval War College, Whitley Smith, Ed Gilsthrop, and the Heritage Flag Company.

Inspiration comes from many places. Even while I was sitting at the computer all of my senses stayed awake thanks to the bowls of mustard greens and slabs of venison supplied by K. D. Kilpatrick, Dot and Rodney Broussard's fresh cracklins, and Kathy and Johnny Richard's boudin. There were the dawn phone calls from Sam Wright with the latest jokes from the night shift at the coal mine. And there was music so powerful that its emotion and passion passed through me and onto the screen over and over and over again—the sounds of the Allman Brothers, Tammy Wynette, Ronnie Milsap, Zachary Richard, Rosanne Cash, Bob Seger, Charlie Daniels, the Chieftains, Melissa Etheridge, the Fabulous Thunderbirds, K. T. Oslin, Run C&W, Reba McEntire, Lyle Lovett, Patsy Cline, Leon Russell, Bruce Springsteen, and Stevie Ray Vaughan. And to Travis, keep on sluggin'.

Many writers thank their family and friends. Mine cooked, sheltered, and supported me through years of frustration and isolation. To their great credit they never succeeded in talking me out of continuing with my adventures in redneck heaven.

And a special note of appreciation for the many acts of kindness from strangers, especially the guy in the pickup who rescued me from the honky-tonk.